A FLORA OF THE WHITE MOUNTAINS,
CALIFORNIA AND NEVADA

Looking north toward White Mountain Peak from the alpine vegetation of the dolomite barrens at 11,700 ft.

A Flora of the White Mountains,
California and Nevada

ROBERT M. LLOYD

Assistant Professor of Botany, Ohio University, Athens, Ohio

and

RICHARD S. MITCHELL

*Assistant Professor of Biology, Virginia Polytechnic Institute and
State University, Blacksburg, Virginia*

UNIVERSITY OF CALIFORNIA PRESS
Berkeley, Los Angeles, London

University of California Press
Berkeley and Los Angeles, California
University of California Press, Ltd.
London, England
Copyright © 1973, by
The Regents of the University of California
ISBN: 0-520-02119-3
Library of Congress Catalog Card Number: 79-172393
Printed in the United States of America

CONTENTS

DEDICATION

This flora of the White Mountains is respectfully dedicated to Mr. Victor Duran, intrepid explorer and collector in these mountains. His specimens form a major contribution to this manual.

Mr. Duran was born on 31 March 1897. He received a master's degree in physics from the University of California in 1925 and shortly thereafter became a student in botany under the guidance of Dr. Willis Linn Jepson. Duran pursued a study of the floristic composition of the White Mountains from 1926 to 1933, making numerous trips to the area, collecting 50 sheets of each plant, and exploring by mule much of the difficult canyon terrain in the northern portion of the range. He was forced to give up the work when he accepted a position in the Scientific Photography Laboratory of the University where he eventually became Scientific Photographer, a position in which he remained until his recent retirement. In his work as Scientific Photographer he maintained the same high degree of scientific procedures and perfectionism which characterized his work in the White Mountains.

At least three insects and two plants have been named in honor of Mr. Duran, including *Heuchera duranii* Bacigalupi and *Streptanthus cordatus* Nutt. var. *duranii* Jepson.

It is with great appreciation for his valuable contributions that we dedicate this manual to Mr. Duran.

Introduction

Although the White Mountains of California and Nevada are of exceptional botanical interest because of the presence of the oldest known living plants (*Pinus longaeva*), they have remained comparatively unknown floristically. This may be due, in part, to their relative isolation and seemingly uninteresting vegetation when viewed from their base. The range is located between 37°13′ and 38° N latitude ande 117° 55′ and 118° 25′ W longitude; it is bounded on the south by Westgard Pass and the Inyo Mountains, on the north by Montgomery Pass, on the east by Deep Springs Valley and Fish Lake Valley, and on the west by the upper Owens Valley region. The range itself comprises about 880 square miles, being about 55 miles long and 20 miles wide at its widest point. The elevation varies from about 4000 feet to 14,246 feet at the summit of the highest point, White Mountain Peak. The highest point in Nevada, Boundary Peak (13,140 feet), is situated near the northern end of the range.

Although separated from the Sierra Nevada by as little as eight miles the vegetation of the White Mountains is distinctly Great Basin in character. The four major vegetation zones include desert scrub (shadscale), pinyon woodland, subalpine forest, and alpine. Within these vegetation zones occur about 815 species of vascular plants.

During the summers of 1963 to 1966 the authors made extensive field collections within the White Mountains. These collections, in addition to those of Victor Duran and Harold A. Mooney, form the nucleus of collections on which this manual is based. It is expected at this time that our catalog of plants is over 90 percent complete. However, most botanical work in the range has been done in the easily accessible southern end, south of White Mountain Peak. Although many of the northern canyons have been collected, especially by Duran, it is expected that they may still harbor some species as yet unknown to the range.

1

ACKNOWLEDGMENTS

The authors are greatly indebted to Dr. Nello Pace and the staff of the White Mountain Research Station for providing basic financial assistance and generous services during our tenure of work. It was primarily his interest which stimulated the production of this floristic list. We are also indebted to the staff of the Herbarium of the University of California at Berkeley for providing space and services during the project. We would very much like to thank the following persons for providing identifications of plant specimens: Loran Anderson (Compositae), Rimo Bacigalupi (Scrophulariaceae), Lyman Benson (Cactaceae), Margaret Bergseng (general), Lincoln Constance (Hydrophyllaceae and Umbelliferae), Theodore Crovello (Salicaceae), Alva Day (Polemoniaceae), Lauramae Dempster (Rubiaceae), J. Robert Haller (Pinaceae), Lawrence R. Heckard (Hydrophyllaceae, Orobanchaceae), John T. Howell (Cyperaceae, Juncaceae), Harold A. Mooney, Peter H. Raven (Onagraceae), James Reveal (Polygonaceae), Reed Rollins (Cruciferae), Herbert Wahl (Chenopodiaceae), and Joyce Zavortink (Loasaceae). We would also like to thank the curators of the following herbaria for making specimens available to us: California Academy of Sciences, San Francisco; Dudley Herbarium, Stanford University; Jepson Herbarium, University of California, Berkeley; Pomona College and Rancho Santa Ana Botanic Garden herbaria, Claremont, California; and the herbaria of the University of California, Berkeley, Davis, and Los Angeles campuses.

This work was supported by funds provided under ONR contract N00014–69–A–0200–1005 and NASA grant NGR 05–003–018 to Dr. Nello Pace and the White Mountain Research Station of the University of California.

HISTORY OF BOTANICAL COLLECTING

Although the White Mountains are relatively isolated and appear botanically uninteresting from a distance, nearly 70 plant collectors have made their way into the range, as far as is known from data compiled from specimens on file in California herbaria. Over half of these collectors concentrated their efforts in the southern quarter of the range, and many are represented only by collections from Westgard Pass. The northern portion of the White Mountains, from White Mountain Peak to Montgomery Pass, is the least collected and least known.

By far the most significant collecting was done by Victor Duran from 1926 to 1933, preparatory to a floristic study of the range which was never completed. The Duran collections, totaling about 1400 numbers, are significant in that they represent the floristic composition of many of the little-visited northern canyons as well as areas in the southern half of the range.

Other significant contributions to the flora have been made by Douglas Powell, a naturalist and plant geographer, who has collected over 3000 plants in nearly every canyon throughout the period from 1950 to 1966, and by Harold A. Mooney and his associates at the University of California, Los Angeles, and Stanford University, who covered the southern portion thoroughly from 1961 to 1966. The authors have done extensive collecting in most parts of the range from 1963 to 1966.

The first botanical exploration in the White Mounains was carried out by William H. Shockley, a mining engineer who resided in Candelaria, Nevada, from 1880 to 1893. From this base Shockley made extensive trips into some of the northern canyons and into the higher regions of Mono County south of White Mountain Peak during 1886 and 1888. Three years later (July 1891) a side party of the Death Valley Expedition, under the leadership of Frederick V. Coville and Frederick Funston, ascended White Mountain Peak and collected in Black Canyon. Coville at this time was in the southern Sierra Nevada and the collections were actually made by Funston. Marcus E. Jones (who collected in Montgomery Pass in 1897) and C. A. Purpus are the only other pre-twentieth-century collectors known to us.

The following list summarizes the significant botanical collecting in the White Mountains.

Collector	Year	Area visited
W. H. Shockley	1886, 1888	Northern canyons, Mono Co.
F. V. Coville and		
F. Funston	1891	Black Canyon
M. E. Jones	1897	Montgomery Pass
	1924	Westgard Pass
	1927	Benton
C. A. Purpus	1898	Inyo Co.
A. A. Heller	1906	Silver Canyon
Katherine Brandegee	1913	Silver and Coldwater canyons
	1916	Silver Canyon
Joseph Grinnell	1917	Silver Canyon, McAfee Meadow
W. L. Jepson	1917	Throughout the range
A. C. Shelton	1917	Peak, McAfee Meadow
Roxanna Ferris	1918	Wyman Creek and Queen Canyon
	1927, 1932	Wyman Creek
Victor Duran	1926–1933	Throughout the range
H. M. Hall	1927	Benton
Jean Linsdale	1927	Indian Creek
C. B. Wolf	1928, 1930	Westgard Pass
	1931	Silver Canyon
Ralph Hoffman	1930	Westgard Pass
D. D. Keck	1930	Westgard Pass
E. I. Applegate	1931	Silver Canyon
Rimo Bacigalupi	1932	Wyman Creek
	1961	Mono Co

Collector	Year	Area Visited
Lyman Benson	1934	Silver Canyon
E. Robinson and B. Lindner	1935	Benton
J. D. Cassel	1936	Black Canyon
Joseph and Hilda Grinnell	1937	Westgard Pass, Benton
W. Hovanitz	1937	Westgard Pass
John Roos	1937	Mustang Peak
I. L. Wiggins	1937	Westgard Pass
W. A. Archer	1938	Indian Creek, Queen Canyon, Chiatovich Creek
E. C. Jaeger	1938	Westgard Pass
	1939	Middle Creek
	1940	Benton and Montgomery Pass
	1949	Trail Canyon
F. W. Peirson	1938	West slope
Percy Train	1940	Trail and Queen canyons
Annie Alexander and Louise Kellogg	1941	Westgard Pass
	1945	Silver Canyon
Alice Eastwood and J. T. Howell	1941	Westgard and Montgomery Pass
Mark Kerr	1941	Westgard Pass
H. D. Ripley and R. C. Barneby	1941	Montgomery Pass
Bassett Maguire and A. H. Holmgren	1945	Wyman Creek, Mono Co.
Peter (Kamb) Ray	1948	Mono Co.
P. A. Munz	1948, 1949	Silver Canyon
	1955	Reed Flat, Wyman Creek
Douglas Powell	1950–1966	Throughout the range
S. F. Cook	1951	White Mountain Road
Freed Hoffman	1951	Silver Canyon
John and Lucille Roos	1951	Mono Co.
	1952	Wyman Creek, Mono Co.
Robert Tofsrud	1951	Crooked Creek
John M. Tucker	1951, 1958	Crooked Creek
A. M. Vollmer and L. Beane	1951	White Mountain Road
Herbert Mason	1953	Mono Co.
Verne and Alva Grant	1954	Westgard Pass
	1955	Montgomery Pass

Collector	Year	Area Visited
Peter H. Raven	1954, 1958, 1959	Westgard Pass, Deep Springs
Richard M. Straw	1954, 1956	Westgard Pass
H. K. Buechner	1955	Deep Springs Valley
Mary DeDecker	1955, 1959, 1960	Throughout the range
E. K. Balls	1956	Westgard Pass
P. C. Everett and E. K. Balls	1956	White Mountain Road
A. A. Beetle	1957	Westgard Pass
Harlan Lewis	1957	Westgard Pass
E. G. Linsley and J. W. MacSwain	1959	Westgard Pass
E. R. Blakley and K. K. Muller	1960	Mono Co.
E. R. Blakley	1961	Schulman Grove
David Gregory	1960	Westgard Pass
Paul Hurd	1960	Antelope Springs
Loran C. Anderson	1961	Silver Canyon
Dennis E. Breedlove	1961	Mono Co.
D. F. Howe	1961	Westgard Pass
Lawrence Heckard	1961	Mono Co.
Harold A. Mooney *et al.*	1961–1966	Throughout the range
Wayne Roderick	1962	White Mountain Road
Larry McHargue	1963	Westgard Pass
Arthur Menzies	1963	Inyo Co.
Charlotte N. Smith	1963	White Mountain Road
R. M. Lloyd and R. S. Mitchell	1963–1966	Throughout the range
T. E. Lankester and P. D. Edwards	1965	White Mountain Road; Indian and Marble Creeks
J. T. Howell	1966	White Mountain Road

TYPE COLLECTIONS IN THE WHITE MOUNTAINS

The following list of type collections was compiled from cards on file at the Botany Department of the California Academy of Sciences.

CALIFORNIA

Inyo County:

Anogra longiflora Heller. Silver Canyon.

Astragalus lentiginosus Dougl. var. *semotus* Jepson. Campito Mt.

Chrysothamnus axillaris Keck. Head of Deep Springs Valley.

Chrysothamnus nauseosus (Pall). Britt. ssp. *viscosus* Keck. 7.7 miles east of Laws, 8000 ft. (Silver Canyon).

Cryptantha hoffmannii Jtn. Westgard Pass.

Eriogonum maculatum Heller. Base of mountains, east of Laws.

Galium matthewsi Gray var. *scabridum* Jepson. Silver Canyon, 7500 ft.

Lomatium foeniculaceum (Nutt.) C. & R. ssp. *fimbriatum* Theobald. O.1 mile northwest of summit of Westgard Pass, 7300 ft.

Lupinus fontis-batchelderi C. P. Smith. Toll House Springs.

Lupinus portae-westgardiae C. P. Smith. West side of Westgard Pass.

Oreocarya lutea Greene. Silver Canyon.

Penstemon scapoides Keck. Westgard Pass.

Phacelia crenulata Torr. var. *funerea* J. Voss ex Munz. Black Canyon, 5700 ft.

Phlox covillei E. Nels. Black Canyon.

Physocarpus alternans (Jones) J. T. Howell var. *annulatus* J. T. Howell. Wyman Creek, 8500 ft.

Scrophularia californica Cham. & Schlecht. var. *desertorum* Munz. Silver Canyon, 7500 ft.

Sisymbrium diffusum Gray var. *jaegeri* Munz. Westgard Pass.

Mono County:

Antennaria scarbra Greene. White Mts. 12,500 ft.

Draba cuneifolia Nutt. ex T. & G. var. *californica* Jepson. North fork of Crooked Creek.

Draba subsessilis Wats. White Mts. 13,000 ft.

Eriogonum gracilipes Wats. White Mts. 13,000 ft.

Gymnosteris minuscula Jepson. Sheep Mt.

Heuchera duranii Bacigalupi. McAfee Meadow, 11,700 ft.

Horkelia hispidula Rydb. White Mts. 3300 m.

Horkelia scandularis Rydb. Mono Co., 12,000 ft.

Lappula coerulescens var. *brevicula* Jepson. Poison Creek, 10,000 ft.

Oxytropis deflexa DC. var. *culminis* Jepson. Cottonwood Creek, 9500 ft.

Penstemon depressus Greene. White Mts. 13,000 ft.

Penstemon monoensis Heller. Near Southern Belle Mine.

Philadelphus stramineus Rydb. Mono Co.

Podistera albensis Jepson. Mono Co. 7–8000 ft.

NEVADA

Arnica chamissonis Less. ssp. *foliosa* (Nutt.) Mag. var. *jepsoniana* Maguire. Esmeralda County, Chiatovich Creek, 8000 ft.

Caulanthus senilis Heller. Mineral County, lower slopes, 7500 ft.

Eriogonum monticola Stokes. Esmeralda County, ridge south of Queen Mine, 10,500 ft.

Gentiana tenella Rottb. var. *monantha* f. *alba* Rouss. & Raym. Esmeralda County, Chiatovich Creek, 8500 ft.

PLANT COMMUNITIES AND VEGETATION

By H. A. Mooney

Although the White Mountain Range lies in close proximity to the central Sierra Nevada, its vegetation bears little resemblance to that found in most parts of the Sierra. It is situated in such a pronounced Sierran rain shadow that water availability is one of the major limiting factors in all vegetation zones. Thus, the White Mountains form a desert mountain range with virtually all of the vegetational affinities lying to the east in the mountains of the Great Basin.

The harsh, arid environments of the White Mountains have produced a small number of simple vegetation types, most of which have relatively few dominants. This is true in spite of the large and topographically diverse land mass which represents a range of elevations from 4000 to 14,246 feet. In regions where temperatures are adequate for tree growth, the amount of precipitation is near the lower limit of sufficiency. Woodlands are depauperate and the forests in many places barely warrant this designation because of their sparse cover.

Details of certain vegetation types of the mountains have been discussed in a number of publications: the pinyon woodland by St. Andre, Mooney and Wright (1965) and Brayton and Mooney (1966); the subalpine forest by Billings and Thompson (1957), Mooney, St. Andre, and Wright (1962), Strain (1964), Wright and Mooney (1965), LaMarche and Mooney (1967), La-Marche (1968, 1969), and Fritts (1969); and the alpine tundra by Mooney *et al.* (1962), Mitchell, LaMarche, and Lloyd (1966), and Mooney (1966).

An attempt is made here to provide a generalized overview of major vegetation units to serve as a background for interpretation of the accompanying flora.

The framework used for reference will be that of plant zones. Recognition of such zones is a convenient means of partitioning the total vegetation into manageable units for discussion. The four major zones—desert scrub, pinyon woodland, subalpine forest, and alpine tundra—may be distinguished basically by the presence or absence of certain woody dominants. The desert scrub lies at elevations below tree growth (less than 6500 ft.). Pinyon woodland is distinguished by the presence of *Pinus monophylla* (6500 to 9500 ft.). The presence of either or both *P. longaeva* and *P. flexilis* characterizes the subalpine forest (9500 to 11,500 ft.). Alpine tundra is located at elevations above tree growth. Generally, there are constellations of species which are unique to these zones; however, certain important species may overlap several zones (e.g., *Artemisia tridentata*). Also, within any given zone, particularly the subalpine, there is considerable community variability which will be discussed.

The main area of concentrated study of the White Mountain vegetation has been on the west slope, south of White Mountain Peak, and within zones above the desert scrub. Hence, these areas are given the greatest emphasis here. Quantitative vegetation data, where given, are derived from simple line transects, 50 meters in length in all zones below the alpine tundra and 25 meters in length in the tundra. Examples of specific samples are used for illustration. Data are also given which reflect conditions in 200 sample stands throughout

the range. Certain growing-season conditions within the four vegetation zones
are also indicated in Table I.

TABLE I

SOME CLIMATIC PARAMETERS WITHIN THE FOUR MAJOR VEGETATION ZONES

For period June through August	Zone			
	Desert* 5,600 ft.	Pinyon 8,600 ft.	Subalpine 10,700 ft.	Alpine 12,700 ft.
Mean weekly maximum Temp. 4 ft. °F				
1961	98.9	86.9	74.5	57.9
1962	93.0	82.4	71.7	58.7
Mean weekly minimum Temp., 4 ft. °F				
1961	62.0	50.5	41.9	30.4
1962	57.0	45.4	37.8	27.9
Total precipitation Inches				
1961	0.94	4.51	6.62	6.57
1962	0.63	1.26	1.55	**
Average miles per hour wind, 18″ ht.				
1961	5.18	1.64	5.23	4.01

* All stations located on west-facing exposures on the west slope of the range.
The subalpine and alpine stations were both at the crest of the range.
** Data not available.

DESERT SCRUB ZONE (4000 TO 6500 FT.)

A desert scrub vegetation covers the base of the mountainsides and the valley floors to an elevation of approximately 6500 feet. The vegetation is monoto-
nously uniform in physiognomy although rather rich in the number of shrubby
components. A few scattered individuals of Mohavian desert species (e.g., *Am-
brosia dumosa, Yucca brevifolia*) are found at the southern end of the range,
indicating the transitional nature of the vegetation. However, the bulk of the
flora is decidedly Great Basin in character. Shadscale (*Atriplex confertifolia*)
dominated scrub is the principal vegetation type (Pl. 1). At the upper elevations below the pinyon zone and at the north end of the range big sagebrush
(*Artemisia tridentata*) predominates.

The shrubby vegetation of the slopes covers, on the average, a little over one-fifth of the soil surface. Herb cover is composed primarily of spring annuals which provide a significant display only in favorable years. There are, however, a number of common and distinctively desert perennial herbs which include *Eriogonum inflatum. Mirabilis bigelovii, Stanleya elata, Hilaria jamesii, Lygodesmia exigua,* and *Machaeranthera* sp.

The shrub composition of a sample of shadscale scrub is indicated in Table II. This vegetation sample was taken at an elevation of 5600 feet on a flat ridgetop on the west slope of the range. Shadscale provides the most cover, as is typical, and *Ephedra* somewhat less. Eleven shrub species were encountered along a 50-meter sample line and two additional shrub species, *Eriogonum fasciculatum* and *Tetradymia axillaris,* were nearby. These species characterize vast expanses of the lowlands.

The desert scrub vegetation is by no means uniform in composition as it changes in character depending on topographic position; the vegetation of washes and the rare springs (Pl. 2) can differ markedly from that of the surrounding slopes. *Encelia virginensis* ssp. *actoni* is particularly common in the dry washes, and *Populus trichocarpa* and *Salix lutea* occur where water is always available.

TABLE II

PERCENT PLANT COVER ON A 50-METER LINE INTERCEPT IN THE SHADSCALE
SCRUB AT 5600 FT. ELEVATION*

Species	Percent cover
Shrubs	
Atriplex confertifolia	4.1
Ephedra nevadensis	3.5
Atriplex polycarpa	2.2
Chrysothamnus teretifolius	1.9
Dead shrubs	1.6
Artemisia spinescens	0.9
Chrysothamnus nauseosus	0.6
Eurotia lanata	0.3
Lepidium fremontii	0.2
Grayia spinosa	0.2
Menodora spinescens	T
Dalea fremontii	T
Total shrub cover	15.2
Total herb cover	1.2
Total cover, all plants	16.7

* Weather data for the desert station given in Table I is for this stand.

PINYON WOODLAND ZONE (6500 TO 9500 FT.)

Pinus monophylla (single-leaf pinyon) is the dominant and virtually only tree species from elevations of 6500 to over 9500 feet. *Juniperus osteosperma* (Utah juniper), however, can be locally important, particularly in alluvial areas, and *Betula occidentalis* forms stands in certain riparian areas.

The pinyon trees form a woodland over extensive areas of the White Mountains (Pl. 3). The mean tree cover within the center of distribution of this species is only about 18 percent; however, in certain localities cover can attain nearly 40 percent (St. Andre *et al.,* 1965). Pinyon trees are relatively short-lived, few attaining ages in excess of 300 years; reproduction is abundant.

Artemisia tridentata (big sagebrush) is by far the most important and abundant shrub within the pinyon zone, attaining mean cover values as high as 17 percent in the altitudes of best development. This species has a relatively broad altitudinal range, extending from the upper edge of the shadscale scrub at 6000 feet to over 10,800 feet, well within the subalpine zone. This species forms the fabric upon which the mosaic pattern of the pinyon woodland is superimposed. In many areas within the elevations of the pinyon zone, particularly on the Wyman Formation, the pine is absent and big sagebrush forms the dominant cover. In areas above the pinyon zone yet below the distribution of limber and bristlecone pine, sagebrush is the dominant cover (the big sagebrush-grass zone of Billings, 1951). The same is true within the subalpine forest zone on the extensive areas with quartzitic sandstone-derived soils, which are in most instances unfavorable for tree growth.

On certain limestone soils, generally deeply weathered, *Artemisia tridentata* is replaced by *A. arbuscula* ssp. *nova,* a small shrub mostly restricted to elevations within the pinyon zone.

Other shrub species of lesser abundance are present within the pinyon woodland. *Purshia glandulosa* (*P. tridentata* to a lesser degree) provides appreciable cover (mean of 6 percent in the region of greatest abundance) throughout the pinyon zone. *Ephedra viridis* is a shrub which typifies the zone although it does not cover much of the soil surface. *Chrysothamnus viscidiflorus* ssp. *puberulus* is quite common everywhere.

On steep limestone outcrops, *Cercocarpus intricatus* forms almost pure stands. The range of this species extends from 6,000 to over 10,000 feet. In many places at elevations above 9000 feet, it hybridizes with *C. ledifolius,* a high-elevation species (Brayton and Mooney, 1966).

Of the many herbs of the pinyon zone (50 were found in the vegetation samples of St. Andre *et al.,* 1965) only five, all perennials, contribute significant amounts of cover: three grasses, *Koeleria cristata, Oryzopsis hymenoides,* and *Sitanion hystrix;* and two forbs, *Phlox stansburyi* and *Eriogonum caespitosum. Koeleria* and *Sitanion* have broad distributions which extend upward into the alpine tundra. Annual herbs, particularly *Phacelia vallis-mortae,* can provide brief periods of substantial cover in certain years.

The relative simplicity of the vegetation of the pinyon zone is indicated by its characteristic species-poor composition as illustrated in two tree-dominated vegetation samples shown in Table III.

TABLE III

PERCENT PLANT COVER ON TWO 50-METER LINE INTERCEPTS IN THE PINYON WOODLAND

Species	Slope habitat at 8,600 ft.*	Alluvium at 7,350 ft.
Trees		
Pinus monophylla	23.2	16.4
Shrubs		
Artemisia tridentata	5.7	18.6
Opuntia erinacea	0.4	0
Purshia glandulosa	0	0.6
Ephedra viridis	0	T
Total herb cover	1.2	0.0
Total cover, all plants	30.5	35.6

*Weather data for the pinyon station given in table I is for this stand.

The pinyon zone as described above is floristically similar to that found throughout Nevada and parts of Utah as well as portions of the eastern slope of the Sierra Nevada. This zone in the White Mountains is of special interest because it occurs at a higher elevation than elsewhere in the Southwest.

In one canyon on the west slope (Lone Tree Creek) trees of *Pinus ponderosa* may be found between the elevations of 7000 and 7800 feet. The presence of this species in such an arid location is anomalous; however, on the east slope of the Sierra individuals of ponderosa pine extend far down into the desert scrub vegetation along well-watered sites.

SUBALPINE FOREST ZONE (9500 TO 11,500 FT.)

The pinyon woodland rarely contacts the subalpine forest. Usually, a treeless, sage-dominated vegetation separates the two communities. This same sage-brush vegetation may continue, in places, uninterrupted by tree cover into areas above the potential limits of tree growth. As stated earlier, between the elevations of 6000 and 10,800 feet (to 12,800 if *Artemisia arbuscula* is considered) sagebrush forms the groundmass upon which other communities are superimposed.

Plate 4 illustrates some of the variability in vegetation found in the lower subalpine landscape. The light, smooth-appearing area is sagebrush-dominated

(*A. tridentata*). In the foreground is a talus slope of quartzitic sandstone. Such rocky, unstable habitats are frequent in the subalpine zone and are usually populated by such shrub species as *Holodiscus microphyllus, Chamaebatiaria millefolium,* and *Ribes cereum.* The dark shrubs (except those on the topmost center which are subalpine pines) on the light soil (Poleta limestone) in the background are *Cercocarpus ledifolius.* This species is abundant on many south-facing slopes in the lower regions of the subalpine zone where it forms almost pure stands.

The White Mountains are most noted because of the subalpine bristlecone-limber pine forest. The bristlecone pine (*P. longaeva*) has proven to be a tree of considerable botanical interest in addition to its utility in bioclimatic interpretation (Schulman, 1958; Fritts, 1966, 1969; LaMarche and Mooney, 1967; Ferguson, 1968).

The bristlecone pine forest is best developed on soils derived from Reed dolomite. This apparent edaphic restriction of the forest is often striking (Pl. 5) and has been the object of recent research (Mooney *et al.,* 1962; Wright, 1963; Wright and Mooney, 1965). There is in general an inverse relationship between

TABLE IV

PERCENT PLANT COVER IN FOUR SUBALPINE PLANT COMMUNITIES

Species	Aspen* forest 9,600 ft.	Bristlecone pine forest on dolomite 11,200 ft.	Bristlecone limber pine on granite 10,500 ft.	Sagebrush community sandstone 10,400 ft.
Trees				
Pinus longaeva	0	29.1	11.1	0
Pinus flexilis	0	0	7.3	0
Populus tremuloides	44.2	0	0	0
Shrubs				
Artemisia tridentata	12.2	0	4.4	15.9
Chamaebatiaria millefolium	0	0	0	0.9
Chrysothamnus viscidiflorus	0	1.0	0	0
Ribes cereum	0	0.2	0	0
Herbs				
Stipa comata	1.1	0	0	0
S. sp.	0.7	0	0	0
Festuca brachyphylla	0.5	0.1	0	0
Senecio integerrimus	0.4	0	0	0
Selaginella watsoni	0.4	0	0	0
Penstemon heterodoxus	0.2	0	0	0
Muhlenbergia richardsonis	T	0.1	0	0
Arabis inyoensis	T	0	0	0
Koeleria cristata	2.7	0.5	T	0.5
Linanthus nuttallii	1.1	0.8	0.4	2.1

Species	Aspen* forest 9,600 ft.	Bristlecone pine forest on dolomite 11,200 ft.	Bristlecone limber pine on granite 10,500 ft.	Sagebrush community sandstone 10,400 ft.
Sitanion hystrix	0.5	T	0	0.8
Poa incurva	0.2	0	0	0
Carex eleocharis	0.1	0	0	0
Gayophytum nuttallii	0.1	0	0	0
Arenaria kingii	0	0.5	1.2	0.9
Phlox covillei	0	0.7	0	0
Antennaria rosea	0	0.1	0	0
Erigeron pygmaeus	0	0.6	0	0
Poa rupicola	0	T	0.1	0
Leptodactylon pungens	0	1.0	0.3	3.2
Cymopterus cinerarius	0	T	0.1	0
Astragalus kentrophyta	0	T	0	0
Haplopappus acaulis	0	0.3	0	0
Oxytropis parryi	0	0.5	0	0
Hymenoxys cooperi	0	0	0.2	0.3
Vegetative grass	0	0	0.3	0.8
Stipa pinetorum	0	0	0.2	0.7
Eriogonum ovalifolium	0	0	0.1	0.8
Erigeron clokeyi	0	0	0.1	0.1
Total cover, all plants	64.4	35.5	25.8	27.0

*Data for this stand from Strain, 1964.

the density of bristlecone pines and the density of sagebrush. On dolomite the pines are well developed and sagebrush is virtually absent. On soils derived from Campito quartzitic sandstone, the reverse is true. A competitive exclusion could, in part, explain this relationship; however, differences in the nutrient requirements and water relations of these species must also be involved in these patterns (Wright and Mooney, 1965).

In the most well-developed bristlecone pine forests on dolomite shrub cover is poor, amounting to an average of less than 7 percent. These "forests" are usually quite open, and the trees generally cover less than one-sixth of the soil surface. Seeds of bristlecone pine are not produced in great profusion every year, and seedlings are even rarer; however, bristlecone pines of all sizes may be found in most stands, indicating adequate reproduction, considering the potential age span of individuals (in excess of 4600 years). The oldest individuals are found on the poorest sites, usually low-elevation, south-facing slope sites with thin soils, a fact noted by Schulman (1954), Wright (1963), and LaMarche (1969).

Herbs which are particularly frequent in this forest on dolomite are *Erigeron clokeyi, Arenaria kingii* var. *glabrescens, Eriogonum gracilipes,* and *Haplopappus acaulis.* Characteristic shrubs in addition to the sparse sagebrush are *Chrysothamnus viscidiflorus* and *Haplopappus suffruticosus.*

Bristlecone pine is also present on soils derived from sandstone and granite. However, on these soils it is poorly developed and usually occurs only on moist north- and west-facing slopes. It is sagebrush that provides the dominant cover on the sandstone and granite soils (an average of 17 percent on the latter). The most abundant herbs of this high-elevation sage community are *Koeleria cristata, Arenaria kingii* var. *glabrescens, Leptodactylon pungens, Linanthus nuttallii,* and *Sitanion hystrix.*

The distribution of limber pine (*Pinus flexilis*) is not entirely coincident with that of bristlecone pine. The greatest abundance of limber pine is on granitically derived soils in favorably moist sites. It is very poorly developed on dolomite. Further, limber pine is not found in abundance above 11,000 feet, whereas bristlecone pine extends as a forest at least to 11,500 feet.

Forests of aspen (*Populus tremuloides*) are also found in certain localities of the subalpine zone (Pl. 6). The great majority of stands are located on the east slope of the range in mesic sites; however, dwarf trees are found in localized exposed sites on the west slope. These latter trees have been found to be genetic dwarfs (Strain, 1964). The moist-site aspen stands are probably one of the most productive communities in the White Mountains (Table IV).

At the north end of the range, on the east slope at the head of Cabin Creek, there is a rather extensive but quite isolated stand of lodgepole pine (*Pinus murrayana*). A detailed study of the restriction of this Sierran species to this particular isolated habitat would be of value.

There is evidence that timberline position has changed in the past several thousands years. The very dry and cold climate of the subalpine zone of the White Mountains does not produce a particularly favorable environment for decomposer organisms. Further, the wood of the slow-growing bristlecone pine is very dense and resinous and is quite resistant, either dead or alive, to attacking organisms. The result of this is that dead trees, standing or fallen, are more subject to erosion by snow blast than to decay. Large trees which died several thousands of years ago can be found at elevations exceeding those where mature living trees now grow—indicating a downward shift of timberline in the recent past, presumably correlated with post-glacial climatic change (Pl. 7) (LaMarche and Mooney, 1967).

The general and average conditions existing within the subalpine zone have been given above. Illustrations of the type of specific variation dependent on such conditions as geological substrate are indicated in Table IV.

ALPINE TUNDRA (11,500 FT. TO THE SUMMIT, 14,246 FT.)

Alpine tundra is generally considered to be the vegetation zone above the limits of tree growth. This definition is somewhat hard to apply in the White Mountains since in many instances the herb and shrub components of the vegetation are quite independent of tree distribution. Shrub and herb elements of the low elevation bristlecone pine forest, for example, can grow considerably above the limits of tree growth on sandstone soils. Further, herbaceous elements which have their centers of distribution at elevations considerably above the limits of tree growth extend down into the forest on dolomite soils. The alpine tundra can be characterized, however, if one recognizes these anomalies and considers primarily centers of distribution rather than limits of tree growth.

One of the most distinctive and extensively represented alpine communities is the dolomitic barren vegetation (Pl. 8). The plant cover on dolomite above tree growth is poor, usually amounting to less than 10 percent. Two predominant species are *Eriogonum gracilipes,* which is characteristic of this community, and *Phlox covillei,* which is also extensively found in alpine communities of other soil types (Table V). *Erigeron pygmaeus* is also generally represented.

Another widely represented community is the fell-field (Pl. 9), which is

TABLE V

PERCENT PLANT COVER IN THREE ALPINE COMMUNITIES

	White Mt. Peak pyramid 13,700 ft.	Dolomite barrens, 11,800 ft.	Fell-field* granite, 12,700 ft.
Herbs			
Erigeron vagus	0.40	0	0.52
Festuca brachyphylla	0.56	0	0
Calyptridium umbellatum	0.24	0	0
Polemonium chartaceum	0.28	0	0
Eriogonum gracilipes	0	1.32	0
Poa rupicola	0	2.00	0
Sitanion hystrix	0	0.36	0.96
Phlox covillei	0	6.52	0
Erigeron pygmaeus	0	0.92	0
Draba sierrae	0	0.28	0.48
Arenaria kingii	0	0.64	0
Castilleja nana	0	0.20	0
Eriogonum ovalifolium	0	0	6.16
Carex helleri	0	0	0.24
Trifolium monoense	0	0	27.64
Selaginella watsoni	0	0	0.68
Haplopappus apargioides	0	0	1.04
Koeleria cristata	0	0	11.12
Lewisia pygmaea	0	0	0.08
Potentilla pennsylvanica	0	0	0.20
Total cover, all plants	1.48	12.24	50.08

*Weather data for the alpine station given in Table 1 is for this stand.

found characteristically on granitic substrates above 12,000 feet elevation. Plant cover can be quite high, covering all of the available soil (Table V). One particularly predominant species is *Trifolium monoense*. This species, so generally abundant in the alpine, is nevertheless not present on the dolomitic barrens. *Eriogonum ovalifolium,* rather than the similar *E. gracilipes* of the barrens, is one of the most common cushion-plants of the fell-fields. Grasses and sedges are abundant. Some of the most numerous grasses are the same species found at elevations as low as the pinyon woodland. (e.g., *Koeleria cristata, Sitanion hystrix*). However, these low- and high-elevation populations are almost certainly physiologically differentiated (Klikoff, 1966).

The alpine vegetation of the peak pyramid is extremely sparse (Table V); however, it is of interest since three of the species found are restricted to elevations above 13,000 feet: *Phoenicaulis eurycarpa, Polemonium chartaceum,* and *Erigeron vagus.* Their presence indicates the high alpine. The sparse soil development and the instability of the substrate preclude a greater development of vegetation.

Active as well as fossil frost features (Mitchell *et al.*, 1966) produce unusual vegetation patterning in limited areas. Other localized alpine habitats have specialized communities; for example, massive rock outcrops, late snowbank areas and springs (*loc. cit.*).

ACKNOWLEDGMENTS

Appreciation is expressed to the National Science Foundation for support of portions of this study. The personnel of the White Mountain Research Station lent generous assistance. G. St. Andre, B. R. Strain, and R. D. Wright collaborated in the field surveys. Albert Hill kindly provided all of the photographs.

Literature Cited

Billings, W. D. 1951. Vegetational zonation in the Great Basin of western North America. Intern. Union Biol. Sc. France, Ser. B, 9: 101–122.

———— and J. H. Thompson. 1957. Composition of a stand of old bristlecone pine in the White Mountains of California. Ecology 38: 158–160.

Brayton, R., and H. A. Mooney. 1966. Population variability of *Cercocarpus* in the White Mountains of California as related to habitat. Evol. 20: 383–391.

Ferguson, C. W. 1968. Bristlecone pine: science and esthetics. Science 159: 839–846.

Fritts, H. C. 1966. Growth-rings of trees: their correlation with climate. Science 154: 973–979.

————. 1969. Bristlecone pine in the White Mountains of California. Growth and ring width characteristics. Papers of the Laboratory of Tree-ring Research, No. 4, Tucson, Ariz.

Klikoff, L. G. 1966. Temperature dependence of the mitochondrial oxidation rates of several plant species found on the west slope of the Sierra Nevada. Bull. Ecol. Soc. Amer. 47: 192.

LaMarche, V. C., Jr. 1964. Recent denudation of the Reed Dolomite, White Mountains, California. Ph.D. Thesis, Harvard Univ., 101 pp.

————. 1968. Rates of slope degradation as determined from botanical evidence, White Mountains, California. U.S. Geol. Surv. Prof. Paper 352–I: 341–377.

————. 1969. Environment in relation to age of bristlecone pines. Ecology 50: 53–59.

———— and H. A. Mooney. 1967. Altithermal timberline advance in western United States. Nature 213: 980–982.

Mitchell, R. S., V. C. LaMarche, Jr., and R. M. Lloyd. 1966. Alpine vegetation and active frost features of Pellisier Flats, White Mountains, California. Amer. Midl. Nat. 75: 516–525.

Mooney, H. A. 1966. Influence of soil type on the distribution of two closely related species of *Erigeron*. Ecology 47: 950–958.

————, G. St. Andre, and R. D. Wright. 1962. Alpine and subalpine vegetation patterns in the White Mountains of California. Amer. Midl. Nat. 68: 257–273.

Schulman, E. 1954. Longevity under adversity in conifers. Science 119: 395–399.

————. 1958. Bristlecone pine, oldest known living thing. Nat. Geogr. Mag. 113: 355–372.

St. Andre, G., H. A. Mooney, and R. D. Wright. 1965. The pinyon woodland zone in the White Mountains of California. Amer. Midl. Nat. 73: 225–239.

Strain, B. R. 1964. Physiological and morphological variability of local quaking aspen clones. Ph.D. Thesis, Univ. of Calif., Los Angeles.

Wright, R. D. 1963. Some ecological studies on bristlecone pine in the White Mountains of California. Ph.D. Thesis, Univ. of Calif., Los Angeles.

Wright, R. D. and H. A. Mooney. 1965. Substrate-oriented distribution of bristlecone pine in the White Mountains of California. Amer. Midl. Nat. 73: 257–284.

PHYTOGEOGRAPHY AND COMPARATIVE FLORISTICS
By Richard S. Mitchell

In the Eocene and Oligocene the vegetation of western North America closely resembled present-day plant assemblages of Central America and Southeast Asia. Genera of warm-temperate and subtropical climates, such as *Sabalites*, *Cinnamonum*, and *Ficus*, were common elements of the flora of the California-Oregon region. Desert and semi-arid regions were not characteristic of inland areas as they are today, but with cooling and drying trends associated with the upper Oligocene (Dorf, 1960), xeromorphic types of vegetation became more prevalent in North America.

During the Miocene, there were two major types of vegetation in western North America (Axelrod, 1950, 1958). The present Great Basin was largely populated by the northern elements of the Arcto-Tertiary flora, whereas the

Sonoran-Mohavean region was vegetated by plants whose ancestors evolved in drier, tropical uplands (Madro-Tertiary flora). Drainage patterns had their origins in areas now in the Sierra Nevada rainshadow, and flow was westward toward the sea across a region of relatively low relief. The drier regions extended westward to the area which now corresponds roughly with the Sierran crest, while more mesic environments extended from there to the Pacific. Axelrod (1950) stated that "In the transition region of central Nevada, species of the Arcto-Tertiary and Madro-Tertiary floras formed an overlapping mosaic of vegetation types in an area of moderate relief." This broad ecotone contained northern elements with modern Sierran and Rocky Mountain distributions super-imposed upon live-oak woodlands and mixed with sclerophylls and subtropical scrub. The area which is now the White Mountains was in the north-south eco-tone and was also at the western border of the drier area with more mesic slopes and hills toward the coast.

The Pliocene brought an increasing trend toward aridity, and although large deserts were not present in the area which they now occupy, many desert genera and species were present in woodland, chaparral, sage, and thorn-scrub associa-tions. It was during this period that most of the eastern genera and those with Asiatic affinities were eliminated from western floras. Much of the woodland and chaparral were also disappearing from the present Great Basin and desert areas. Many forest elements characteristic of the Rocky Mountains, which had been wider ranging, either became restricted to higher elevations and riparian areas or died out. Two such species persisting in the White Mountains are *Populus angustifolia* and *Betula occidentalis*. Oak woodland became restricted to areas to the south and the east, and toward the California coast. In the Great Basin it was largely replaced by pinyon-juniper, sagebrush, and grassland.

With the onset of the Pleistocene, factors affecting plant distribution in the California-Nevada region became increasingly complex. The uplift of the Sierra Nevada (including the rise of the Inyo-White Mountain ranges) provided a highly diversified terrain and new, high-elevation habitats in which relics of mesic environments could survive. Northern species then migrated southward at higher elevations, extending their ranges up to 800 miles. The influx of north-ern elements was largely in the Sierra Nevada, as its western slopes were re-ceiving most of the precipitation which had formerly been distributed over the Southwest. Since their origin, the White Mountains, only 30–40 miles east across the Owens Valley from the Sierra Nevada, have been under the severest influence of the Sierran rainshadow. Thus, it is not surprising that some of the most common elements of the eastern Sierran flora, such as *Pinus jeffreyi*, can grow within 25 miles of the White Mountains and yet not occur there.

In the White Mountains, as well as in adjacent transmontane ranges such as the Inyo and Sweetwater mountains, extinction rates and evolutionary processes were undoubtedly accelerated during extreme environmental changes. In addi-tion to the oscillation of pluvial periods, accompanied by glaciation at high levels, the restriction of precipitation almost entirely to alpine snow must have created habitats unlike any to which the vegetation had previously been exposed. The proximity of these young ranges to the Sierran escarpment predisposed great loss in the diversity of their vegetation, and brought about the characteristic zonation of vegetation seen there today.

There are striking omissions in the flora of the White Mountains, which must be attributed to the severity of past and present climatic and physiographic conditions. Among these are the lack of *Abies,* and the complete absence of members of Fagaceae, Ericaceae, Verbenaceae, Cucurbitaceae, Lauraceae, Berberidaceae, Limnanthaceae, Oxalidaceae, Hippocastanaceae, Rhamnaceae, Guttiferae, and Pyrolaceae. In addition, the truly aquatic flora of the range is limited to three species.

COMPARATIVE FLORISTICS
ALPINE ZONE

The alpine vegetation zone of the White Mountains is perhaps the most interesting in terms of plant migration. Since alpine habitats were lacking in the region prior to the Pleistocene, a high percentage of species presently occurring above timberline must have migrated in from other areas. The two largest and most likely sources of alpine immigrants are the Sierra Nevada and the Colorado Rockies. It is fortunate that good checklists of alpine plants are available from these areas for comparison (Sharsmith, 1940; Weber and Scott-Williams, 1965).

Timberline in most parts of the White Mountains is at approximately 11,500 feet, the upper altitudinal distribution of *Pinus longaeva* and *P. flexilis.* Although the alpine zone has many characteristic species, a number of its shrubs and cespitose perennials are also present in the bristlecone forest, but in smaller numbers. In the White Mountains there are approximately 125 species and varieties which are characteristically alpine, and there are some 75 more which are frequently found above timberline. These 200 taxa have been used as a basis for the comparative study which follows.

The number of taxa in the checklists for the Sierra Nevada and Colorado Rockies is strikingly similar. Sharsmith (1940) recognizes about 200 truly alpine plants in his text on the Sierra Nevada but reports over 325 taxa in the annotated checklist. Weber and Scott-Williams report 313 alpine taxa from Colorado, and the numbers of families and genera are also equivalent to the Sierran study (Table VI). The White Mountains, with 200 alpine species, show considerable floristic diversity considering their smaller size and more recent orogeny.

Boreal element. Species with montane-boreal affinities are not conspicuous in the White Mountain alpine flora, but two common grasses which might be categorized in this way are *Deschampsia caespitosa* and *Phleum alpinum.* The ubiquitous fern, *Cystopteris fragilis,* reaches what is probably its altitudinal extreme at 13,000 feet on Pellisier Flats, where the rhizomes grow under the southeast faces of boulders and the fronds die back for much of the year. A number of montane-boreal elements reach their upper limits well above treeline (e.g., species of *Ribes, Potentilla, Pedicularis,* etc.).

Arctic-alpine elements. There has long been controversy over the usefulness and historical accuracy of separating arctic elements from northern Cordilleran ones (Hultén, 1937); however, this alpine flora will be even further broken down in hopes of reflecting more recent origins of the floristic components. In Table VIII, species with alpine distributions are listed either as "Arctic-Alpine," "Sierran," "Northwestern," or as occurring from the Rocky Mountains westward. These species occupy part of the range of Chaney's (1944) "West American element," which extends from near the Bering Straits down the west coast of Canada and follows the Sierra Nevada and Rocky Mountain chains southward nearly to Mexico. Taxa which are listed as strictly "Arctic-Alpine" are those with arctic tolerance whose origins and evolutionary affinities lie with circumpolar stock. Some of these have broad ranges extending across the Bering Straits to Eurasia.

Two Arctic-alpine species which clearly have Asian centers of distribution are *Androsace septentrionalis* and *Sedum rosea*. These species should probably be considered more Asiatic-alpine than arctic, and their present distribution is most easily explained by a Bering land-bridge hypothesis. Among the truly Arctic elements of the flora which may have had alpine origins are: *Festuca ovina* var. *brachyphylla, Carex capitata, Oxyria digyna, Sibbaldia procumbens,* and *Gentiana tenella*.

The Cordilleran species considered here may be roughly divided into a western coastal assemblage, extending from the Bering Straits south to the Sierra Nevada of California, and a group with continental affinities centering in the Rocky Mountains.

Western Cordilleran elements. Three species of probable Beringian origin which occur in California's White Mountains are: *Cerastium beeringianum, Stellaria crispa,* and *Draba stenoloba*. A list of other arctic and sub-arctic Cordilleran species includes: *Calamagrostis purpurascens, Carex albo-nigra, Draba oligosperma, Potentilla diversifolia, Erigeron compositus,* and *Antennaria rosea*.

Some characteristic Pacific Cordilleran elements extending down the Sierra to the White Mountains are: *Phoenicaulis eurycarpa, Potentilla flabelliformis, Astragalus whitneyi, Gentiana newberryi, Penstemon confertus, Mimulus primuloides,* and *M. coccineus*. Of these, *Phoenicaulis* has a curious discontinuous distribution to Idaho, and several of the other species occur also in the Rocky Mountains.

The following species may have northern ancestors but are characteristically Sierran and are found only in the Sierra Nevada and adjacent ranges. Several of these were thought to be Sierran endemics until discovered in the White mountains. They are: *Carex helleri, C. subnigricans, Draba sierrae, Lupinus breweri, Dodocatheon redolens, Erigeron pygmaeus, Raillardella argentea,* and *Hulsea algida*.

Continental Cordilleran elements. Continental alpine species, with distributions from the Rocky Mountains westward, are of three general types. First, there are the widespread species common in most alpine regions of the west. Examples are: *Sitanion hystrix, Calyptridium umbellatum* var. *caudiciferum, Astragalus lentiginosus, Leptodactylon pungens,* and *Linanthus nuttallii*.

Plants probably of Great Basin origin are: *Selaginella watsoni, Ivesia gordonii, I. lycopodioides, Podistera nevadensis, Cryptantha nubigena,* and numerous others.

Finally, there are species which are typically of the Rocky Mountains, but which have outliers that reach their western limits in the White Mountains and the alpine Sierra Nevada. A partial list of these species follows: *Poa rupicola, Stipa pinetorum, S. occidentalis, Carex vernacula, C. phaeocephala, C. haydeniana, C. festivella, Rumex pauciflorus, Eriogonum ovalifolium, Lewisia pygmaea, Arabis lyallii, Ribes cereum, Astragalus kentrophyta, Linum lewisii, Phlox caespitosa, Mimulus tilingii, Agoseris glauca, Erigeron vagus, Haplopappus macronema, Antennaria media.*

Alpine endemics. Half of the endemic taxa of the White Mountains are found in the alpine zone. The following is a list of alpine elements endemic to the White Mountain and Inyo ranges, with the exception of *Trifolium monoense* which is also found north to the Bridgeport area: *Eriogonum gracilipes, Heuchera duranii, Horkelia hispidula, Ivesia lycopodioides* var. *scandularis, Astragalus lentiginosus* var. *semotus,* and *Trifolium monoense.*

Derivation of the alpine flora. Sixty-two percent of the alpine taxa of the White Mountains may be found in the Sierra Nevada. By contrast (Table VI), only 28 percent of White Mountain alpine plants are present in the Rocky Mountains, and only 11 percent are common to all three regions. Since the 11 percent common to all could have migrated via the Sierra Nevada, only 17 percent of the White Mountain alpine flora needs explanation in terms of dispersal across the Great Basin. Indeed, a higher percentage of the alpine flora may have reached the White Mountains by this route, since Rocky Mountain elements are found commonly throughout the Great Basin ranges. It is probable, however, that the White Mountains received the greatest number of alpine species (up to 65 percent) from the nearby Sierra Nevada, once both ranges had attained a height to be invaded by north-Cordilleran and arctic-alpine species.

TABLE VI

ALPINE FLORAS. COMPARISON OF THE SIERRA NEVADA AND COLORADO ROCKIES ALPINE FLORAS AND THEIR RELATIONSHIP TO THAT OF THE WHITE MOUNTAINS.

	Sierra Nevada	Colorado Rockies
Families	34	36
Genera	127 ± 3	128
Species and varieties	328 ± 5	313
Taxa in common with White Mountains	125	57
Percent White Mountain alpine elements shared	62%	28%
White Mountain taxa characteristic of each area	51%	17%

Taxa common to all three ranges: 23 = 11% of the White Mountains alpine flora.

WOODLAND AND DESERT FLORAS

Comparison with the Charleston Mountains. Clokey (1951) provided a comprehensive flora of a Great Basin range in his treatment of the Charleston Mountains of Nevada. This range, north of Las Vegas, predates the Sierra Nevada by about four million years (Clokey, *ibid.*). Older inland ranges such as the Charleston Mountains were relatively dry during the Pliocene but have served as refugia for coniferous and oak forests up to the present. Except for relatively brief spans of Pleistocene cooling, when lakes occurred in the area, the Charleston Mountains flora has remained isolated in an island-like fashion since the Pliocene. With their mixture of North American and Mexican Cordilleran elements, this range and others like it have undoubtedly been "spawning grounds" for new montane-desert species which are now more widespread.

Since the area covered by the Charleston Mountains flora is about four times that of the White Mountains, it would be expected that the total number of taxa present would also be greater. This turns out not to be the case. The numbers of families and genera represented in the Charleston Mountains are slightly higher, but the number of species and varieties is over 100 fewer than in the White Mountains (Table VII). The White Mountains undoubtedly owe a much richer high-montane flora to their proximity to the Sierra Nevada, as discussed above, and this group of taxa alone accounts for a large share of the difference in species numbers between the ranges.

TABLE VII

COMPARISON OF THE FLORISTIC COMPOSITIONS OF THE WHITE MOUNTAINS OF CALIFORNIA AND NEVADA, THE CHARLESTON MOUNTAINS OF NEVADA, AND KERN COUNTY, CALIFORNIA.

	White Mountains	Charleston Mountains	Kern County
Families	76	82	120
Genera	298	324	573
Species and varieties	811	699	1875
White Mtn. taxa shared	811	279	331
Percent White Mtn. flora	100%	31%	40%
Number of endemics	13	31	17

The flora of the Charleston Mountains has few components from the much younger Sierra Nevada. Its floristic affinities lie with the Rocky Mountains and Great Basin desert ranges, as well as with the Mexican Cordillera. Of the 30 percent of the White Mountain flora shared with the Charleston Mountains, many species are desert and sagebrush-associated taxa of wide distribution in the western United States, while a few are relics of a widespread inland Pliocene flora which reached its western limits in eastern California.

The coniferous flora of the Charleston Mountains is richer than that of the White Mountains in having *Abies concolor* and four juniper species rather than one. The greater diversity of gymnosperms and the persistence of oak woodland both point to more mesic and ancient habitats at middle and upper altitudes in the Charleston Mountains.

The distribution of *Abies* alone, however, would not be sufficient to warrant such a statement, since it is known to occur in California's Chocolate Mountains and some other very dry ranges.

Examples of striking parallels in species from the Great Basin and desert areas are found between the Charleston and White Mountains in the Boraginaceae: *Cryptantha barbigera, C. circumscissa, C. confertiflora, C. echinella, C. flavoculata, C. gracilis, C. jamesii, C. micrantha, C. nevadensis, C. pterocarya, C. recurvata, C. utahensis, C. virginensis, Pectocarya setosa,* and *Plagiobothrys jonesii;* in the Cactaceae: *Echinocactus polyancistrus, Echinocereus engelmannii, E. triglochidiatus, Opuntia basilaris,* and *O. erinacea;* and in the Rosaceae: *Cercocarpus intricatus, C. ledifolius, Chamaebatiaria millefolium, Cowania mexicana, Holodiscus microphyllus, Peraphyllum ramosissimum, Petrophytum caespitosum, Purshia glandulosa, P. tridentata,* and *Rosa woodsii.*

A number of the species listed above extend to the Rocky Mountains, and some of them are characteristic of the drier Rockies and their foothills. Although the Charleston Mountains could possibly have served as an intermediate station for dispersal between the Rocky Mountains and the southern Sierra Nevada, it is far more likely that species common to all three areas were once widespread and are now extinct in intervening areas. The flora of the White Mountains has apparently increased in diversity through recent immigration of species, whereas the Charleston Mountains flora has retained more relics and nearly three times the number of endemics.

Comparison with Kern County. Kern County, California, in addition to being a much larger area than the White Mountains, is far from wholly montane. The larger number of taxa in this flora (Table VII) reflects the extent and diversity of terrain covered. In his treatment of Kern County, Twisselmann (1967) lists five floras which comprise the larger part of its vegetation. These are: the Sierra Nevada flora, southern California mountain flora, San Joaquin Valley flora, Coast Range flora, and Mojave Desert flora (including Sonoran elements). Under these headings are also found some Great Basin species.

Although the White Mountains share 40 percent of their flora with Kern County, the floristic provinces are quite unlike. Only Mohavean and Sierran elements are shared to any great extent. Because of transverse ranges, such as the Tehachapi Mountains, many elements of the Coast Range and San Joaquin Valley floras occur there, which are totally absent from the White Mountains. The three major associations shared by these areas are shadscale, pinyon-juniper, and sagebrush. Many plants common to both areas are listed in the Kern flora as characteristically occurring with woody dominants absent from the White Mountains. For example, some species listed as typical of Jeffrey pine forest are: *Muhlenbergia asperifolia, Carex douglasii, Astragalus whitneyi, Leptodactylon pungens* var. *hallii,* and *Chrysothamnus viscidiflorus* ssp. *pumilus.* In the White Mountains these same species are to be found in habitats as unlike as alkali sink (*Muhlenbergia*) and alpine meadow (*Carex*). A large number of species listed in the Kern County flora as typical of creosote bush scrub are also common in the White Mountains where creosote bush is absent. Thus, a number of species are held in common by the two floras, but the associations in which they are found are different.

Some important plant associations present in Kern County but missing in the White Mountains are: Jeffrey and yellow pine forest, freshwater marshes and vernal pools, creosote bush scrub, red fir forest, chaparral, oak woodland, and Sonoran grassland. The zone of importance in the White Mountains which is not shared with Kern County is the bristlecone pine forest.

ORIGIN OF THE WHITE MOUNTAINS FLORISTIC ASSEMBLAGE

Present species distributions do not, of course, give many reliable clues to past distributions. Modern habitat preferences, however, coupled with both physiological and morphological adaptations to environment, may often link a species to certain known conditions and associations of the past. The tabulation in Table VIII was derived in part from paleobotanical information (Axelrod, 1958; Chaney, 1940; Wolfe, 1969) but is mostly a reflection of present centers of distribution. Species of the White Mountains flora were considered individually and indicated under the distributional heading considered most likely to reflect the area from which they came. Some headings, such as "Cosmopolitan" and "Rockies west," are necessarily vague, as past migration routes of such species are always highly questionable. An explanation of each of the distribution headings in Table VIII follows:

Cosmopolitan species. Those which range widely over the United States and frequently to other continents.

Rockies west. Species found characteristically in the Rocky Mountains but which also range north or across the Great Basin to California's Sierra Nevada. Western Cordilleran elements are excluded.

Arctic-Alpine. Plants from known circumpolar stock which occur only at high altitudes. This category includes only a small portion of the total alpine flora of the White Mountains.

Northwestern. Western Cordilleran elements which range northward along the Sierra Nevada into Oregon, Washington, Canada, or even to the Bering Straits. Some of these also reach the Rocky Mountains, but are not centered there.

Sierran. Species characteristic of the Sierra Nevada of California. Some are endemics, but most extend into adjacent ranges.

Cismontane California. All species concentrated on the west side of the Sierra Nevada including Coast Ranges, San Joaquin Valley, and western foothill species.

Great Basin. Species from several plant associations including sagebrush, shadscale, montane coniferous forest, and alpine meadows, but all characteristic of the cool-desert, interior drainage system of western North America.

Sonoran-Mohavean. Warm desert species which may have invaded the

White Mountains before the relatively recent differentiation of the Sonoran and Mojave deserts.

Desert ranges. Montane species which do not center in the Sierra Nevada or the Rocky Mountains. They may range from southern California mountains to Texas and Mexico, but most are restricted to a few warm-desert ranges.

Inyo-Mono. Endemics in the two-county area bordering the Nevada line. Some of them extend into Esmeralda County, Nevada, in the White Mountains near Montgomery Pass. Most are centered around the Owens Valley on the eastern slopes of the Sierra Nevada and the western slopes of the White Mountains.

White Mountains endemics. Species known only from the White Mountain range with the possible exception of a few outliers in the Inyo Mountains a few miles away.

Introduced. Foreign adventives, planted trees, or American weedy species known to have spread into California from other regions.

TABLE VIII

PRESENT CENTERS OF DISTRIBUTIONS OF WHITE MOUNTAINS SPECIES. NUMERALS REPRESENT THE NUMBER OF SPECIES PER GENUS WHICH IS CHARACTERISTIC OF EACH GENERALIZED DISTRIBUTION PATTERN.

	Cosmopolitan	Rockies West	Arctic-Alpine	Northwestern	Sierran	Cismontane Calif.	Great Basin	Sonoran-Mohavean	Desert Ranges	Inyo-Mono	Endemic-White Mtn.	Introduced	Rare in Calif.
Botrychium	1												
Pellaea		1											
Cheilanthes								3					2
Cystopteris	1												
Woodsia	1												
Equisetum	1	1											
Selaginella							1						1
Pinus		3					2						1
Juniperus							1						
Ephedra							1	1					
Agropyron	2	1											1
Agrostis					1							1	
Blepharidachne							1						

	Cosmopolitan	Rockies West	Arctic-Alpine	Northwestern	Sierran	Cismontane Calif.	Great Basin	Sonoran-Mohavean	Desert Ranges	Inyo-Mono	Endemic-White Mtn.	Introduced	Rare in Calif.
Bouteloua	1												
Bromus		3										5	2
Calamagrostis			1										
Deschampsia				1									
Distichlis		1											
Elymus							2						
Festuca	2		1										
Glyceria	1												
Hesperochloa							1						
Hilaria							1						1
Holcus												1	
Hordeum				1	1							1	
Koeleria	1												
Melica		1			1								
Muhlenbergia	2	1											
Oryzopsis		1					2						1
Phleum			1									1	
Phragmites	1												
Poa		4	2	3	2		1					3	2
Polypogon												2	
Pucciniella												1	
Sitanion		3											
Sporobolus	1	1						1					
Stipa		2	1	1	2					1		1	
Tridens							1						
Trisetum			1										
Carex	4	7	4	7	2		1					3	
Eleocharis	3												
Scirpus	2			1									
Lemna	1												
Juncus	2			5	2		1	1					
Luzula	1												
Asparagus												1	
Calochortus		1								1			1
Fritillaria				2									
Smilacina	1												
Veratrum				1									

	Cosmopolitan	Rockies West	Arctic-Alpine	Northwestern	Sierran	Cismontane Calif.	Great Basin	Sonoran-Mohavean	Desert Ranges	Inyo-Mono	Endemic-White Mtm.	Introduced	Rare in Calif.
Zygadenus							1						
Allium							1	1					
Yucca								1					
Iris	1												
Sisyrinchium				1									
Epipactis		1											
Habenaria				1									
Populus	1			1			1					1	
Salix		2		1		1	3						
Betula		1											
Ulmus												1	
Urtica						1							
Phoradendron							2						
Chorizanthe							1	2					2
Eriogonum		2			6		5	9	5		1		5
Oxyria			1										
Oxytheca							1	1					
Polygonum	1	1											
Rumex		1			2						1	1	
Atriplex		2					3						
Chenopodium	2	2					2		1			1	2
Eurotia		1											
Grayia							1						
Kochia							1						
Monolepis	1												
Salsola												1	
Sarcobatus							1						
Amaranthus	1												
Abronia				1									
Hermidium							1						
Mirabilis							3	1					1
Oxybaphus								1					
Calyptridium		2											
Lewisia		1					1						
Montia					3								1
Arenaria					1	3		1					1
Cerastium			1										

	Cosmopolitan	Rockies West	Arctic-Alpine	Northwestern	Sierran	Cismontane Calif.	Great Basin	Sonoran-Mohavean	Desert Ranges	Inyo-Mono	Endemic-White Mtn.	Introduced	Rare in Calif.
Sagina				1									
Silene					3		1	1					1
Stellaria				2									
Aconitum				2	1								
Aquilegia				1				1					
Clematis		1											
Delphinium					1			1					
Myosorus				1									
Ranunculus		2	1	1									
Thalictrum			2										
Argemone								1					
Eschscholzia								1					
Corydalis	1												
Arabis	1	5		2	1		2	1		5			3
Barbarea	2												
Brassica												1	
Cardamine	1												1
Caulanthus							2	1	1				2
Descurainia				2									
Draba	1	3	1	3			2	1					4
Erysimum							1						1
Halimolobus									2				1
Hutchinsia	1												
Lepidium		1					1	2					
Lesquerella									2				2
Phoenicaulis				1									
Physaria							1						
Rorippa	1	1										1	
Sisymbrium												1	
Stanleya							1	1					1
Streptanthella							1						
Streptanthus							1						
Thelypodium								1	1				
Cleome							1						
Sedum			1										
Heuchera		1									1		1
Parnassia				1									
Philadelphus									1				

	Cosmopolitan	Rockies West	Arctic-Alpine	Northwestern	Sierran	Cismontane Calif.	Great Basin	Sonoran-Mohavean	Desert Ranges	Inyo-Mono	Endemic-White Mtn.	Introduced	Rare in Calif.
Ribes		1		1			3						
Amelanchier					1								
Cercocarpus		1						1					
Chamaebatiaria		1	1										
Cowania		1											
Geum				1									
Holodiscus		1											
Horkelia											1		1
Ivesia							2				1		2
Peraphyllum							1						
Petrophytum		1											1
Physocarpus							1						1
Potentilla	2	1		2	2		4						2
Prunus		1							1				
Purshia							2						
Rosa							1						
Sibbaldia			1										
Astragalus				1	3		4	2	4	1	1		5
Dalea							1	2					
Glycyrrhiza												1	
Lupinus				1			6	2			1		2
Medicago												1	
Melilotus												2	
Oxytropis				2			2						2
Robinia												1	
Trifolium		1		2	1						1	2	1
Vicia		1											
Erodium												1	
Tribulus												1	
Ailanthus												1	
Polygala							1						
Euphorbia		2										1	
Callitriche	1												
Linum	1												
Forsellesia							1	1					1
Acer							1						
Vitis												1	
Malva												1	

	Cosmopolitan	Rockies West	Arctic-Alpine	Northwestern	Sierran	Cismontane Calif.	Great Basin	Sonoran-Mohavean	Desert Ranges	Inyo-Mono	Endemic-White Mtn.	Introduced	Rare in Calif.
Sphaeralcea							1	1					1
Viola	1												
Mentzelia		2			1			2					
Petalonyx								1					1
Sclerocactus								1					1
Echinocereus								1	1				1
Opuntia		1						4					1
Shepherdia		1											
Camissonia							7	2	1				2
Epilobium	2	2		2									
Gayophytum	1	2											
Oenothera					1		1	1			1		1
Angelica							1	1					1
Berula	1												
Cymopterus					1			1	2				1
Lomatium							2	1		1			1
Oxypolis					1								
Podistera							1						
Pteryxia							1						
Sphenosciadium					1								
Cornus				1									
Androsace			1										
Dodocatheon					1								
Menodora								1					
Frasera										1			1
Gentiana	2	1	1										
Apocynum	1			1									
Asclepias	1			1									
Convolvulus												1	
Cuscuta		1		1	1								
Collomia	1												
Eriastrum							1	1	1				
Gilia		1						8	2				2
Gymnosteris				1									
Ipomopsis		1			1			1					
Langloisia								1					
Leptodactylon					1			1					

	Cosmopolitan	Rockies West	Arctic-Alpine	Northwestern	Sierran	Cismontane Calif.	Great Basin	Sonoran-Mohavean	Desert Ranges	Inyo-Mono	Endemic-White Mtn.	Introduced	Rare in Calif.
Linanthus		2						2					
Navarretia							1						
Phlox			1		1		2		1				1
Polemonium					1								1
Emmenanthe						1							
Eucrypta								1					
Hesperochiron							2						
Nama					1		1	1					1
Phacelia		1		1		1	4	4		1			3
Tricardia								1					
Amsinckia						1							
Coldenia								1					
Cryptantha		1			3		4	6	3		1		3
Hackelia				1			1						1
Heliotropium							1						
Lappula	1						1						
Mertensia					1								
Pectocarya							1						
Plagiobothrys									2	1			2
Mentha	1												
Monardella		1			2				1				
Salvia							1	1					1
Stachys					1								
Lycium								1					
Nicotiana		1											
Solanum												1	
Antirrhinum									1				
Castilleja		1		1	2		2						2
Collinsia		1											
Cordylanthus									1				1
Mimulus		4			3			2	1				2
Pedicularis					1								
Penstemon				1	1		2	1	2	4	1		6
Scrophularia									1				
Verbascum												1	
Veronica	3											1	
Orobanche	2							1					1

	Cosmopolitan	Rockies West	Arctic-Alpine	Northwestern	Sierran	Cismontane Calif.	Great Basin	Sonoran-Mohavean	Desert Ranges	Inyo-Mono	Endemic-White Mtn.	Introduced	Rare in Calif.
Plantago												1	
Galium	1	1							3	1			
Sambucus				1									
Symphoricarpos		2											
Valeriana				1									
Nemacladus								2	1				1
Acamptopappus								1					
Achillea		1											
Agoseris		2		1									
Ambrosia	1							1	1				1
Aniscoma								1					
Antennaria		1	1										
Arnica			2	1						1			
Artemisia	1	2		1	1		3	2					
Aster	1		2	2			1						
Bebbia								1					
Brickellia								1	1				1
Calycoseris								1					
Chaenactis		1		1			2	3					3
Chaetadelpha								1					
Chrysothamnus		2	1				1	4		1	2		3
Cirsium		1						1					
Conyza	1												
Crepis		1	1		1					1			1
Eatonella								1					
Encelia								1					
Erigeron		2	2	2			1	1	4				4
Eupatorium			1										
Eriophyllum		1											
Glyptopleura									1				
Gnaphalium		1	1				1						1
Gutierrezia									1				
Haplopappus		1			1		2	2					
Helianthus												1	
Hulsea					1								
Hymenoclea							1						
Hymenopappus						1							

	Cosmopolitan	Rockies West	Arctic-Alpine	Northwestern	Sierran	Cismontane Calif.	Great Basin	Sonoran-Mohavean	Desert Ranges	Inyo-Mono	Endemic-White Mtn.	Introduced	Rare in Calif.
Hymenoxys							1						
Iva	1								1				1
Lactuca												1	
Laphamia										1			1
Layia							1						
Lepidospartum									1				
Leucelene								1					
Lygodesmia								1					
Machaeranthera		1						1	1				1
Malacothrix		1											
Pericome							1						
Psathyrotes								2					
Raillardella			1										
Senecio		2		1	3	1	1	1	1				1
Solidago			1				1	1					
Sonchus												1	
Stephanomeria		3											
Taraxacum												1	
Tetradymia						1	1	1	1				1
Townsendia							1		1				1
Viguiera		1											

It may be seen from Table VIII that White Mountain representatives of some genera have come largely from the Northwest and the Rocky Mountains, whereas species of other genera have strong affinity with southern desert floras. Such genera are often chosen as representatives of Arcto-Tertiary and Madro-Tertiary elements whose species are now found to overlap in range. Among the larger genera with predominantly northern species in the White Mountains are: *Poa, Stipa, Carex, Ranunculus, Draba, Trifolium, Epilobium, Gentiana,* and *Senecio.* Some genera strongly represented by southern desert elements are: *Eriogonum, Astragalus, Gilia, Cryptantha, Penstemon,* and *Chrysothamnus* (Table VIII).

A numerical tabulation of floristic elements of the White Mountains (Table IX) shows that 8 percent of the flora is cosmopolitan and 6 percent is introduced. The combined figure added to 3 percent for species with anomalous distributions gives a total of 17 percent of the flora. For this group it would be extremely difficult to speculate upon geographic routes of dispersal. Of the re-

TABLE IX

NUMERICAL TABULATION OF WHITE MOUNTAINS TAXA IN RELATION TO OVERALL DISTRIBUTION PATTERNS.

Area	Pterid.	Gymnosp.	Monocots	Dicots	Total	Percent Flora
Cosmopolitan	4	0	26	40	70	8%
Rockies West	2	3	27	91	123	15%
Arctic-Alpine	0	0	11	12	23	3%
Northwestern	0	0	25	57	82	10%
Sierran	0	0	10	65	75	9%
Cismontane California	0	0	0	8	8	1%
Great Basin	1	4	13	130	148	18%
Sonoran-Mohavean	3	1	3	116	123	15%
Desert Ranges	0	0	3	60	63	8%
Inyo-Mono	0	0	0	19	19	2%
White Mtns.	0	0	0	13	13	2%
Introduced	0	0	17	31	48	5%
Total Taxa	10	8	135	634	787	97%
				not treated—	24	3%
					811	100%

maining 83 percent the bulk of the species seem to have come from three major distribution centers. Great Basin elements are most prevalent, comprising 18 percent of the flora, whereas species ranging from the Rocky Mountains westward also represent 15 percent of the total number of taxa. If the Sonoran-Mohavean elements (15 percent) are added to related taxa restricted to desert ranges, however, this combined "Madro-Tertiary element" exceeds the Great Basin element alone in its contribution to the White Mountains flora. In sharp contrast to our previous consideration of the alpine zone, the total flora has only 9 percent Sierran elements and 10 percent Northwest Cordilleran. The combination of northwestern, Sierran and arctic-alpine elements yields 22 percent of the total flora which is probably of northern origin. Southern desert elements, including Sonoran-Mohavean neo-endemic and desert range species, total 27 percent. Finally, the largest floristic component represented by combined figures is that which is mostly present farther east. The combined influences of present and past Great Basin floras, including Rocky Mountain species, have undoubtedly been the greatest forces structuring the modern flora of the White Mountains. Although some species ranging from the Rockies westward may have come to the White Mountains via the Sierra Nevada, 33 percent of the flora is represented in the Great Basin and on the slopes of the Rocky Mountains.

In spite of the proximity of the Sierra Nevada, the White Mountains must truly be called a Great Basin desert range whose flora may be characterized in general terms as follows: Sonoran-Mohavean at low altitudes and in the southern part; Great Basin with Rocky Mountain elements from mid-altitudes to the subalpine; and North Cordilleran at high altitudes. Sierran elements are scattered throughout, but are most prevalent in subalpine and alpine areas toward the north end of the range.

One may speculate that the Rocky Mountain elements are mostly relictual from Pliocene times and that northern elements are more recent immigrants from the Sierra Nevada. It is also tempting to postulate that Sonoran-Mohavean elements are recent immigrants from the south.

Thus, the flora of the White Mountains presents the picture of a much depleted Pliocene flora surviving at mid-altitudes, superimposed by a northwestern flora at high altitudes, and encroached upon by warm-desert elements from below.

LITERATURE CITED

Axelrod, D. I. 1950. Evolution of desert vegetation in western North America. (in Studies in Late Tertiary Botany) Carnegie Inst. Wash. Publ. 590: 217–306.

————. 1958. Evolution of the Madro-Tertiary Geoflora. Bot. Rev. 24: 433–509.

Chaney, R. W. 1944. Pliocene floras of California and Oregon. Carnegie Inst. Wash. Publ. 553, 407 p.

Clokey, I. W. 1951. Flora of the Charleston Mountains, Clark County, Nevada. Univ. Calif. Publ. in Botany. 24, 274 p.

Dorf, E. 1960. Climatic changes of the past and present. Am. Sci., 48: 341–364.

Hultén, E. 1937. Outline of the history of arctic and boreal biota during the Quaternary period. Stockholm Press, Stockholm. 168 p.

Sharsmith, C. W. 1940. A contribution to the history of the alpine flora of the Sierra Nevada. Ph.D. Thesis, Univ. of Calif., Berkeley.

Twisselmann, E. C. 1967. A flora of Kern County, California. Wassman Jour. Biol. 25: 1–395.

Weber, W. A., and Elizabeth Scott-Williams. 1965. Checklist of alpine tundra species of vascular plants found in Colorado. Mimeographed. 13 p.

Wolfe, J. A. 1969. Neogene floristic and vegetational history of the Pacific Northwest. Madroño 20: 83–110.

GUIDE TO THE GEOLOGY
By Valmore C. LaMarche Jr.

This section is primarily a guide to published reports, geologic maps, and geologic work in progress. It includes general descriptions of the rock types, their distribution, origin, and geological history, along with discussion of recent events and present-day processes.

GENERAL FEATURES

The White Mountains are formed from a triangular fault block that was elevated and tilted eastward in relatively recent geological time. The block is made up of sedimentary, metamorphic, and coarse-grained igneous rocks, with a thin, patchy cover of lava flows. The steep flanks of the range are abutted by gently sloping alluvial fans that merge downward into the sediments in the adjoining basins.

Two main groups of rocks make up the bedrock core. In the southern part of the range, sedimentary sandstone, shale, limestone, and dolomite are abundant. These rocks are similar to the rocks of the Great Basin ranges to the south and east. In the northern part there are large bodies of granitic rocks. These occur along with metamorphic rocks derived from volcanic deposits and from chert, shale, and sandstone beds. Similar rocks are found in the Sierra Nevada and associated ranges to the north and west.

The major internal structural feature of the range is a broad, south-plunging anticline formed in pre-Cretaceous sedimentary strata. However, there are numerous smaller folds with different orientations. The structure is further complicated by closely spaced faults of several different ages.

Younger rocks of volcanic origin occur mainly on the eastern side and at the extreme northern end of the White Mountains. Basalt flows rest on the eroded surface of the older core rocks, or on lighter-colored flows and ashfall deposits that are interbedded with alluvium and lake deposits.

Superficial deposits in the White Mountains include relatively homogeneous soils, scree, and colluvium derived mainly from underlying and adjacent rocks,

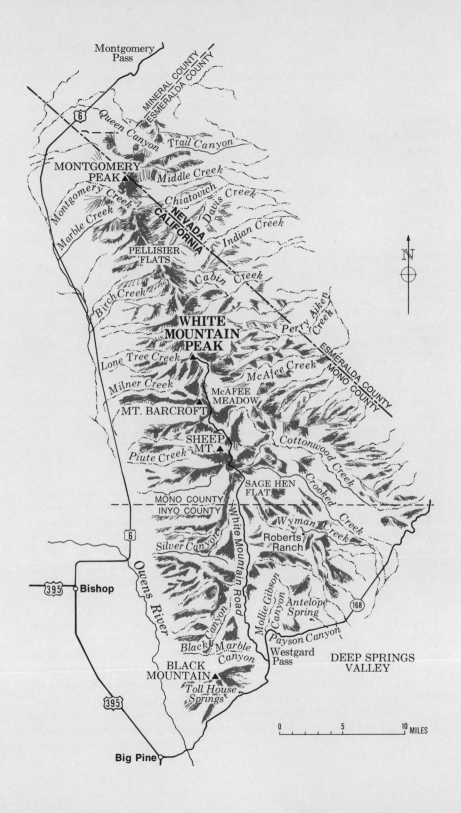

and more heterogeneous stream deposits and glacial till that have been transported considerable distances from their places of origin.

Present-day erosional and depositional processes are conditioned by the high
relief of the range, by the arid to semiarid climate, by the general sparseness of
vegetation, and at high elevations by the low seasonal temperatures. Chemical
weathering and soil formation proceed slowly under these conditions. Mechan-
ical breakdown and transportation of rock debris are relatively important.

GEOLOGICAL MAPS AND REPORTS

A small scale (1:250,000) but up-to-date geological map covering all of the
California portion of the White Mountains is available (California Division of
Mines and Geology, 1967). Adjacent areas in Nevada have also been mapped at
similar scales (Ross, 1961; Albers and Stewart, 1965).

Geological maps of U.S. Geological Survey 15-minute topographic quadrangles (Fig. 1) at a scale of 1:62,500 are available for the southern part of the
range, including the Soldier Pass quadrangle (McKee and Nelson, 1967), the
Blanco Mountain quadrangle (Nelson, 1966*a*), the Waucoba Mountain quadrangle (Nelson, 1966*b*), and the Bishop and the Big Pine quadrangles (Bateman, 1965). A larger-scale (1:48,000) but uncolored version of the Blanco
Mountain map has also been published (Nelson, 1963).

Coverage of the northern half of the range is less complete. A generalized
geologic map of the Mt. Barcroft quadrangle, emphasizing the granitic rocks,
has been published by Emerson (1966). A more detailed map of this quadrangle is in preparation by K. B. Krauskopf (written comm. 1970) and will be
released in the U.S. Geological Survey Geological Quadrangle series. Other
maps in this series are being prepared by D. F. Crowder, M. F. Sheridan, and
P. T. Robinson for the White Mountain Peak, Davis Mountain, and Benton
quadrangles (D. F. Crowder, written comm. 1970). Geological maps at a scale
of 1:24,000 for the west half of the White Mountain Peak quadrangle are available in the U.S. Geological Survey open files (Sheridan and Crowder, 1964).

Other potentially useful maps include older, small-scale geologic maps which
cover the southern (Knopf, 1918) and northern (Anderson, 1937) parts of the
range. Anderson's map is also available at a larger scale (Anderson, 1933).
Geologic maps showing smaller areas have been included in various publications
(Miller, 1928; LaMarche, 1967; McKee and Nash, 1967) and theses (Blanc,
1958; Bryson, 1937; Gallick, 1964; Gangloff, 1963; Hall, 1963; Harris, 1967;
Nash, 1962; Perry, 1955).

The sedimentary strata of the southern White Mountains and northern Inyo
Mountains are geologically important because they include the type section for
rocks of Waucoban (Lower Cambrian) age. The current stratigraphic terminol-
ogy and age assignments for these rocks are based in part on Walcott's (1908)
description, and in part on later additions and modifications by Kirk (*in* Knopf,
1918), Maxson (1935), Nelson (1962), and Stewart (1965, 1966). The Knopf
report remains an excellent general description of the geology of this region,
and contains the most detailed descriptions of many of the stratigraphic units.

The metamorphic rocks of the northern White Mountains have been little studied until very recently, and published information is scarce. The granitic rocks have received more attention. Anderson's (1937) paper invoked a process of "granitization" to explain what he interpreted as relict sedimentary features in some of these rocks, and his conclusions have been widely cited to support this concept. More recently, a magmatic origin has been proposed for the same rocks by Emerson (1966). Krauskopf (1968) has emphasized the complexity of the plutonic history in this area. The younger volcanic and sedimentary rocks of the northern White Mountains are described by Ross (1961).

The White Mountains have not produced important amounts of mineral products. However, small mines have been operated for lead, zinc, gold, silver, mercury, and other metals, and andalusite (for ceramic insulators) was mined near White Mountain Peak. Among the reports dealing with mines and mineral resources of this area are those by Kerr (1932), Norman and Stewart (1951), Ross (1961), Sampson (1940), Tucker and Sampson (1939), and Woodhouse (1951).

AGE RELATIONSHIPS

The rocks of the White Mountains can be divided into three groups on the basis of age: (1) pre-Cretaceous sedimentary, volcanic, and metamorphic rocks; (2) granite rocks, which were emplaced mainly in Jurassic and Cretaceous time; (3) younger volcanic and sedimentary rocks and unconsolidated or semi-consolidated deposits of Tertiary to Recent age.

The pre-Cretaceous rocks include a thick succession of strata of late Precambrian and early Cambrian age. These rocks are exposed throughout the southern part of the range and extended in a discontinuous belt, bordering the granitic batholith along its northeastern margin. The stratigraphic units (with approximate thickness in parentheses) are the Wyman (greater than 9000 feet), the Reed (2000 feet), and the Deep Spring (1500 feet.) Formations of probable Precambrian age, the Campito Formation (3500 feet) of probable Precambrian through Early Cambrian age, and the Early Cambrian Poleta (1200 feet) and the Harkless (2000 feet) Formations (Nelson, 1962).

A group of pre-Cretaceous metamorphic rocks is exposed along the western margin of the range north of Milner Creek, and in a belt extending from Milner Creek through White Mountain Peak to Indian Creek. A small area near the northeastern corner of the range is underlain by the Ordovician Palmetto Formation (Albers and Stewart, 1965).

Granitic rocks from the southeastern White Mountains have been dated by radiometric methods (McKee and Nash, 1967). The results indicate that the main body of granitic rock was emplaced in Early to Middle Jurassic time, and that the isolated intrusive bodies (Sage Hen Flat and Birch Creek plutons) are of Cretaceous age.

The oldest post-Cretaceous stratigraphic unit in the White Mountains may be represented by a small body of volcanic breccia of Oligocene or Miocene age at the northeast end of the range (Albers and Stewart, 1965). More extensive deposits of Late Miocene to Early Pliocene age in the same area include the Esmeralda Formation (Ross, 1961) and the overlying lava flows and ash deposits. A basalt flow and underlying rhyolitic ash at the north end of Deep Springs Valley can also be assigned to Early Pliocene time on the basis of concordant radiometric dates (Dalrymple, 1963).

There are several types of deposits of Pleistocene to Recent age in the White Mountains. Indurated alluvial fan deposits (fanglomerates) along the western margin of the range may be of Middle Pleistocene age (Bateman, 1965). Glacial till, pond sediment, and proglacial terrace gravels in the major east-draining streams in the northern part of the range are of Pleistocene age (La-Marche, 1965a), as are the lake beds on the margin of Deep Springs Valley (Nelson, 1966a), Certain periglacial phenomena at intermediate elevations (8000–12,000 ft.) within the range, such as solifluction terraces, large-scale inactive patterned ground, and vegetated talus slopes, may also be relicts of Late Pleistocene age.

ROCK TYPES

Carbonate Rocks. Limestone and dolomite are abundant in the southern White Mountains. The Wyman Formation contains discontinuous carbonate beds in its upper part, one of which can be seen along Crooked Creek about a mile east of Crooked Creek Laboratory. The Reed Formation, named for exposures east of Reed Flat, in this area consists almost entirely of massive, fine-grained, white to grey dolomite. About half of the Deep Spring Formation is dolomite and limestone, ranging from beds of limestone a few inches thick and interbedded with sandstone and shale to massive dolomite in units up to 200 feet thick. These rocks outcrop in a north-trending belt to the west of the Reed Formation from Reed Flat to Sheep Mountain as well as in other areas. The lower half of the Poleta Formation consists of thickly bedded blue-grey fossiliferous limestone, and two limestone units are included in the upper half. Most of the limestone in the Westgard Pass area and in Silver Canyon is in the Poleta Formation. Some limestone is present near the base and near the top of the predominantly shaly Harkless Formation, which occurs in the same general areas.

Clastic Rocks. Sandstone, siltstone, and shale are probably the most wide-spread sedimentary rock types in the White Mountains. The Wyman Formation, exposed over a wide area in the Wyman Creek drainage, consists of thin-bedded shale, siltstone and fine-grained sandstone that characteristically weather to yield small, platy fragments. The Deep Spring Formation contains a thick, light-grey quartzite near the base that weathers to reddish blocks. This outcrops prominently on the northeast side of Reed Flat. A darker grey quartzite occurs in some areas toward the top of the unit. The lower part of the Campito Formation consists of dark greenish-grey, thickly bedded sandstone, interbedded with siltstone and shale. The purple-to-black color of weathered surfaces and the blocky fracturing are distinctive. The upper part of this unit is dark grey-to-green shale, with beds of siltstone and sandstone. The "narrows" on the road south of Westgard Pass and in Payson Canyon to the east are cut in the Campito Formation. This unit also underlies Campito Mountain and other prominent peaks. The upper part of the Poleta Formation contains light grey-green shale interbedded with limestone. More grey-green shale, interbedded with siltstone and sandstone, makes up most of the overlying Harkless Formation.

Metamorphic Rocks. All of the pre-Cretaceous rocks of the White Mountains have been somewhat affected by low-grade regional metamorphism. However, extreme changes from original texture and mineralogical composition are found mainly in the vicinity of the granitic bodies. Assemblages of calcium-silicate minerals were locally formed where granitic rocks contacted carbonate beds in the southern part of the range (Nash, 1962). Schist, hornfels and marbles also occur in this area. The original sandstone, chert, volcanic rocks, and shales in the northern White Mountains have been transformed to quartzite, greenstone, phyllite, schist, and hornfels.

Granitic Rocks. The granitic rocks of the White Mountains vary in composition from diorite to granite, but granodiorite and quartz monzonite (adamellite) are most abundant (Emerson, 1966). These rocks are generally light-colored, medium-grained, and massive. They consist of varying proportions of feldspar, quartz, and dark-colored mafic minerals, mainly hornblende and/or biotite. The large continuous body of granitic rock along the east side and on the northern end of the White Mountains has been termed the Inyo Batholith, and consists mostly of rocks of Jurassic age (McKee and Nash, 1967). To the south and west granitic rocks occur in small, discrete plutonic bodies, two of which have been dated as Cretaceous.

Younger Rocks and Unconsolidated Deposits. The low hills at the extreme north end of the White Mountains are composed of sedimentary and volcanic rocks of Tertiary age. The Esmeralda Formation is composed mainly of bedded tuff and tuffaceous sedimentary rocks. Light-colored, felsic volcanic rocks, including rhyolitic and dacitic flows, ash flows, and welded tuffs, overlie the Esmeralda Formation in most of the area. Small areas of older andesitic breccia, and younger andesitic intrusive rocks also occur in this area.

Younger lava flows cap ridges and buttes in the east-central and extreme northern parts of the White Mountains. These rocks are dark greenish-grey and some are scoriaceous. Flows in the Deep Springs Valley area are described as basalt (Nelson, 1966a; Dalrymple, 1963) and rest locally on thin beds of rhyolitic tuff and gravels. The flows on the north end of the range mainly overlie felsic volcanic rocks. Some of these dark flow rocks are potassium-rich and have been described as trachybasalts and trachyandesites (Ross, 1961). Much of the present relief of the White Mountains has developed since these mafic volcanic flows occurred.

More recent volcanic activity is also recorded in deposits in the White Mountains. The basal rhyolite pumice unit of the Bishop Tuff of Middle Pleistocene age (Bateman, 1965), occurs locally along the west flank of the range at elevations up to 6000 feet, in part interbedded with older alluvial fan deposits. Rhyolite pumice layers are found in relatively recent stream deposits near the west edge of the range. These may be related to volcanic activity in the Inyo Crater area to the northwest. Scoriaceous fragments and bombs of mafic volcanic rock, found on the ground surface in the southern White Mountains, may be products of volcanic eruptions in the Owens Valley south of Big Pine.

Alluvium is not abundant in the White Mountains. Much of the sediment carried by the stream channels has been transported to the adjacent basins to form deep and extensive alluvial fan and basin deposits (Lustig, 1965; Kesseli and Beaty, 1959). Within the range, most of the west-draining streams have only narrow alluvial flats or flow directly on bedrock. Broader valleys with deeper alluvial fills are characteristic of the east- and southeast-draining streams on the opposite side of the range. The stream deposits consist mainly of gravel and coarse sand, but deposits of silt and fine sand occur in some reaches.

The White Mountains have a long history of alluvial fan formation. Older consolidated fan deposits have been uplifted by faulting along the west side of the range, and deeply dissected by subsequent erosion. These are probably of middle Pleistocene age and are at least 600 feet thick (Bateman, 1965). The modern streams flow in trenches cut into these older deposits and are now building alluvial fans at lower elevations. Similar relationships can be seen in Deep Springs Valley and along the northeast margins of the range bordering Fish Lake Valley.

Thin layers of fossiliferous fresh-water limestone and calcareous shale are interbedded with the consolidated alluvial fan deposits along the west side of the White Mountains (Bateman, 1965). Thick and extensive lacustrine deposits, probably correlative in age, occur in the Waucoba Embayment in the Inyo Range (Walcott, 1897) to the south. Thin and discontinuous lake deposits are found on the alluvial fans along the west side of Deep Springs Valley (Nelson, 1966a), indicating that a lake (perhaps as much as 500 feet deep) occupied this basin at one or more times during the Pleistocene.

LANDFORMS, WEATHERING, AND SOILS

Soil profile development is weak or nonexistent in most areas of the White Mountains. Surficial material as a rule closely resembles the parent rock. A profile description and classification for a soil on the Reed Dolomite is given by Fritts (1969). Mineralogical and textural descriptions of other dolomite and limestone soils are given by LaMarche (1967, 1968). Mooney and others (1962) have published textural data for a variety of soils in the White Mountains.

The White Mountains exemplify "Basin and Range" topography, in which relief is closely related to vertical fault movements (Hinds, 1952). However, many of the internal topographic features of the range reflect the underlying rocks. The Campito Formation and the Reed Formation in the southern White Mountains, and the quartzites, greenstones, and some of the granitic rocks to the north are relatively resistant rocks that usually form the high ridges and peaks. The Wyman, Deep Springs, Poleta and Harkless Formations, and some granitic rocks are less resistant and commonly underlie basins and valleys.

Some of the topographic features of the White Mountains appear to be of great age. The rolling surface of the northern part of the range, including Pellisier and Chiatovich Flats, as well as small "flats" and meadows farther south, may be derived from a surface which existed prior to the most recent uplift of the range. The relief on the surface that is present beneath Pliocene lava flows on the east side of the range is much less than that which exists today.

Weathering, mass-movement, and erosion are active in the White Mountains today. Rates and processes of slope erosion on the Reed Dolomite are discussed in detail by LaMarche (1968). The importance of cloudburst floods in gullying and stream-channel erosion and deposition are emphasized by Beaty (Kesseli and Beaty, 1959; Beaty, 1959, 1960, 1963, 1968). Frost action is important over a large area of the White Mountains, with active large-scale, patterned ground features at high elevations (Mitchell *et al.*, 1966), and miniature frost features at lower elevations.

The eastward-draining canyons in the northern White Mountains have been extensively glaciated in the past, and contain such typical glacial features as cirques, moraines, and ephemeral ponds (LaMarche, 1965a). Small areas near the heads of some canyons on the west side of the range also contain small deposits (C. B. Beaty pers. comm., 1970). Although persistent snowbanks and semipermanent ice bodies do exist at high elevations, there are no glaciers in the White Mountains today.

Most of the canyons on the west side of the White Mountains are short, deep, and narrow and have very high gradients. Some are virtually inaccessible due to numerous dry waterfalls. The streams draining the east side of the range are longer and have lower gradients and wider valleys than those on the west side. Only the largest canyons contain permanent streams. The rest have only intermittent or ephemeral flow during most years. Rare but destructive flash floods may be accompanied by deep erosion or deposition on the canyon floors. Some other floods extend as debris-laden mudflows onto the alluvial fans bordering the mountains. The history of flooding in the White Mountains is well documented by Kesseli and Beaty (1959).

Barnes (1965) and Slack (1967) have investigated in great detail the chemistry and biology of Birch Creek—a travertine-depositing stream in the southeastern White Mountains. The chemistry and mineralogy of Deep Springs Lake and some aspects of the hydrology of the White Mountains are reported on by Jones (1965).

SELECTED REFERENCES

Albers, J. P., and J. H. Stewart. 1962. Precambrian and Cambrian stratigraphy in Esmeralda County, Nevada. U.S. Geol. Survey Prof. Paper 450–D: 24–26.
————. 1965. Preliminary Geologic Map of Esmeralda County, Nevada. U.S. Geol. Survey Min. Inv. Field Studies Map MF–298.
Anderson, G. H. 1933. Geology of the north half of the White Mountain quadrangle. Ph.D. Thesis. Calif. Inst. of Tech.
————. 1937. Granitization, albitization, and related phenomena in the

northern Inyo Range of California-Nevada: Geol. Soc. Am. Bull. 48: 1–74.

———, and J. H. Maxon. 1935. Physiography of the northern Inyo Range (abstract): Geol. Soc. Am. Proc. for 1934: 318.

Barnes, Ivan. 1965. Geochemistry of Birch Creek, Inyo County, California— A travertine depositing creek in an arid climate. Geochim. Cosmochim. Acta. 29: 85–112.

Bateman, P. C. 1965. Geology and tungsten mineralization of the Bishop district, California, with a section on gravity study of Owens Valley by L. C. Pakiser and M. F. Kane, and a section on Seismic Profile by L. C. Pakiser. U.S. Geol. Survey Prof. Paper 470. 208 p.

Beaty, C. B. 1959. Slope retreat by gullying. Geol. Soc. Am. Bull. 70: 1479–1482.

———. 1960. Gradational processes in the White Mountains of California and Nevada. Ph.D. Thesis, Univ. of Calif.., Berkeley. 260 p.

———. 1963. Origin of alluvial fans, White Mountains, California and Nevada. Assoc. Am. Geog. Ann. 53: 516–535.

———. 1968. Sequential study of desert flooding in the White Mountains of California and Nevada. U.S. Army Natick Laboratories, Natick, Mass., Tech. Rep. 68–31–ES. 96 p.

Blackwelder, Elliot. 1931. Pleistocene glaciation of the Sierra Nevada and Basin Ranges. Geol. Soc. Am. Bull. 42: 856–922.

———. 1934. Supplementary notes on Pleistocene glaciation in the Great Basin. Wash. Acad. Sci. J. 24: 217–222.

Blanc, R. P. 1958. Geology of the Deep Spring Valley area, White-Inyo Mountains, California. M. A. Thesis. Univ. of Calif., Los Angeles.

Bryson, R. P. 1937. Faulted fanglomerates at the mouth of Perry Aiken Creek, Northern Inyo Range, California-Nevada. M. S. Thesis. Calif. Inst. of Tech.

California Division of Mines and Geology. 1967. Geologic map of California: Mariposa Sheet. Calif. Div. Mines and Geology, San Francisco.

Cloud, P. E., and C. A. Nelson. 1966. Pteridinium and the Precambrian-Cambrian boundary. Science 154: 766.

Crowder, D. F., and M. F. Sheridan. In preparation. Geologic map of the White Mountain Peak quadrangle, California. U.S. Geol. Survey Geol. Quad. Map GQ ——.

Dalrymple, G. B. 1963. Potassium-argon dates of some Cenozoic volcanic rocks of the Sierra Nevada, California. Geol. Soc. Am. Bull. 74: 379–390.

DeLisle, Mark. 1963. Lead retention of zircons under conditions of dynamothermal contact metamorphism, White Mountains, California (abs). Geol. Soc. Am. Special Paper 73: 33 p.

Emerson, D. O. 1966. Granitic rocks of the Mt. Barcroft quadrangle, Inyo batholith, California-Nevada. Geol. Soc. Am. Bull. 77: 127–152.

Fritts, H. C. 1969. Bristlecone pine in the White Mountains of California: Growth and ring-width characteristics. Univ. of Ariz. Press, Tucson. 44 p.

Gallick, C. M. 1964. The geology of a part of the Blanco Mountain quadrangle, Inyo County, California. M.A. Thesis. Univ. of Calif., Los Angeles.

Gangloff, R. A. 1963. Archaeocyatha from Westgard Pass area, Inyo-White Mountains, California. M.A. Thesis. Univ. of Calif., Los Angeles.

Gilbert, C. M. 1941. Late Tertiary geology southeast of Mono Lake, California. Geol. Soc. Am. Bull. 52: 781–815.

Hall, M. L. 1963. Intrusive truncation of the Precambrian-Cambrian succession in the White Mountains, California. M.A. Thesis. Univ. of Calif., Berkeley.

Harris, D. L. 1967. Petrology of the Boundary Peak adamellite pluton, in the Benton quadrangle, Mono and Esmeralda Counties, California and Nevada. M.S. Thesis. Univ. of Calif., Davis.

Harris, W. S. 1958. Geology of the southwestern portion of the Blanco Mountain quadrangle, Inyo County, California. M.A. Thesis. Univ. of Calif., Los Angeles.

Hinds, N. E. A. 1952. Evolution of the California landscape. Calif. Div. of Mines Bull. 158: 249 p.

Jones, B. F. 1965. The hydrology and mineralogy of Deep Springs Lake, Inyo County, California. U.S. Geol. Survey Prof. Paper 502–A, 56 p.

Kerr, P. F. 1932. Andalusite and related minerals at White Mountain, California. Econ. Geol. 27: 614–643.

Kesseli, J. E., and C. B. Beaty. 1959. Desert flood conditions in the White Mountains of California and Nevada. Quart. Res. and Engin. Comm., U.S. Army Environment Prot. Res. Div. Tech. Rept. EP–108. 107 p.

Knopf, Adolf. 1918. A geological reconnaissance of the Inyo Range and the eastern slope of the southern Sierra Nevada, *with* a section on the stratigraphy of the Inyo Range by Edwin Kirk. U.S. Geol. Survey Prof. Paper 110. 130 p.

Krauskopf, K. B. 1968. A tale of ten plutons. Geol. Soc. Am. Bull. 79: 1–18.

————. In preparation. Geologic map of the Mt. Barcroft quadrangle, California-Nevada. U.S. Geol. Survey Geol. Quad. Map GQ ——.

LaMarche, V. C., Jr. 1963. Origin and geologic significance of buttress roots of bristlecone pines, White Mountains, California. U.S. Geol. Survey Prof. Paper 475–C: C148–C149.

————. 1965a. Distribution of Pleistocene glaciers in the White Mountains of California and Nevada. U.S. Geol. Survey Prof. Paper 525C: C146–C147.

————. 1965b. Determination of denudational rates from measurements of root exposure. Geol. Soc. Am. Special Paper 82: 117 p.

————. 1967. Spheroidal weathering of thermally metamorphosed limestone and dolomite, White Mountains, California. Geol. Survey Prof. Paper 575–C: C32–C37.

————. 1968. Rates of slope degradation as determined from botanical evidence, White Mountains, California. U.S. Geol. Survey Prof. Paper 352–I: 341–377.

Lustig, L. K. 1965. Clastic sedimentation in Deep Springs Valley, California. U.S. Geol. Survey Prof. Paper 352–F: 131–192.

Maxson, J. A. 1935. Pre-Cambrian stratigraphy of the Inyo Range (abstract). Geol. Soc. Am. Proc. for 1934.

McKee, E. H., and D. B. Nash. 1967. Potassium-argon ages of granitic rocks in the Inyo batholith, east-central California. Geol. Soc. Am. Bull. 78: 669–680.

———— and C. A. Nelson. 1967. Geologic map of the Soldier Pass quadrangle, California and Nevada. U.S. Geol. Survey Geol. Quad. Map GQ–654.

Miller, W. J. 1928. Geology of the Deep Springs Valley. J. Geol. 36: 510–525.

Mitchell, R. S., V. C. LaMarche Jr., and R. M. Lloyd. 1966. Alpine vegetation and active frost features of Pellisier Flats, White Mountains, California. Am. Midl. Nat. 75: 516–525.

Mooney, H. A., G. St. Andre, and R. R. Wright. 1962. Alpine and subalpine vegetation patterns in the White Mountains of California. Am. Midl. Nat. 68: 257–273.

Nash, D. B. 1962. Contact metamorphism at Birch Creek, Blanco Mountain quadrangle, Inyo County, California. M.S. Thesis. Univ. of Calif., Berkeley.

Nelson, C. A. 1957. Lower Cambrian-Waucoban stratigraphy, Inyo Mountains, California (abstract). Geol. Soc. Am. Bull. 68: 1838.

————. 1962. Lower Cambrian-Precambrian succession, White–Inyo Mountains, California. Geol. Soc. Am. Bull. 73: 139–144.

————. 1963. Preliminary geologic map of the Blanco Mountain quadrangle, Inyo and Mono Counties, California. U.S. Geol. Survey Investigations Field Studies Map MF–256.

————. 1966a. Geologic map of the Blanco Mountain quadrangle, Inyo County, California. U.S. Geol. Survey Geol. Quad. Map GQ–529.

————. 1966b. Geologic map of the Waucoba Mountain quadrangle, Inyo County, California. U.S. Geol. Survey Geol. Quad Map GQ–528.

———— and L. J. Perry. 1955. Late Pre-Cambrian–early Cambrian strata, White–Inyo Mountains, California (abstract). Geol. Soc. Am. Bull. 62: 1508.

Nevin, A. E. 1963. Late Cenozoic stratigraphy and structure of the Benton area, Mono County, California. M.A. Thesis. Univ. of Calif., Berkeley.

Norman, L. A. Jr., and R. M. Stewart. 1951. Mines and mineral resources of Inyo County. Calif. J. Mines and Geol. 47: 17–223.

Perry, L. J. 1955. Geology of the portion of the Blanco Mountain quadrangle, Inyo County, California. M.S. Thesis. Univ. of Calif., Los Angeles.

Petersen, M. N. A., and C. S. Bien. Radiocarbon age determination of recent dolomite from Deep Springs Lake, California (abstract). Am. Geophys. Union Trans. 44: 108.

Powell, D. R. 1963. Physical geography of the White Mountains, California–Nevada. M.A. Thesis, Univ. of Calif., Berkeley.

Robinson, P. T., and D. F. Crowder. In preparation. Geology of the Davis Mountain quadrangle, Nevada-California. U.S. Geol. Survey Geol. Quad Map GQ ——.

Ross, D. C. 1961. Geology and mineral deposits of Mineral County, Nevada. Nevada Bur. Mines Bull. 58: 98 p.

Sampson, R. J. 1940. Mineral resources of Mono County, California. Calif. J. Mines and Geol. 36: 116–156.

Sheridan, M. F., and D. F. Crowder. 1964. Geologic map of the southwest quarter of the White Mountain Peak quadrangle, Mono County, California. U.S. Geol. Survey Open-File Rept.

————. 1964. Geologic map of the northwest quarter of the White Mountain Peak quadrangle, Mono County, California. U.S. Geol. Survey Open-File Rept.

Slack, K. V. 1967. Physical and chemical description of Birch Creek, a travertine-depositing stream in Inyo County, California. U.S. Geol. Survey Prof. Paper 549–A. 19 p.

Stewart, J. H. 1965. Precambrian and lower Cambrian formations in the Last Chance Range area, Inyo County, California. p. 60–70 *in* Cohee, G. V. and W. S. West. Changes in stratigraphic nomenclature by the U.S. Geological Survey, 1964. U.S. Geol. Survey Bull. 1224A.

————. 1966. Correlation of lower Cambrian and some Precambrian strata in the southern Great Basin, California and Nevada. U.S. Geol. Survey Prof. Paper 550–C: C66–C72.

Trent, D. D. 1955. The physiography of Mono County, California. Compass. 32: 247–259.

Tucker, W. B., and R. J. Sampson. 1939. Mineral resources of Inyo County, California. Calif. J. Mines and Geol. 34: 368–500.

Walcott, C. D. 1897. The post-Pliocene elevation of the Inyo Range and the lake beds of the Waucobi Embayment, Inyo County, California. J. Geol. 5: 346–348.

————. 1908. Cambrian sections of the Cordilleran area. Smithson. Inst. Misc. Coll. 53: 167–230.

Woodhouse, C. D. 1951. The Mono County Andalusite Mine (California). Rocks and Minerals 26: 486–493.

VASCULAR PLANTS OF THE WHITE MOUNTAINS

The following treatment is intended for use as an identification manual for the flora of the White Mountains. Diagnostic keys, field data, and citation of examined herbarium specimens are listed for all species now known to occur in the range. Further information on these taxa can be obtained by consulting *A California Flora* by P. A. Munz (University of California Press, 1959). About 50 percent of the species listed here have been previously reported from the range by the authors in a mimeographed plant list prepared for the White Mountain Research Station (1964, 1966).

Families of pteridophytes are arranged according to the system of Copeland (*Genera Filicum*, 1947). Angiosperm families are arranged according to Cronquist, *The Evolution and Classification of Flowering Plants* (Houghton Mifflin Co., 1968). Complete first sets of specimens collected by the authors and by Victor Duran are on file in the Herbarium of the University of California, Berkeley. Collections made by H. A. Mooney are on file in his personal ecology herbarium housed at Stanford University. In the following lists these collections are cited as follows: D = Duran, HM = H. A. Mooney, L = Lloyd, M = Mitchell. Where specimens of Duran have been observed in other herbaria this listing follows the collection number. All other collections made in the White Mountains are cited by individual collectors, followed by herbarium abbreviations of their location according to those given in Lanjouw and Stafleu (Index Herbariorum, Regnum Veg. 31. 1964).

A reference collection for use in the field has been established at the Crooked

Creek Laboratory of the White Mountain Research Station. Arrangements for use of that collection can be made through that organization.

Keys for the plants are either original or, mostly, have been modified from existing keys from Munz (*A California Flora*) or Abrams (*Flora of the Pacific Northwest*). Some treatments and keys have been provided by other people. These are cited where they occur in the text.

Families

KEY TO FAMILIES

A. Plants truly aquatic; leaves submerged or floating.
  B. Leaves submerged, opposite on a tufted stem .... 55. *Callitrichaceae*
  BB. Leaves floating: tiny budding fronds with no obvious stem structure
                                             69. *Lemnaceae*
AA. Plants not truly aquatic; leaves and stems emergent if in water.
  B. Reproduction by single-celled spores, seedless (PTERIDOPHYTA).
    C. Leaves entire with a single vein, less than 2 cm. long.
      D. Sporangia single in the axils of microphylls; stems not jointed or
        ribbed .... 2. *Selaginellaceae*
      DD. Sporangia clustered on sporangiophores in a dense strobilus; stems
        jointed and ribbed .... 1. *Equisetaceae*
    CC. Leaves lobed or compound, multinerved, more than 2 cm. long.
      D. Sporangia minute, borne singly or in sori on the underside of
        the fronds.
        E. Sporangia never in distinct sori, marginal ...... 4. *Pteridaceaé*
        EE. Sporangia in distinct sori away from the margins of the pinnae
                                          5. *Aspidiaceae*
      DD. Sporangia large, borne on a stalked panicle .. 3.*Ophioglossaceae*
  BB. Reproduction by seeds from cones or ripened ovaries (fruit).
    C. Seeds produced in cones (sometimes berrylike) or clusters of scaly
      bracts (GYMNOSPERMAE).
      D. Stems jointed; seeds formed within fleshly to scaly bracts; strag-
        gling, wiry shrubs .... 8. *Ephedraceae*
      DD. Stems not jointed; seeds formed within a woody or fleshy strobilus,
        trees.
        E. Female cones woody; leaves needlelike .... 6. *Pinaceae*
        EE. Female cones berrylike; leaves flattened, decurrent
                                        7. *Cupressaceae*
    CC. Seeds produced in ripened ovaries, not in cones
                             (ANGIOSPERMAE).
      D. Major veins with few anastomoses, appearing parallel before con-

49

verging at the leaf tip; floral parts usually in 3's or multiples of 3
(MONOCOTYLEDONEAE).
E. Perianth absent or reduced to scarious scales or bristles.
    F. Perianth parts 6, subequal, not concealed within bracts or
        glumes .... 66. *Juncaceae*
    FF. Perianth parts unequal or reduced to bristles, often concealed
        in sterile bracts or glumes.
        G. Stems hollow, terete; leaf sheath tending to split longitu-
            dinally opposite the blade, fruit a caryopsis 68. *Gramineae*
        GG. Stems usually solid, angled; leaf sheath continuous around
            the stem, fruit an achene .... 67. *Cyperaceae*
EE. Perianth petaloid, not scalelike.
    F. Stems woody, forming straggling trees with spine-tipped
        leaves .... 73. *Agavaceae*
    FF. Stems herbaceous; leaves not spiny.
        G. Inflorescence a distinct umbel; fresh plants with onion odor
            71. *Amaryllidaceae*
        GG. Inflorescence not an umbel; onion odor absent.
            H. Flowers zygomorphic, spurred; stamen 1
                74. *Orchidaceae*
            HH. Flowers actinomorphic; stamens 3 or more.
                I. Stigmas petaloid, purple; perianth epigynous
                    72. *Iridaceae*
                II. Stigmas not petaloid; perianth hypogynous
                    70. *Liliaceae*
DD. Major veins of leaves with divergent or reticulated branching pat-
    terns; floral parts in 4's, 5's (3's) or many
    (DICOTYLEDONEAE).
    E. Carpellate flowers without an apparent perianth (in some cases
        enclosed in an involucre or foliaceous bracts).
        F. Leaves pinnately compound ....39. *Aceraceae*
        FF. Leaves simple.
        G. Plants parasitic on the branches of trees or shrubs
            36. *Loranthaceae*
        GG. Plants neither parasitic nor epiphytic.
            H. Herbs or shrubs of dry or alkaline places.
                I. Gynoecium of 3 fused carpels in a common involucre
                    with jointed stamens (male flowers) 38. *Euphorbiaceae*
                II. Gynoecium of 1 carpel; flowers unisexual or perfect
                    19. *Chenopodiaceae*
            HH. Trees or scandent shrubs of riparian areas.
                I. Flowers borne in catkins.
                  J. Plants monoecious; bark dark bronze, shining; sti-
                    pules deciduous; leaves broadly ovate, sharply serrate
                    14. *Betulaceae*
                JJ. Plants dioecious; bark various, if reddish-brown then
                  stipules persistent or leaves not as above
                  25. *Salicaceae*
                II. Flowers in fascicles .... 12. *Ulmaceae*
EE. Carpellate (or perfect) flowers with a true perianth.
    F. Leaves and stems covered with stinging hairs; coarse herbs of
        watercourses .... 13. *Urticaceae*
    FF. Leaves and stems not covered with stinging hairs.

G.   Flowers clustered in dense heads or umbels which are subtended by a common involucre.

   H.   Corolla papilionaceous . . . . 32. *Leguminosae*

   HH. Corolla not papilionaceous.

      I.   Flowers in umbels.

         J.   Corolla gamopetalous; ovary superior

                           28. *Primulaceae*

         JJ. Corolla choripetalous; ovary inferior

                           45. *Umbelliferae*

      II. Flowers in dense heads.

         J.   Perianth epigynous . . . . 65. *Compositae*

         JJ. Perianth hypogynous.

            K.   Calyx absent; ovary unlobed 15. *Nyctaginaceae*

            KK. Calyx present; ovary 4-lobed . . . .56. *Labiatae*

GG. Flowers not in clusters subtended by a common involucre.

   H.   Perianth parts similar in color and texture, not in two distinct whorls.

      I.   Perianth epigynous or perigynous.

         J.   Woody shrubs or small trees.

            K.   Flowers perfect, style plumose; fruit an achene

                         31. *Rosaceae*

            KK. Flowers unisexual, style filiform; fruit a drupe

                         34. *Elaeagnaceae*

         JJ. Herbs with 4-angled stems . . . . 62. *Rubiaceae*

      II. Perianth hypogynous.

         J.   Carpels separate or slightly fused at base.

            K.   Leaves succulent; perianth dark purple-brown to yellowish . . . . 29. *Crassulaceae*

            KK. Leaves not succulent; perianth greenish or brightly colored . . . . 9. *Ranunculaceae*

         JJ. Carpels 1, or several fused into a single compound ovary.

            K.   Stamens more than twice the number of perianth lobes . . . . 10. *Papaveraceae*

            KK. Stamens fewer than twice the number of perianth lobes.

               L.   Stipules present at nodes . . 21. *Polygonaceae*

               LL. Stipules absent from nodes.

                  M.   Perianth lobes and stamens 5 or less. (Go to N.)

N.   Floral bracts scarious; plants neither mealy nor scurfy 20. *Amaranthaceae*

NN. Floral bracts not scarious; plants mealy or scurfy . . . .19. *Chenopodiaceae*

                  MM. Perianth lobes 6; stamens 6

                         21. *Polygonaceae*

   HH. Perianth parts in two morphologically distinct whorls (simulated in *Mirabilis froebelii* by involucre and petaloid calyx).

      I.   Corolla choripetalous. (**II on page 53**).

         J.   Stamens twice or more than twice the number of petals.

            K.   Perianth hypogynous.

               L.   Sepals 2, joined into a pointed cap, early deciduous .... 10. *Papaveraceae*

LL. Sepals more than 2, not deciduous.

  M.   Stamens united into a tube around the ovary and styles .... 22. *Malvaceae*

  MM. Stamens not united into a common tube. (Go to N.)

N.   Flowers bisexual; herbs or shrubs .... 31. *Rosaceae*

NN. Flowers polygamo-dioecious; trees .... 40. *Simaroubaceae*

KK. Perianth perigynous or epigynous.

  L.   Stems succulent, spiny; leaves wanting

16. *Cactaceae*

  LL. Stems not succulent; leaves present.

  M.   Leaf margins entire .. 30. *Saxifragaceae*

  MM. Leaf margins serrate, dentate, or lobed. (Go to N.)

N.   Ovary 1-loculed; plants with rough, barbed hairs .... 24. *Loasaceae*

NN. Ovary more than 1-loculed; plants without barbed hairs .... 31. *Rosaceae*

JJ. Stamens fewer than twice the number of petals.

  K.   Carpels more than 1, separate.

  L.   Stipules absent; carpels fewer than the sepals (or rarely the same number)

30. *Saxifragaceae*

  LL. Stipules present; carpels as many as the sepals

31. *Rosaceae*

KK. Carpels 1 or several fused into a single compound ovary.

  L.   Styles more than 1, united only at the base.

  M.   Plants woody: shrubs or trees.

N.   Ovary inferior, fruit a berry; shrubs .... 30. *Saxifragaceae*

NN. Ovary superior, fruit a samara; trees .... 39. *Aceraceae*

  MM. Plants herbaceous. (Go to N.)

N.   Perianth hypogynous.

  O.   Leaves succulent, in rosettes or cauline .... 18. *Portulacaceae*

  OO. Leaves not succulent, cauline.

  P.   Petals blue, entire, 1 cm. or longer .... 43. *Linaceae*

  PP. Petals white or pink-tinged, 1 cm. long and lacerate or less than 1 cm.

17. *Caryophyllaceae*

NN. Perianth epigynous ... . 30. *Saxifragaceae*

  LL. Styles 1, or several, united nearly to the stigmas.

  M.   Perianth epigynous. (Go to N.)

N.   Plants woody with fleshy fruit.

  O.   Inflorescence cymose; stamens 4 .... 35. *Cornaceae*

  OO. Inflorescence racemose or flowers solitary, stamens (4) 5-many

30. *Saxifragaceae*

NN. Plants herbaceous; fruit dry, dehiscent .... 33. *Onagraceae*

MM. Perianth hypogynous. (Go to N.)
N.   Petals 3, the upper one hooded; lateral calyx lobes petaloid
                                  44. *Polygalaceae*
NN. Petals 4 or more, calyx not petaloid.
  O.   Plants woody.
    P.   Flowers papilionaceous .... 32. *Leguminosae*
    PP. Flowers actinomorphic, not papilionaceous.
      Q.   Flowers 5-merous; intricately branched shrubs .. 37. *Celastraceae*
      QQ. Flowers 4-merous; plants with few branches and a basal rosette
  OO. Plants herbaceous.
    P.   Sepals 2 .... 18. *Portulacaceae*
    PP. Sepals 4 or more.
      Q.   Corolla zygomorphic.
        R.   Flowers papilionaceous, fruit a legume ...... 32. *Leguminosae*
        RR. Flowers not papilionaceous, fruit an ovoid capsule
                              23. *Violaceae*

      QQ.Corolla actinomorphic
        R.   Perianth 5-merous.
          S.   Flowers purple-pink; branches unarmed .... 42. *Geraniaceae*
          SS. Flowers yellow; branches armed with short spines
                             41. *Zygophyllaceae*
        RR. Perianth 4-merous.
          S.   Leaves trifoliate; ovary stalked .... 26. *Capparidaceae*
          SS. Leaves not trifoliate; ovary sessile .... 27. *Cruciferae*
          II. Corolla gamopetalous. (**continued from I, page 51**).
          J.   Plants lacking chlorophyll, cream, yellow, to deep
              rose-purple, parasitic.
            K.   Corolla zygomophic; root parasites
                             69. *Orobanchaceae*
            KK. Corolla actinomorphic; stems slender, twining
                               51. *Cuscutaceae*
          JJ. Plants green, possessing chlorophyll, at least in the
             leaves.
            K.   Perianth epigynous or perigynous.
              L.   Stamens 1–3; herbs to 6 dm. tall
                             64. *Valerianaceae*
            LL. Stamens 4–5.
              M.   Shrubs .... 63. *Caprifoliaceae*
              MM. Small annuals to 2.5 cm. tall
                             61. *Campanulaceae*
          KK. Perianth hypogynous.
            L.   Corolla zygomorphic, bilateral or with sub-
              equal lobes.
            M.   Petals fused only at the base, papiliona-
              ceous .... 32. *Leguminosae*

      MM. Petals fused laterally or forming a complete
        corolla tube. (Go to N.)

N. Stamens 6, petals 4, sepals 2 .... 11. *Fumariaceae*
NN. Stamens 5 or less; perianth 5-merous.
 O. Ovary 4-lobed; fresh foliage with mint odor .... 56. *Labiatae*
 OO. Ovary unlobed; mint odor lacking .... 59. *Scrophulariaceae*
      LL. Corolla actinomorphic, definitely radial in sym-
        metry.
     M. Carpels 2, separate, although the styles and
        stigmas may adhere. (Go to N.)
N. Corolla more than 5 mm. in diameter, a crown of concave hoods
              48. *Asclepiadaceae*
NN. Corolla less than 4 mm. in diameter, urn-shaped ...... 47. *Apocynaceae*
      MM. Carpels 1 or several, fused in a single com-
        pound ovary. (Go to N.)
N. Corolla dry, membranous, unveined .... 57. *Plantaginaceae*
NN. Corolla not membranous, veined.
 O. Ovary 4-lobed, forming nutlets at maturity .... 54. *Boraginaceae*
 OO. Ovary not lobed; fruit a capsule or berry.
  P. Stamens 2; capsule circumscissile .... 58. *Oleaceae*
  PP. Stamens more than 2; capsule not circumscissile.
   Q. Stigmas 3, style 3-cleft .... 52. *Polemoniaceae*
   QQ. Stigmas and styles 1 or 2.
    R. Calyx of 5 distinct lobes or fused only at base.
     S. Plants twining or trailing; inflorescence not coiled
        50. *Convolvulaceae*
     SS. Plants spreading or erect; inflorescence a cyme, often coiled
        53. *Hydrophyllaceae*
    RR. Calyx lobes fused above the base.
     S. Leaves opposite .... 46. *Gentianaceae*
     SS. Leaves alternate .... 49. *Solanaceae*

PTERIDOPHYTA
FAMILY 1. EQUISETACEAE
1. Equisetum

A. Aerial stems dimorphic; sterile stems profusely branched .. 1. *E. arvense*
AA. Aerial stems monomorphic, rarely branched .... 2. *E. laevigatum*

 1. **E. arvense** L. Usually near streams, moist canyons of the central portion of the range, 6000–8500 ft.: Wyman Creek: 7900 ft., *M 2052*; 8300 ft., *L 2782*; also reported in Middle Creek, Lone Tree Creek, and Milner Creek.

 2. **E. laevigatum** A. Br. Common, riparian areas throughout the range, 5600–9200 ft.: spring northeast of Antelope Springs, 5680 ft., *L 3018*; Montenegro Springs, 7050 ft., *L 3125*; Wyman Creek, 2 miles below Roberts Ranch, 7500 ft., *D s.n.*; Cottonwood Creek, 8900 ft., *L 2936*.

FAMILY 2. SELAGINELLACEAE
1. Selaginella

1. **S. watsoni** Underw. Usually in moist places at the base of rocks, throughout the range, 8000–13,500 ft.: northeast corner of Sagehen Flat, 10,250 ft., *L 3162*; hill east of Crooked Creek lab, 10,200 ft., *Bacigalupi et al., 8046* (JEPS); White Mountain Road, 13,400 ft., *HM 519*; Pellisier Flats, 1 mile south of Jump-Off, 13,400 ft., *M 2172*; Chiatovich Creek, 8000 ft., D *s.n.*

FAMILY 3. OPHIOGLOSSACEAE
1. Botrychium

1. **B. simplex** E. Hitchc. var. **compositum** (Lasch) Milde. Rare, hummocks of damp open meadows, glaciated east-facing canyons, 8000–9000 ft.: Chiatovich Creek: 8000 ft., *D 3080*; 8900 ft., frequent, *D 2535*.

FAMILY 4. PTERIDACEAE

A. Sporangia confluent; pinna margins reflexed, segments not beadlike
2. *Pellaea*

AA. Sporangia mostly interrupted; pinna margins not reflexed, or, if reflexed, then segments beadlike . . . . 1. *Cheilanthes*

1. Cheilanthes

A. Sori naked; leaf margin scarcely or not at all reflexed.
B. Fronds neither hairy nor scaly . . . . 2. *C. jonesii*
BB. Fronds hairy . . . . 3. *C. parryi*
AA. Sori covered with the reflexed pinna margin; pinnules beadlike.
B. Rhizome slender, widely creeping; undersides of pinnae scaly
4. *C. wootonii*
BB. Rhizome stout, branched, short-creeping to ascending; undersides of pinnae tomentose . . . . 1. *C. feei*

1. **C. feei** T. Moore. Rare, on limestone, rocky crevices in southern canyons, 5000–9500 ft.: Marble Canyon of Black Canyon, 5700 ft., *D 2632*; Wyman Creek, 9450 ft., *L 2814*.

2. **C. jonesii** (Maxon) Munz. Rare, rock crevices; known only from Marble Canyon of Black Canyon, 5700 ft., *D 2633*.

3. **C. parryi** (D.C. Eat.) Domin. Rare, rock crevices 5500–10,000 ft.: Marble Canyon of Black Canyon, 5700 ft., *D s.n.*; Wyman Creek, 9700 ft., *L 2823*.

4. **C. wootoni** Maxon. To be expected below 8000 ft. in rock crevices and rocky areas, especially east of Benton.

2. Pellaea

1. **P. breweri** D.C. Eat. Exposed rocky areas or near base of rocks, throughout the range, 7900–12,000 ft.: road from Crooked Creek to Cottonwood Creek, 10,000 ft., *HM 441*; McAfee Meadow, 11,500 ft., *D 2811*; Chiatovich Creek, 7900 ft., *D 3081*.

FAMILY 5. ASPIDIACEAE

A. Indusium roundish or ovate-acuminate .... 1. *Cystopteris*
AA. Indusium divided into lanceolate segments .... 2. *Woodsia*

1. Cystopteris

1. **C. fragilis** (L.) Bernh. Common, moist areas and under rocks, throughout the range, pinyon woodland to alpine fell-fields, 8000–13,900 ft.: Crooked Creek, 10,100 ft., *M 2013*; Cottonwood Creek, 8900 ft., *L 2937*; Cottonwood Creek, 11,700 ft., *D 2583*; McAfee Meadow, 11,600 ft., *D s.n.*; south of White Mountain Peak, 13,700 ft., *HM 560*; head of north fork of Perry Aiken Creek, 13,200 ft., *Tucker 3434* (DAV); Pellisier Flats, 12,800 ft., *M 2217*.

2. Woodsia

1. **W. scopulina** D.C. Eat. Rock crevices, meadows, and talus slopes where moist; pinyon woodland to subalpine forest, throughout the range, 8000–11,000 ft.: Silver Canyon, 8800 ft., *L 3885*; 1/2 mile south of Mexican Mine, 9550 ft., *Blakley 4649* (CAS); Big Prospector Meadow, 10,700 ft., *Munz 21065* (UC); Station Peak (Crooked Creek), 10,000 ft., *D 1588*; south fork, Chiatovich Creek, ca. 8000 ft., *D 3363*.

SPERMATOPHYTA
GYMNOSPERMAE
FAMILY 6. PINACEAE
1. Pinus

A. Needles 5 per fascicle.
    B. Umbos terminal, unarmed; needles 2.5–7.0 cm. long; young bark gray to white .... 2. *P. flexilis*
    BB. Umbos dorsal, with slender incurved prickles; needles 2.5–3.5 cm. long; young bark reddish-brown .... 1. *P. longaeva*
AA. Needles 1–3 per fascicle.
    B. Needles mostly one per fascicle .... 3. *P. monophylla*
    BB. Needles 2 or 3 per fascicle.
        C. Needles 2 per fascicle .... 4. *P. murrayana*
        CC. Needles mostly 3 per fascicle .... 5. *P. ponderosa*

1. **P. longaeva** D. K. Bailey. Of sporadic distribution, forming large stands on dolomite and limestone, less frequently on other substrates, subalpine forest, more common in southern portion of the range, 8600–11,600 ft.: 9 miles north of Westgard Pass on White Mountain Road, 10,000 ft., *Everett & Balls 21929* (RSA); Wyman Creek, 9700 ft., *L 2822*; Crooked Creek lab, 10,200 ft., *Tucker 3437* (DAV); Cottonwood Creek, 10,500 ft., *D 1644*. D. K. Bailey has recently segregated out these distinct Great Basin bristlecone pine populations as a new species, *P. longaeva*, from the Rocky Mountains *Pinus aristata* complex. (see Ann. Missouri Bot. Gard. 57: 210–249).

2. **P. flexilis** James. Forming pure stands or mixed with *Pinus longaeva*, throughout the range, 6800–11,400 ft.: 8.4 miles north of Westgard Pass on White Mountain Road, 9700 ft., *Everett & Balls 21919* (RSA); Wyman Creek, 8500 ft., *D s.n.*; Station Peak (Crooked Creek), 10,000 ft., *D 1585*; slope just south of Crooked Creek lab, 10,200 ft., *Tucker 3436* (DAV); there are about 15 trees at 6800 ft., in Lone Tree Creek.

3. **P. monophylla** Torr. & Frem. Common, dry ridges, slopes, and flats, forming woodlands throughout the range, 5900–9500 ft.: 4 miles west of White Mountain Road on Westgard Pass, 6400 ft., *L 2716*; Cedar Flat, 7200 ft., *D s.n.*

4. **P. murrayana** Grev. & Balf. Sporadic distribution in a few of the northern canyons, 9000–10,500 ft. Perhaps best represented on Chiatovich Flats and the glacial moraines of Perry Aiken Creek: Cabin Creek, 10,000 ft., *Kliethforth s.n.* (LA); also reported from Milner Creek and Montgomery Creek.

5. **P. ponderosa** Dougl. ex P. & C. Lawson. Known only from Lone Tree Creek, 7000 ft., *Powell 2184* (UCSB).

FAMILY 7. CUPRESSACEAE
1. **Juniperus**

1. **J. osteosperma** (Torr.) Little. Sporadic populations distributed throughout the pinyon woodland; most common on alluvial flats, 6800–10,300 ft.: Westgard Pass, just above the Narrows, 6950 ft., *L 2759*; Cedar Flat, 7200 ft., *D s.n.*; Roberts Ranch, Wyman Creek, 8000 ft., *D 1691*; isolated plants have been observed above Crooked Creek lab at 10,300 ft.

FAMILY 8. EPHEDRACEAE
1. **Ephedra**

A.   Branchlets yellow-green; leaf-bases brown ... . 2. *E. viridis*
AA. Branchlets gray-green, ± glaucous; leaf-bases gray .... 1. *E. nevadensis*

1. **E. nevadensis** Wats. Dry flats, canyons and slopes, desert scrub, 4500–6500 ft.: first canyon south of Silver Canyon, 5200 ft., *HM 245*; Wyman Creek, 1 mile above mouth, ca. 6000 ft., *D 3171*; mouth of Milner Creek, 5500 ft., *D 3235*.

2. **E. viridis** Cov. Common, dry flats, canyons, and slopes, throughout the range, desert scrub to subalpine forest, 4500–9500 ft.: Black Canyon, 9500 ft., *Tucker 3438* (DAV); Silver Canyon, 7000 ft., *M 2300*; Cottonwood Creek, 9500 ft., *D 1602*; Trail Canyon, 8000 ft., *D s.n.*

ANGIOSPERMAE
DICOTYLEDONEAE
FAMILY 9. RANUNCULACEAE

A.   Pistils with few to several ovules; fruit a berry or follicle; flowers blue, purplish-blue, or red and yellowish.
B.   Flowers irregular, blue to purplish-blue.

58

    C.   Upper sepal spurred; petals 4 .... 4. *Delphinium*
    CC. Upper sepal hooded; petals 2 or 5 .... 1. *Aconitum*
  BB. Flowers regular, red and yellow or green .... 2. *Aquilegia*
AA. Pistils with one ovule; fruit an achene; flowers whitish to yellow or greenish-yellow.
    B.   Stem leaves opposite; woody vine .... 3. *Clematis*
    BB. Stem leaves alternate or none.
      C.   Petals present.
        D.   Sepals spurred; leaves basal and linear .... 5. *Myosurus*
        DD. Sepals not spurred; leaves usually basal and cauline, not linear
                                        6. *Ranunculus*
      CC. Petals absent; flowers usually unisexual .... 7. *Thalictrum*

1. Aconitum

1. **A. columbianum** Nutt. Sporadic, moist areas, throughout northern canyons and Silver Canyon, 7500–9000 ft.: Chiatovich Creek, ca. 8300 ft., *D M75*.

2. Aquilegia

A.   Basal leaves biternate; sepals red .... 1. *A. formosa*
AA. Basal leaves mostly triternate; sepals red or with some green or yellow
                                        2. *A. shockleyi*

1. **A. formosa** Fisch. Common along streams, 5000–10,000 ft.: at forks of Silver Canyon, 6700 ft., *Wolf 2596* (UC); Wyman Creek, 7800 ft., *L 2767*; Old Ranger Station, road north of Crooked Creek, 9800 ft., *L 2889*; Cottonwood Creek, 8900 ft., *L 2832*; Lone Tree Creek, 6800 ft., *M 2244*.
2. **A. shockleyi** Eastw. Sporadic, along streams, wet places, 4900–9700 ft.: Toll House Springs, 5971 ft., *Blakley 4632* (CAS); Antelope Springs, 4900 ft., *Raven 7044* (CAS), *Munz 21,000* (CAS); Cottonwood Creek, 9700 ft., *HM 248*; Chiatovich Creek, 8000 ft., *D 3091*.

3. Clematis

1. **C. ligusticifolia** Nutt. Common vine, riparian areas below 7500 ft.: spring northeast of Antelope Spring, Deep Springs Valley, 5680 ft., *L 3020*; Black Canyon between Marble Canyon and Black Canyon Springs, 5700 ft., *D 2620*; Silver Canyon, 7000 ft., *HM 484*; Roberts Ranch, Wyman Creek, 7500 ft., *D 1716*.

4. Delphinium

A.   Leaves glabrous; flowers deep-blue to bluish-purple .. 2. *D. polycladon*
AA. Leaves pubescent; flowers light bluish or violet .... 1. *D. parishii*

1. **D. parishii** Gray. Washes and canyon bottoms, desert scrub to pinyon woodland, throughout the range, 5000–7500 ft.: Westgard Pass Road, 7.4 miles west of White Mountain Road, 5000 ft., *L 2655*; Black Canyon at Marble

Canyon, 5700 ft., *D 2650*; Silver Canyon, 7350 ft., *HM 106*; also reported in Indian Creek at 6000 ft.

2. **D. polycladon** Eastw. Moist glaciated canyons and wet meadows, along streambanks, 8500–11,500 ft.: Crooked Creek Ranger Station, 9500 ft., *D 1576*; Poison Creek, ca. 1½ mile north of junction with Cottonwood Creek, 10,000 ft., *Tucker 3416* (UC); McAfee Creek, 11,500 ft., *L 3324*; also observed in Milner Creek.

5. Myosurus

1. **M. aristatus** Benth. ex Hook. ssp. **montanus** (Campb.) Stone. Meadows and along streambanks, 10,000–11,000 ft.: head of Crooked Creek, westsouthwest of lab buildings in meadow, 10,200 ft., *L 3137*; Campito Meadow, 11,000 ft., *Tucker 3430* (DAV).

This is *M. minimus* L. ssp. *montanus* Campb. in Munz.

6. Ranunculus

A. Basal leaves 3-lobed or parted . . . . 3. *R. eschscholtzii*
AA. Basal leaves entire or shallowly lobed.
    B. Basal leaves elliptic to oblanceolate or lanceolate; petals usually 5; receptacle glabrous.
        C. Sepals tinged lavender, 5–8 mm. long; achenes 75–150, usually pubescent; petals 6–15 mm. long . . . . 4. *R. glaberrimus*
        CC. Sepals yellowish-green, 3–5 mm. long; achenes 10–30, glabrous; petals ca. 6 mm. long . . . . 1. *R. alismaefolius*
    BB. Basal leaves cordate, ovate, to reniform; petals 5–12; receptacle pubescent . . . . 2. *R. cymbalaria*

1. **R. alismaefolius** Geyer ex Benth. var. **alismellus** Gray. Known only from about rocks in damp grassland of McAfee Meadow, 11,800 ft., *D 1668*.

2. **R. cymbalaria** Pursh var. **saximontanus** Fern. Common, moist areas and streambanks, throughout the range, 6000–10,500 ft.: Wyman Creek, 8300 ft., *L 2783*; Crooked Creek, 10,000 ft., *Cook s.n.* (UC); Cottonwood Creek, 9500 ft., *D 1605*; Chiatovich Creek, 8000 ft., *D 3094*; also reported in Indian Creek at 6000 ft.

3. **R. eschscholtzii** Schlecht var. **oxynotus** (Gray) Jeps. Meadows and moist seepages beside snowbanks, upper subalpine and alpine, throughout the range, 11,400–14,000 ft.; Sheep Meadow, 11,400 ft., *HM 839*; White Mountain Peak: 13,300 ft., *D 2822*; 14,000 ft., *HM 489*; Pellisier Flats, 1 mile south of Jump-Off, 13,400 ft., *M 2169*.

4. **R. glaberrimus** Hook var. **ellipticus** (Greene) Greene. Meadows and glaciated canyons, upper elevations: road to Barcroft, 11,600 ft., *HM 136*.

7. Thalictrum

A. Plants 10–25 cm. high; stem scapose; flowers racemose . . . . 1. *T. alpinum*
AA. Plants 30–120 cm. high; stem leafy; flowers paniculate . 2. *T. sparsiflorum*

1. **T. alpinum** L. Moist meadows and springs by snowbanks, 10,500–12,000 ft.: Sheep Meadow, 11,400 ft., *HM 837;* Cottonwood Creek, 10,500 ft., *D 1625;* McAfee Meadow, 11,700 ft., *D 2615.*

2. **T. sparsiflorum** Turcz. Moist places in northern canyons, 8000–10,000 ft.; Chiatovich Creek, 8300 ft., *D 3075;* Trail Canyon, 9800 ft., *D 3354.*

FAMILY 10. PAPAVERACEAE

A. Plants with numerous prickles; petals several cm. long, white. 1. *Argemone*
AA. Plants glabrous; petals ca. 8 mm. long, yellow . . . . 2. *Eschscholzia*

1. Argemone

1. **A. munita** Dur. & Hilg. ssp. **rotundata** (Rydb.) Ownbey. Canyons and hillsides, desert scrub and pinyon woodland, below 8500 ft.: Westgard Pass Road, 5.4 miles west of White Mountain Road, 5900 ft., *L 2669;* Silver Canyon, 7350 ft., *HM 104;* Roberts Ranch, Wyman Creek, 8000 ft., *D 1712.*

2. Eschscholzia

1. **E. minutiflora** Wats. var. **darwinensis** Jones. Frequent, desert scrub and pinyon woodland, below 6000 ft.: below Toll House Springs, *Eastwood & Howell 9577* (CAS); 2.7 miles east of road to Saline Valley on Westgard Pass Road, *Lewis 1084* (UC); Black Canyon at Marble Canyon, 5700 ft., *D 2668;* mouth of Silver Canyon, *Heller 8195* (UC).

FAMILY 11. FUMARIACEAE
1. Corydalis

1. **C. aurea** Willd. Known only from Chiatovich Creek and Trail Canyon, 7500–8500 ft.: Chiatovich Creek, 8250 ft., *D 3069.*

FAMILY 12. ULMACEAE
1. Ulmus

1. **U. carpinifolia** Gleditsch. Cultivated in front of old shack, Toll House Springs, Westgard Pass Road, 5971 ft. *L 3328a.*

FAMILY 13. URTICACEAE
1. Urtica

1. **U. holosericea** Nutt. Extremely common, riparian areas throughout the range, below 9000 ft.: Silver Canyon, 7000 ft., *D 1524;* Wyman Creek, 1 mile below Roberts Ranch, 8000 ft., *D 1703;* Chiatovich Creek, 8000 ft., *D 3098;* also collected by Lankester in Indian Creek at 6000 ft.

FAMILY 14. BETULACEAE
1. Betula

1. **B. occidentalis** Hook. Forming scattered, discontinuous stands in riparian areas throughout the range, 5000–8000 ft.: Silver Canyon, 5500 ft., *Heller 8266* (UC); Wyman Creek, 7650 ft., *L 2808;* Trail Canyon, 8000 ft., *D 2698.*

FAMILY 15. NYCTAGINACEAE

A. Stigma fusiform, linear; perianth salverform . . . . 1. *Abronia*
AA. Stigma subglobose to globose; perianth campanulate to funnelform.
  B. Involucre of distinct bracts . . . . 2. *Hermidium*
  BB. Involucre of united bracts.
    C. Fruit 5-ribbed; involucre enlarged in fruit; leaf-blades deltoid to ovate-deltoid, succulent . . . . .4. *Oxybaphus*
    CC. Fruit ± smooth; involucre not much enlarged in fruit; leaf-blades ovate to reniform-ovate, not succulent . . . . 3. *Mirabilis*

1. Abronia

1. **A. turbinata** Torr. Open dry washes and sandy places, below 6500 ft.: north of Pinyon Hill, 6500 ft., *D 2873*; also reported from Benton, near Bishop, and in Deep Springs Valley (*Purpus 5822*, UC).

2. Hermidium

1. **H. alipes** Wats. Sporadic, dry slopes and flats, throughout the range, below 6500 ft.: highway near Basalt, 6000 ft., *DeDecker 1027* (CAS); between B & B Mine and Pinchot Creek, 6500 ft., *D M48*; 5 miles south of Basalt near mouth of Pinchot Creek, 6500 ft., *D 3256*; also reported near Laws at 4000 ft.

3. Mirabilis

A. Perianth white to pale pink 8–13 mm. long; involucre 1-flowered
                                                1. *M. bigelovii*
AA. Perianth deep pink to rose-purple, 3.5–4.5 cm. long; involucre 3- or more-flowered . . . . 2. *M. froebelii*

1. **M. bigelovii** Gray.
A. Stems subglabrous below, scabrous-puberulent above with short retrorse hairs . . . . 1c. var. *retrorsa*
AA. Stems villous and viscid.
  B. Fruit subglobose with 10 pale vertical lines . . . . 1b. var. *aspera*
  BB. Fruit ovoid, elongate, without 10 vertical lines . . . . . .1a. var. *bigelovii*

1a. Var. **bigelovii**. Desert scrub, throughout the range: 4500–7200 ft.: 4 miles east of Zurich on Westgard Pass Road, 4500 ft., *Straw s.n.* (RSA); east side of Westgard Pass, *Peirson 7540* (RSA); Silver Canyon, 5800 ft., *L 2866*; north fork of Silver Canyon, 7200 ft., *Wolf 2579* (RSA).

1b. Var. **aspera** (Greene) Munz. With the species in the southern portion of the range, below 6500 ft.: west base of Westgard Pass Road on desert slopes and washes, 4500–5000 ft., *HM 781*; Silver Canyon, 6500 ft., at base of cliff, *Munz 13556* (RSA).

1c. Var. **retrorsa** (Heller) Munz. Frequent in southern portion of the range below 6000 ft.: 8.5 miles west of summit on Westgard Pass Road, 4600 ft., *L 2636*; Birch Creek Canyon, 4.8 miles north of Payson Canyon Road, 6000 ft., *L 2983*; Silver Canyon, 6000 ft., *HM 132*.

62

2. **M. froebelii** (Behr) Greene. Dry hillsides and washes, 5000–8000 ft.: Westgard Pass, 6000 ft., *L 2895;* upper part of Marble Canyon of Black Canyon 7300 ft., *D 2883;* Silver Canyon, 5400 ft., *M 2065;* 1 mile below Roberts Ranch, Wyman Creek, 8000 ft., *D 1706.*

4. Oxybaphus
1. **O. pumilus** (Standl.) Standl. Southern canyons around 6000 ft.: Toll House Springs, 5971 ft., *Howell 41586* (CAS); 4.8 miles north of Payson Canyon in Birch Creek, 6000 ft., *L 2983A.*

FAMILY 16. CACTACEAE
A. Stems jointed; areoles with glochids . . . . 2. *Opuntia*
AA. Stems not jointed; arreoles without glochids.
B. Flowers lateral; fruits spiny . . . . 1. *Echinocereus*
BB. Flowers nearly terminal; fruits not spiny . . . . 3. *Sclerocactus*

1. Echinocereus
A. Plants cespitose forming clumps or mounds; flowers dull scarlet; radial spines nearly as long as the central spine . . . . 2. *E. triglochidiatus*
AA. Plants with stems 1–3 dm. high; flowers crimson-magenta or paler; radial spines much shorter than the central spine . . . . 1. *E. engelmannii*

1. **E. engelmannii** (Parry) Ruempl. Dry slopes, known only from Black Canyon, 5700 ft., *D 2726.*
2. **E. triglochidiatus** Engelm. var. **mohavensis** (Engelm. & Bigel.) L. Benson. Rocky slopes and alluvia, desert scrub and pinyon woodland, below 8500 ft.: Black Canyon, 5700 ft., *D 2636;* near Black Canyon Sprng, 8500 ft., *D 3018;* north fork, Silver Canyon, 7200 ft., *Wolf 2583* (RSA); pass between Deep Springs Valley and Fish Lake Valley, 6000 ft., *Balls 19000* (RSA).

2. Opuntia
A. Joints terete, tuberculate.
B. Petals greenish-yellow; stems erect . . . . 2. *O. echinocarpa*
BB. Petals purplish; stems low . . . . 4. *O. pulchella*
AA. Some joints flat or compressed, not tuberculate.
B. Flowers reddish; plants spineless . . . . 1. *O. basilaris*
BB. Flowers yellow to reddish; plants spiny . . . . 3. *O. erinacea*

1. **O. basilaris** Engelm. & Bigel. Infrequent, dry slopes and alluvium, below 6000 ft.: Antelope Springs, Deep Springs Valley, 5600 ft., *D 3027.*
2. **O. echinocarpa** Engelm. & Bigel., Desert scrub along northern base of range, below 7000 ft.: near mouth of Chiatovich Creek, 6700 ft., *D M31;* near Benton Station, *D M32.*
3. **O. erinacea** Engelm. & Bigel.

A. Flowers yellow; nearly all areoles with 4–9 spines . . . . 3a. var. *erinacea*
AA. Flowers reddish, salmon-yellow to yellow; areoles of lower joints spineless;

upper areoles with 1–4 spines . . . . 3b. var. *xanthostema*
3a. Var. **erinacea.** Dry slopes, desert scrub and pinyon woodland, below 7500 ft.: Marble Canyon at Black Canyon, 5700 ft., *D 3001*; Chiatovich Creek, 7500 ft., *D 2773*.
3b. Var. **xanthostema** (K. Schum.) L. Benson. Sporadically common on dry slopes: Chiatovich Creek, 8000 ft., *D 2547*.
4. **O. pulchella** Engelm. Dry slopes and flats; known only from near Pinyon Hill, 6500 ft., *D 2872*.

3. Sclerocactus
1. **S. polyancistrus** (Engelm. & Bigel.) Britt. & Rose. Dry slopes and flats, especially along eastern flank of range, below 6500 ft.: Payson Canyon Road, 6100 ft., *M 2443-A*; near Pinyon Hill, 6500 ft., *D 2761*.

FAMILY 17. CARYOPHYLLACEAE
A.   Sepals more or less distinct; petals without claws.
  B.   Capsule ovoid or ellipsoid.
    C.   Styles alternate with sepals, 4–5; petals ca. 1 mm. long . . 3. *Sagina*
    CC. Styles opposite sepals, 3; petals 2–6.5 mm. long or wanting.
      D.   Petals deeply notched or bifid . . . . 5. *Stellaria*
      DD. Petals more or less entire . . . . 1. *Arenaria*
  BB. Capsule cylindrical; petals 6–8 mm. long . . . . 2. *Cerastium*
AA. Sepals united into a tubular or cuplike calyx; petals clawed . . 4. *Silene*

1. Arenaria
A.   Entire plant glandular-pubescent.
  B.   Capsule valves entire; sepals 4–5 mm. long . . . . 3. *A. nuttallii*
  BB. Capsule valves 2-toothed; sepals 2.5–4.5 mm. long . . . . . . 1. *A. kingii*
AA. Plants glabrous or slightly glandular-pubescent in inflorescence.
  B.   Leaves 3–8 mm. long; flowers solitary to 2 or 3.
    C.   Sepals 2–2.5 mm. long; flowers solitary to 2 or 3 . . . . . . 4. *A. rossii*
    CC. Sepals 2.5–3.5 mm. long; flowers solitary
                                      la. *A. kingii* ssp. *compacta*
  BB. Leaves 1–6 cm. long; few- to several-flowered.
    C.   Leaves 1–2 cm. long; sepals 2.5–4.5 mm. long . . . . 1. *A. kingii*
    CC. Leaves 2–6 cm. long; sepals 5.5–6.5 mm. long . . . . 2. *A. macradenia*
1. **A. kingii** (Wats.) Jones
A.   Stems 10–20 cm. high; leaves 1–2 cm. long; cymes few- to several-flowered
                                      lb. var. *glabrescens*
AA. Stems 2–6 cm. high; leaves 3–6 mm. long; flowers solitary
                                      la. ssp. *compacta*

la. Ssp. **compacta** (Cov.) Maguire. Frequent, slopes, flats, and meadows, subalpine and alpine, 9800–12,500 ft.: head of Silver Canyon, 10,650 ft., *Kamb 1233* (UC); 1 mile north of Sheep Mountain, 11,800 ft., *J & L Roos 5161*

(UC); head of south fork of Cottonwood Creek, 11,700 ft., *Maguire & Holmgren 26153* (UC); McAfee Meadow, 11,700 ft., *D M85*; Barcroft lab, 12,500 ft., *Cook s.n.* (UC).

lb. Var. **glabrescens** (Wats.) Maguire. Frequent, dry slopes, throughout the range, abundant at higher elevations, 6000–12,600 ft.: White Mountain Road at "Sierra Viewpoint", 9500 ft., *L 2901*; Silver Canyon, 10,000 ft., *HM 238*; southeast slope of Sheep Mountain, 11,450 ft., *L 3179*; Cottonwood Creek on south ridge at 10,250 ft., *HM 266*; McAfee Meadow, 11,700 ft. *D 2807*; also reported from Indian Creek, Nev., at 6000 ft.

2. **A. macradenia** Wats. var. **parishiorum** Rob. Sporadic, desert scrub of the southern half of the range, below 6000 ft.: 5.4 miles west of White Mountain Road on Westgard Pass Road, 5900 ft., *L 2684*.

3. **A. nuttallii** Pax ssp. **gracilis** (Gray) Maguire. Known only on talus slopes at 11,200 ft., Sheep Mountain, *HM 848*.

4. **A. rossii** R. Br. Known only from sandy wet places in McAfee Meadow at ca. 11,700 ft., *D 2829*.

2. Cerastium

1. **C. beeringianum** Cham. & Schlecht. Frequent, slopes and meadows in moist areas above 12,500 ft.: near spring near Mt. Barcroft at ca. 12,500 ft., *HM 895*; road to White Mountain Peak: 13,200 ft., *D 1673*; 14,100 ft., *M 2228*; 1 mile south of Jump-Off, Pellisier Flats, 13,300 ft., *M & L 2182*.

3. Sagina

1. **S. saginoides** (L.) Karst. var. **hesperia** Fern. Infrequent, Meadows and moist rocky places at higher elevations: just below Barcroft lab at 12,450 ft., *Bacigalupi et al 8141*. (JEPS); Chiatovich Creek, *D2801*.

4. Silene

A.   Corollas usually less than 10 mm. long; calyx 5–8 mm. long
                                                                   2. *S. menziesii*
AA. Corollas usually more than 10 mm. long; calyx 8–18 mm. long.
  B.   Basal leaves usually less than 2 cm. long and 1–4 mm. wide.
    C.   Blades of petals equally 4-lobed, 4–6 mm. long; calyx 13–16 mm.
         long .... 1. *S. bernardina*
    CC. Blades of petals 2-lobed, each lobe with a small lateral tooth
                                                                   3. *S. sargentii*
  BB. Basal leaves usually more than 3 cm. long and 4 mm. wide.
    C.   Blades of petals with 4 subequal linear lobes .... 1. *S. bernardina*
    CC. Blades of petals with 2 lobes with appendages .... 4. *S. verecunda*
1. **S. bernardina** Wats.
A.   Plants glandular to base; leaves linear-lanceolate to linear-oblanceolate,
     1.5–3 mm. broad .... la. ssp. *bernardina*
AA. Plants glandular above only; leaves oblanceolate to lance-linear, 2–6 mm.
     broad .... lb. ssp. *maguirei*

la. Ssp. **bernardina** (= S. *montana* Wats. ssp. *bernardina* Wats. in Munz). Rocky slopes and flats, 10,000–12,600 ft.: 17 miles up Wyman Creek in bristlecone forest, *Maguire & Holmgren 26046* (UC); saddle north of intersection of White Mountain Road and Crooked Creek Road on east side of Campito Mountain, 10,800 ft., common, *L 3176*; northeast slope of Sheep Mountain, 12,100 ft., *M 2222*; north of Barcroft Lab, 12,600 ft., *Bacigalupi et al. 8130* (JEPS).

lb. Ssp. **Maguirei** Bocquet (S. *montana* Wats. in Munz): Rocky soils and talus slopes, throughout the range, 8500–10,700 ft.: basalt atop Bucks Peak, 10,700 ft., *M 2237*; Crooked Creek, 3 miles below lab, 9600 ft., *HM 879*; ridge between Crooked Creek and Cottonwood Creek, 10,000 ft., *HM 442*; Chiatovich Creek, 8500 ft., *D 2540*.

2. **S. menziesii** Hook. ssp. **dorrii** (Kell.) Hitchc. & Maguire. Dry soils, streambanks and moist canyons, 8000–10,000 ft.: Roberts Ranch, Wyman Creek, 8000 ft., *D 3138*; Cottonwood Creek, 9200 ft., *L 3301*; south fork of Cottonwood Creek in aspens, 9800 ft., *HM 458*.

3. **S. sargentii** Wats. Rocky slopes at upper elevations. Known only from upper Cottonwood Creek drainage at 11,800 ft., *D 2599*.

4. **S. verecunda** Wats. ssp. **andersonii** (Clokey) Hitchc. & Maguire. Uncommon, 5300–7500 ft.: Wyman Creek, 7500 ft., *D 3159*; Benton Station, *Jones s.n.* (POM).

5. Stellaria

A. Leaves ovate; petals shorter than sepals or wanting . . . . . . 1. S. *crispa*
AA. Leaves lance-linear; petals equal to or longer than sepals . . 2. S. *longipes*

1. **S. crispa** Cham. & Schlecht. Damp meadows and along streams, upper elevations. Known only from Chiatovich Creek, 10,300 ft., *D 3122*.

2. **S. longipes** Goldie. Meadows and streambanks throughout the range, 6000–11,500 ft.: Crooked Creek, 9000 ft., *L 2870*; Cottonwood Creek, 9000 ft., *D 1595*; McAfee Creek, 11,500 ft., *L 3323*; Big Meadows, Chiatovich Creek, 8800 ft., *D 3330*.

FAMILY 18: PORTULACACEAE

A. Capsule circumscissle; sepals 2–8; stamens 5–many . . . . . . 2. *Lewisia*
AA. Capsule dehiscent by 2–3 valves; sepals 2; stamens 1–5.
B. Style simple with 2 stigmas; capsule 2-valved; stamens 1–3
1. *Calyptridium*
BB. Style branches 3; capsule 3-valved; stamens 2–6 . . . . 3. *Montia*

1. Calyptridium

A. Style short; petals 2 . . . . 1. C. *roseum*
AA. Style long-filiform; petals 4 . . . . 2. C. *umbellatum*

1. **C. roseum** Wats. Open, sometimes moist places in washes and disturbed areas, throughout the range, 8500–12,000 ft.: White Mountain Road, 8500 ft., *HM 771*; Crooked Creek Ranger Station, 9500 ft., *D 1568*; McAfee Meadow, 11,700 ft., *D 2805*; Cabin Creek, 10,300 ft., *D 2550*.

2. **C. umbellatum** (Torr.) Greene var. **caudiciferum** (Gray) Jeps. Fell-fields and rocky slopes, 12,500–14,100 ft.: McAfee Meadow, 12,500 ft., *Tucker 2264* (DAV); White Mountain Peak, common among rocks, 14,100 ft., *L 3241*; Pellisier Flats, 1 mile south of Jump-Off, 13,300 ft., *M 2192*.

2. Lewisia

A. Sepals herbaceous or hyaline; petals 7–18 mm. long; seeds 1–1.2 mm. long
1. *L. pygmaea*

AA. Sepals petaloid, scarious in age; petals 15–25 mm. long; seeds 2–2.5 mm. long .... 2. *L. rediviva*

1. **L. pygmaea** (Gray) Rob.
A. Marginal gland of sepals light in color, not stipitate
1a. ssp. *pygmaea*
AA. Marginal gland of sepals dark, stipitate .... 1b. ssp. *glandulosa*

1a. Ssp. **pygmaea.** Meadows, slopes and ridges in seepage and other damp areas, alpine areas, 11,900–14,100 ft.: north slope of Sheep Mountain, 11,900 ft., *M 2131*; McAfee Meadows, 12,000 ft., *D 1676A*; ridge south of White Mountain Peak, 12,000 ft., *D 1639*; White Mountain Peak, 14,050 ft., *Bacigalupi et al. 8176* (JEPS); Pellisier Flats, north of Mt. Dubois, 13,200 ft., *M & L 2180*.

1b. Ssp. **glandulosa** (Rydb.) Ferris. Meadows and rocky slopes, alpine areas above 12,000 ft.: north of Barcroft Peak, 12,500 ft., *HM 605-A*; White Mountain Road, 13,500 ft., *L 3247*.

2. **L. rediviva** Pursh var. **minor** (Rydb.) Munz. Infrequent, pinyon woodland, throughout the range, 7300–9200 ft.: Westgard Pass, 7300 ft., *Grinnell 1048A* (UC); weasel turnaround, Silver Canyon, 9200 ft., *HM 744*; Trail Canyon, 8000 ft., *D. s.n.*

3. Montia

A. Stem leaves 2–several pairs.
B. Annual; petals 1–3 mm. long .... 2. *M. funstonii*
BB. Perennial; petals 5–8 mm. long .... 1. *M. chamissoi*
AA. Stem leaves 1 pair, united into a suborbicular disc .... 3. *M. perfoliata*

1. **M. chamissoi** (Ledeb.) Dur. & Jacks. Streamsides and wet meadows, throughout the range, 7000–11,000 ft.: White Mountain Road at Campito Meadow, 10,600 ft., *L 3173*; Cabin Creek, 10,300 ft., *D 2554A*; Chiatovich Creek, 8000 ft., *D 3079*.

2. **M. funstonii** Rydb. Moist banks and edges of streams, 8400–10,500 ft.: south fork, Creeked Creek, 10,300 ft., *M 2236*; Chiatovich Creek, 8400 ft., *M 2080*.

3. **M. perfoliata** (Donn) Howell. Shaded damp places, below 7000 ft.: Marble Canyon of Black Canyon, 5800 ft., *D 2724*. Ours is forma *parviflora* (Doubl.) Howell.

FAMILY 19. CHENOPODIACEAE

A. Leaves flattened, not scaly or fleshy.
  B. Flowers perfect or female, not enclosed in bracts.
    C. Calyx with 3–5 segments; stamens 4–5 . . . . 2. *Chenopodium*
    CC. Calyx with 1 segment; stamen 1 . . . . 6. *Monolepis*
  BB. Flowers imperfect, the female enclosed in two bracts.
    C. Fruiting bracts glabrous; leaves not revolute.
      D. Bracts compressed, the margins not entirely united; leaves linear
          to triangular, spatulate, ovate or oblong, ± farinose . . 1. *Atriplex*
      DD. Bracts obcompressed, united entirely into a sac; leaves oblanceo-
          late to oblong, usually glabrate in age . . . . .4. *Grayia*
    CC. Fruiting bracts hairy; leaves linear to lanceolate, the margins revolute
                                                                        3. *Eurotia*
AA. Leaves fleshy and sublinear or scaly and spiny.
  B. Plants with perfect or perfect and female flowers, mostly herbs.
    C. Leaves not spine- or bristle-tipped; perennial . . . . 5. *Kochia*
    CC. Leaves spine- or bristle-tipped; annual . . . . 7. *Salsola*
  BB. Plants with male flowers in terminal spikes and female flowers solitary
      in leaf axils, spiny shrubs . . . . 8. *Sarcobatus*

1. Atriplex

A. Plants herbaceous, 1.5–6 dm. tall; monoecious; leaves petioled, blades 2–5
    cm. long . . . . 1. *A. argentea*
AA. Plants woody, mostly taller than 4 dm. (except sometimes in *A. conferti-
    folia*); dioecious; leaves sessile to subsessile (short-petioled in *A. torreyi*)
    blades 1.5–3 cm. long (–5 cm. in *A. canescens*).
  B. Leaves linear-spatulate to narrowly oblong, 1.5–5 cm. long; fruiting
      bracts with second pair of wings arising from middle of each bract
                                                                  2. *A. canescens*
  BB. Leaves elliptic to ovate, oblong, or spatulate, 0.3–3 cm. long; fruiting
      bracts without second pair of wings.
    C. Fruiting bracts 6–12 mm. long, spine present . . . . 3. *A. confertifolia*
    CC. Fruiting bracts 2–4 mm. long.
      D. Leaves 0.3–2 cm. long, usually sessile; twigs not spinelike
                                                                  4. *A. polycarpa*
      DD. Leaves 1.5–3 cm. long, short-petioled; twigs acutely angled into
          spines . . . . 5. *A. torreyi*

1. **A. argentea** Nutt. On alluvia and in alkaline places, desert scrub and pinyon woodland, 5000–7700 ft.: above Westgard Pass on White Mountain Road,
7700 ft., *HM 358*; Silver Canyon, 7000 ft., *M 2335*; Fish Lake Valley, 5000 ft.,
D 3320 (CAS).

2. **A. canescens** (Pursh) Nutt. Dry slopes and washes, desert scrub and pinyon woodland, below 6500 ft.: 7.4 miles west of White Mountain Road on

Westgard Pass Road, 5000 ft., *L 2668*; Payson Canyon, 6400 ft., *Wolf 3229* (CAS); Black Canyon at Marble Canyon, 5700 ft., *D 2646*.

3. **A. confertifolia** (Torr. & Frem.) Wats. Dry flats and canyon bottoms and alkaline places, desert scrub below 6500 ft.: Westgard Pass Road, 5.4 miles west of White Mountain Road, 5900 ft., *L 2673*; Black Canyon at Marble Canyon, 5700 ft., *D 2695*; Silver Canyon, 6500 ft., *L 2837*.

4. **A. polycarpa** (Torr.) Wats. Slopes and washes, desert scrub below 6000 ft.: Toll House Springs, 5971 ft., *HM 82, L 2696*; ridge north of Silver Canyon on west slope, 5800 ft., *HM 200*.

5. **A. torreyi** (Wats.) Wats. Occasional, canyons and flats of the desert scrub of the southwestern portion of the range; below 6000 ft.: Silver Canyon, 5525 ft., *D 3154*; also reported from near Zurich.

2. Chenopodium

A. Plants glandular-villous . . . . 3. *C. botrys*
AA. Plants not glandular-pubescent but mostly mealy or farinose or glabrous.
  B. Seeds mostly horizontal.
  C. Leaf-blades ± cordate at base . . . . 6. *C. gigantospermum*
  CC. Leaf-blades rounded to truncate, attenuate, or hastate at base.
    D. Leaf-blades linear to narrow-lanceolate, to oblong or oval, with short petioles.
      E. Leaves linear, 2–3 mm. wide . . . . 8. *C. leptophyllum*
      EE. Leaves narrowly lanceolate to oblong or oval, the lower 4–18 mm. wide; pericarp free . . . . 4. *C. dessicatum*
    DD. Leaf-blades lance-ovate to ovate to triangularly hastate or elliptic-oblong; short- to long-petioled.
      E. Main leaf-blades definitely longer than wide.
        F. Plants few-branched or simple; flowers in paniculate spikes.
          G. Stems 10–50 cm. tall; pericarp free . . . . 1. *C. atrovirens*
          GG. Stems 30–150 cm. tall; pericarp adherent.
            H. Stems 40–80 cm. tall; plants ill-scented; branches farinose, seeds nearly smooth . . . . 7. *C. hians*
            HH. Stems 30–150 cm. tall, plants not ill-smelling, glabrous; seeds minutely roughened . . . . .2. *C. berlandieri*
        FF. Plants much branched; flowers in diffuse cymose panicles
            9. *C. nevadense*
      EE. Main leaf-blades not longer than wide . . . . . . 5. *C. fremontii*
  BB. Seeds mostly vertical.
  C. Perianth at maturity conspicuously bright red and fleshy
            10. *C. overi*
  CC. Perianth at maturity not bright red or fleshy, stems red
            11. *C. rubrum*

1. **C. atrovirens** Rydb. Common, dry open areas, desert scrub to subalpine, 5500–10,200 ft.: Antelope Springs, 5600 ft., *Raven 7049* (CAS); Crooked Creek, 10,000 ft., *L 3266*; Trail Canyon, 8300 ft., *D 2521*.

2. **C. berlandieri** Moq. var. **zschackei** (Murr) Murr. Known only from Toll House Springs, Westgard Pass Road, 5971 ft., *L 3327*.

This is a distinctive and infrequent form with little farinosity, prominently green and with nearly trilobed leaves; essentially identical with material from Mt. Laguna, San Diego Co. (*Wahl 21813*, PAC).

3. **C. botrys** L. Deserts and canyon bottoms in sandy places, below 7000 ft.: near the cabins on valley floor, Black Canyon at Marble Canyon, 5700 ft., *D 2858*; Silver Canyon, 4.7 miles east of Laws, 7000 ft., *Munz 12716* (RSA).

4. **C. dessicatum** A. Nels.

A.   Plants low, 1–3 dm. high; leaves oblong to oval .... 4a. var. *dessicatum*
AA. Plants erect, 2–8 dm. high; leaves narrow-lanceolate to oblong
                                      4b. var. *leptophylloides*

4a. Var. **dessicatum**. Occasional, in dry areas, 7700–10,500 ft.: White Mountain Road, above Westgard Pass, on sandstone, 7700 ft., *HM 357*; north end of Sagehen Flat, 10,500 ft., *HM 542*.

4b. Var. **leptophylloides** (Murr) H. A. Wahl. Known only from Toll House Springs, Westgard Pass Road, 5971 ft., *L 3327*.

5. **C. fremontii** Wats. Locally common in dry places below 8000 ft.: White Mountain Road, 7700 ft., *L 3029*; also reported by Lankester from Fish Lake Valley at 4900 ft.

6. **C. gigantospermum** Aellen. Known only from the summit of Westgard Pass, under pinyons at 7800 ft.: *Jaeger s.n.* (POM).

7. **C. hians** Standley. Known only from open field, Crooked Creek lab, 10,200 ft.: *Tucker 2250* (UC).

8. **C. leptophyllum** Nutt. Dry alkaline places and sandy soils, slopes and canyons, throughout the range, 4300–10,500 ft.: edge of Reed Flat, 10,300 ft., *Munz 21017* (UC); near mouth of Silver Canyon, 4300 ft., *D 3460*; head of Wyman Creek, 10,000 ft., *Munz 21060* (UC); head of Crooked Creek, *Maguire & Holmgren 26158* (UC); Cottonwood Creek, 8900 ft., *L 2928*; Indian Creek (Nev.), 7400 ft., *Archer 7227* (UC).

9. **C. nevadense** Standley. Rare, 4900–6500 ft.: Deep Springs Valley, *Raven 7049* (CAS); near mouth of Pinchot Creek, 6500 ft., *D 3273*; also collected by Lankester (*791*) from Fish Lake Valley at 4900 ft.

10. **C. overi** Aellen. Dry soil, rocky slopes among sagebrush, 9000–11,000 ft.: Crooked Creek Ranger Station, 9500 ft., *D 1544*.

11. **C. rubrum** L. Subalpine forest, 9500–11,000 ft.: on basalt capped ridge of Buck's Peak, 10,800 ft., *M 2230*; also reported from Crooked Creek Ranger Station, 9500 ft.

3. Eurotia

1. **E. lanata** (Pursh) Moq. Common, flats and slopes and dry washes, desert scrub and pinyon woodland, throughout the range, 4000–8000 ft.: west side of Westgard Pass, *Eastwood & Howell 9582* (CAS); mouth of Birch Creek at

Payson Canyon Road, 5050 ft., *L 2977*; Trail Canyon, on rocky slopes at 8000 ft., *D 3356*; Queen Canyon, 7000 ft., *Archer 7172* (UC).

4. Grayia

1. **G. spinosa** (Hook.) Moq. Common, desert scrub and lower parts of the pinyon woodland, southern end of the range, below 7200 ft.: 2.3 miles southwest of Westgard Pass on Westgard Pass Road, 6600 ft., *HM 61*; mouth of Mollie Gibson Canyon, 6960 ft., *L 2950*; Black Ace Mine, Cedar Flats, 7200 ft., *HM 805*; Black Canyon at Marble Canyon, 5700 ft., *D 2677*; Silver Canyon, 5700 ft., *M 1499*; Wyman Creek, 6800 ft., *L 2812*.

5. Kochia

1. **K. americana** Wats. var. **vestita** Wats. Dry areas, hillsides and flats. Known only from near Pinyon Hill, 6500 ft., *D 2867*.

6. Monolepis

1. **M. nuttalliana** (Schult.) Greene. Occasional in meadows, dry sandy areas, or disturbed habitats, subalpine, ca. 10,000 ft.: head of Wyman Creek, 10,000 ft., *Munz 21046* (RSA); Crooked Creek lab, 10,150 ft., *L 3113*.

7. Salsola

1. **S. kali** L. var. **tenuifolia** Tausch. Open valley floors, washes, and roadsides, throughout the range, below 7000 ft. (9000): Westgard Pass Road, 7.4 miles west of White Mountain Road, 5000 ft., *L 2653*; Black Canyon at Marble Canyon, 5700 ft., *D 2855*; Silver Canyon, 7000 ft., *M 2325*.

8. Sarcobatus

1. **S. vermiculatus** (Hook.) Torr. Sporadic in lower canyons and alkaline places, throughout the range, below 7000 ft.: Antelope Springs, 5600 ft., *L 2999, M & L 1751*; Black Canyon, 6500 ft., *D 1754*; also reported from Queen Canyon and near Zurich.

FAMILY 20. AMARANTHACEAE
1. Amaranthus

1. **A. blitoides** Wats. Dry soils, canyons and washes. Known only from Wyman Creek, above Roberts Ranch, ca. 8000 ft., *D 3166*.

This species is *A. graecizans* L. in Munz. Sauer reports that *A. blitoides is* distinct from *A. graecizans* (Flora of Wisc. Cont.).

FAMILY 21. POLYGONACEAE
A. Leaves without stipules.
    B. Involucre with spine- or bristle-tipped teeth.
        C. Involucre usually 1-flowered (2–3) and 3, 5, or 6-toothed; the tube cylindrical or 3-angled . . . . 1. *Chorizanthe*
        CC. Involucre usually 2–several flowered, the tube turbinate, with 4–5

lobes .... 4. *Oxytheca*
BB. Involucre with 3–8 lobes or teeth, not spine- or bristle-tipped
2. *Eriogonum*
AA. Leaves with stipular sheaths; involucres lacking.
  B.   Calyx 4- or 6-parted.
      C.   Leaves reniform; sepals 4 .... 3. *Oxyria*
      CC. Leaves narrow to broadly lanceolate .... 6. *Rumex*
  BB. Calyx 5-parted .... 5. *Polygonum*

1. Chorizanthe
A.   Involucre 6-toothed and ribbed; leaves 2–5 cm. long, broadly spatulate
1. *C. brevicornu* ssp. *spathulata*
AA. Involucre 3- or 5-toothed
  B.   Involucre with straight spines or teeth; leaves ovate to obovate, 1–3 cm.
      long, glabrous above .... 2. *C. rigida*
  BB. Involucre with 5 teeth, 4 of which are recurved or hooked and 1 leaflike;
      leaves oblanceolate, 2–3 cm. long, villous above ...... 3. *C. watsonii*

1. **C. brevicornu** Torr. ssp. **spathulata** (Small ex Rydb.) Munz. Common, desert and sagebrush-covered flats, alluvia and hillsides, below 7500 ft.: 2.9 miles east of Big Pine on Westgard Pass Road, 4200 ft., *HM 12*; Black Canyon at Marble Canyon, 5700 ft., *D 2738*; first canyon south of Silver Canyon, 5000 ft., *HM 722*.

2. **C. rigida** (Torr.) Torr. & Gray. Desert and sagebrush-covered hillsides and flats, below 6000 ft.: 2.9 miles east of Big Pine on Westgard Pass Road, 4200 ft., *HM 13*; first canyon south of Silver Canyon at 5600 ft., *HM 778*.

3. **C. watsonii** Torr. & Gray. Sporadic on alluvia, throughout the range, below 7500 ft.: Westgard Pass, 7300 ft., *D 2794*; first canyon south of Silver Canyon, 5000 ft., *HM 723*; Birch Creek, 5300 ft., *D M68*.

2. Eriogonum
Text contributed by James L. Reveal
A.   Plants annuals.
  B.   Involucres turbinate to campanulate, not ribbed, mostly peduncled.
      C.   Calyx-segments pubescent or puberulent.
         D.   Leaves basal and also on the lower nodes.
            E.   Basal leaves lanceolate to obovate, 1–1.5 cm. wide, tomentose;
               calyx-segments with outer inflated segments distinctly spotted,
               glandular-puberulent .... 16. *E. maculatum*
            EE. Basal leaves linear, 0.5–3 mm. wide, pilose; calyx-segments not
               inflated, sparsely pubescent .... 26. *E. spergulinum*
         DD. Leaves strictly basal.
            E.   Involucres glabrous; calyx-segments short-hirsute; leaves hispid;
               perennials but flowering the first year, stems often inflated
12. *E. inflatum*

       EE. Involucres and calyx-segments glandular-puberulent; leaves densely tomentose below; strictly annual, stems never inflated

                                   22. *E. pusillum*

CC. Calyx-segments glabrous.

    D.   leaves densely tomentose below.

       E.   Outer calyx-segments panduriform, crisped, not cordate; peduncles slender, 3–5 mm. long . . . . 5. *E. cernuum*

       EE. Outer calyx-segments cordate at the base.

          F.   Stems glabrous.

             G.   Involucres narrowly turbinate to turbinate; peduncles usually obvious, up to 15 mm. long; calyx-segments white

                                       6. *E. deflexum*

             GG. Involucres hemispheric; peduncles lacking; calyx-segments yellow . . . . 11. *E. hookeri*

          FF. Stems glandular; calyx-segments white . . 3. *E. brachypodum*

    DD. Leaves pilose or pilose-hispid, not tomentose.

       E.   Leaves strictly basal, round-obovate, 4–20 mm. wide, pilose-hispid . . . . 7. *E. esmeraldense*

       EE. Leaves basal and cauline, linear, 0.5–3 mm. wide, pilose

                                   26. *E. spergulinum*

BB. Involucres narrowly cylindrical, erect, angled or ribbed, not peduncled.

    C.   Outer calyx-segments fan-shaped, their sides incurved below the broad truncate apices, yellowish to reddish; branches usually incurved at the summit in age; involucres few-flowered . . 18. *E. nidularium*

CC. Outer calyx-segments plane, not distinctly fan-shaped, white or distinctly yellow; branches open, not incurved at the summit.

    D.   Calyx-segments 1.5–2 mm. long, white.

       E.   Stems densely tomentose; flowers 3–10 per involucre; plants rather densely branched . . . . 20. *E. palmerianum*

       EE. Stems glabrous or merely floccose at the very base; flowers more than 10 per involucre; plants mostly open and erect

                                     1. *E. baileyi*

    D.   Calyx-segments 0.6–1 mm. long, yellow . . . . 2. *E. brachyanthum*

AA. Plants perennials.

    B.   Involucres on capillary peduncles 5–20 mm. long; calyx-segments short-hirsute; stems inflated . . . . 12. *E. inflatum*

BB. Involucres sessile, or if peduncled, then these not capillary.

    C.   Flowers with a stipitate base.

       D.   Calyx-segments pubescent externally; inflorescences capitate.

          E.   Flowering stems less than 1 dm. long; leaves densely tomentose, up to 1 cm. long . . . . 4. *E. caespitosum*

          EE. Flowering stems 1.5–3 dm. long; leaves subglabrous to short-pilose, 1–3 cm. long . . . . 15. *E. latens*

       DD. Calyx-segments glabrous externally; inflorescences not capitate.

E. Leaves spatulate to elliptic, tomentose below or subglabrous to glabrate on both surfaces; calyx-segments yellowish
27. *E. umbellatum*

EE. Leaves obovate to orbicular, densely white felty-tomentose throughout; calyx-segments whitish .... 25. *E. saxatile*

CC. Flowers not stipitate at the base.

D. Inflorescences capitate, plants cespitose or nearly so.

E. Calyx-segments dissimilar, the outer whorl of segments mostly twice as wide as the inner whorl; leaves thinly tomentose, not at all glandular .... 19. *E. ovalifolium*

EE. Calyx-segments similar or nearly so.

F. Calyx-segments glabrous or glandular, not villous.

G. Involucres forming a distinct rigid tube 3–4 mm. long.

H. Calyx-segments white; leaf-blades mostly less than 5 mm. long, densely white-tomentose on both surfaces, not glandular .... 14. *E. kennedyi*

HH. Calyx-segments yellowish; leaf-blades 4–10 (15) mm. long, greenish-tomentose and glandular on both surfaces
23. *E. rosense*

GG. Involucres membranaceous and indistinctly forming a tube 2–3 mm. long; calyx-segments rose to red; leaves 1–2 cm. long, tomentose and glandular throughout
9. *E. gracilipes*

FF. Calyx-segments villous within and without; leaves 3–8 mm. long, densely tomentose; achenes slightly villous; lower elevations on the eastern slope of the White Mountains, but not found in our immediate area .... *E. shockleyi*

DD. Inflorescences cymose or racemose, open and not capitate, or if so, then plants shrubby.

E. Inflorescences with involucres racemosely arranged along the upper branches; involucres tomentose.

F. Plants shrubby, up to 12 dm. high; leaves mostly elliptic to oblong, 2–3 cm. long, scattered along the lower stems, soon deciduous .... 13. *E. kearneyi*

FF. Plants low subshrubs or herbaceous perennials less than 3 dm. high.

G. Plants suffrutescent and much branched at the base, spreading; leaves narrowly elliptic, 2–5 mm. wide
28. *E. wrightii*

GG. Plants not suffrutescent at the base; leaves oblong to rounded, 1–3 cm. wide.

H. Basal leaves roundish to broadly ovate, 1.5–4 cm. long, 1–2.5 cm. wide; plants from a highly branched woody caudex; involucres 3–5 mm. long . . 21. *E. panamintense*

74

HH. Basal leaves oblong to oblong-ovate, 2.5–3.5 cm. long,
1.5–2.5 cm. wide; plants arising from a single, woody,
little branched caudex; involucres 3–4 mm. long
24. *E. rupinum*
EE. Inflorescences with involucres arranged in cymes or panicles;
involucres thinly pubescent or glabrous.
F. Plants herbaceous, not shrubby.
G. Leaves oblong, densely tomentose below; calyx-segments
white or more commonly yellow; probably on the lower
slopes, but not definitely known from the White Mountains
E. nudum
GG. Leaves lanceolate to lance-ovate, thinly pubescent below;
calyx-segments white; to be expected on the northern
foothills of the White Mountains . . . . *E. elatum*
FF. Plants shrubby, woody at the base and with the lower stems
leafy.
G. Calyx-segments glabrous.
H. Inflorescence a compact terminal cyme; involucres mostly sparsely pubescent, turbinate; calyx-segments 2–3
mm. long, oblong, subcordate at the base; leaves densely
tomentose below, floccose or sparsely pubescent above,
persistent . . . . 17. *E. microthecum*
HH. Inflorescence a divaricately branched panicle; involucres glabrous, mostly campanulate; calyx-segments 3–4
mm. long, orbicular or nearly so, cordate at the base;
leaves sparsely floccose below, glabrous above, quickly
deciduous . . . . 10. *E. heermannii*
GG. Calyx-segments pubescent; leaves canescent to hoary above
8. *E. fasciculatum*

1. **E. baileyi** S. Wats. Infrequent, in dry washes on the lower foothills, desert
scrub, below 6000 feet elevation. Observed south of Benton.
2. **E. brachyanthum** Cov. Infrequent, sandy or gravelly soils, scrub and pinyon
woodlands below 7500 ft. Known only from Post Meadow, Indian Creek, 7500
ft., *Archer 7231* (UC). More common on the lower foothills along the western
side of the White Mountains.
3. **E. brachypodum** Torr. & Gray. Common, dry washes and disturbed gravelly soils, desert scrub and pinyon woodland in southern portion of the range,
below 7000 ft.: Westgard Pass Road, 7.4 miles west of White Mountain Road,
5000 ft., *L 2644*; Black Canyon, 6000 ft., *D 1755*; Silver Canyon at ca. 4600
ft., *D s.n.*; Silver Canyon, 4.7 miles east of Laws, 7000 ft., *Munz 12714* (CAS).
Care must be taken not to confuse this species with the closely related *E. deflexum* as the two will occasionally be found growing together.
4. **E. caespitosum** Nutt. Common, sagebrush scrub and pinyon woodland,
throughout the range, 7000–10,000 ft.; Cedar Flat, 7000 ft., *D 3289*; Black

Mountain Road, 8100 ft., *HM 387a*; Silver Canyon, 9750 ft., *L 2855*; mouth of Queen Canyon, 7000 ft., *D 3254*.

5. **E. cernuum** Nutt. Infrequent but locally common, sandy, gravelly, or rocky soils, in a wide variety of habitats ranging from sagebrush scrub to alpine fell-fields, 8000–10,500 ft.: Wyman Creek, Roberts Ranch, 8000 ft., *D 1697*; Wyman Creek, 1 mile east of White Mountain Road, 10,000 ft., *L 3054*; Crooked Creek, vicinity of White Mountain Research Station, 10,200 ft., *Tucker 2228* (UC); McCloud Camp, Cottonwood Creek, ca. 9000 ft., *D s.n.*; Chiatovich Creek, 8700 ft., *D 3118*. Our plant is the var. *cernuum* and includes as a synonym the taxon *tenue*.

6. **E. deflexum** Torr.
A.   Peduncles 1.5–2 mm. long; involucres turbinate . . . . . . 6a. var. *deflexum*
AA. Peduncles mostly 5–15 mm. long; involucres narrowly turbinate
$\qquad\qquad\qquad\qquad\qquad\qquad\qquad$ 6b. var. *baratum*

6a. Var. **deflexum.** Infrequent, gravelly soils, Westgard Pass and along the highway on both slopes, sagebrush scrub: Westgard Pass, 6000 ft., *Jaeger s.n.* (DS).

6b. Var. **baratum** (Elmer) Reveal. Common, on gravelly basaltic or sandy soils, pinyon woodland, 4500–7500 ft.: "The Narrows," Westgard Pass Road, 2.2 miles west of White Mountain Road, 7000 ft., *Bacigalupi et al. 8217* (JEPS); Molly Gibson Canyon mine road at mouth of canyon, 6800 ft., *M & L 1727*; Black Canyon, 5700 ft., *D s.n.*, 9 June, 1930; Silver Canyon, 4500 ft., *L 2851*; Chiatovich Creek, 2 miles west of Kellogg Ranch, 5100 ft., *Archer 7216* (UC); near Pinyon Hill, Esmeralda Co., 7000 ft., *D s.n.*

7. **E. esmeraldense** S. Wats. Rare or infrequent, washes and on gravelly soils, pinyon woodland, 7000–10,300 ft.: head of Silver Canyon, 10,300 ft., *HM 671*; Crooked Creek, 10,000 ft., *L 3283*; near Pinyon Hill, 7000 ft., *D 2750*. Our plant is var. *esmeraldense*.

8. **E. fasciculatum** Benth. var. **polifolium** (Benth. in DC) Torr. & Gray. Common, gravelly and rocky slopes and canyons, sagebrush scrub and pinyon woodland, 5000–7500 ft.: Westgard Pass Road, 7.4 miles west of White Mountain Road, 5000 ft., *L 2658*; Black Canyon at Marble Canyon, 5600 ft., *D 3020*; second ridge south of Silver Canyon, 5500 ft., *HM 140*; Roberts Ranch, Wyman Creek, 7500 ft., *D 1717*.

9. **E. gracilipes** S. Wats. Infrequent, dry rocky soils, alpine fell-fields, 10,000–13,000 ft.: north of Schulman Grove, 10,000 ft., *HM 394*; southeast slope of Sheep Mountain, White Mountain Road, 11,450 ft., *L 3184*; head of south fork of Cottonwood Creek, 11,700 ft., *Maguire & Holmgren 26154* (UC); White Mountain Road above Barcroft Laboratory, 12,700 ft., *HM 851*. Endemic to the White Mountains.

10. **E. heermannii** Dur. & Hilg.
A.   Stems and branches glabrous; shrubs to 8 dm. high . . 10a. var. *humilius*

AA. Stems and branches scabrous; subshrubs to 4 dm. high

10b. var. *argense*

10a. Var **humilius** (S. Stokes) Reveal. Common on the west side of the White Mountains, sandy to gravelly soils or broken talus slopes, sagebrush, shadscale shrub, and pinyon woodland, 5000–8000 ft.: Toll House Springs, Westgard Pass Road, 5971 ft., *L 3330*; upper end of Marble Canyon of Black Canyon, 7000 ft., *D 2844*.

10b. Var. **argense**(M.E. Jones)Munz. Rare to infrequent along the eastern slope and southern end of the White Mountain. Rarely on the west slope, below 8500 ft.: 1.2 miles below forks of Silver Canyon, scattered throughout the canyon at 6200 ft., *Wolf 2599* (UC); reported by J. T. Howell from the fossil outcrop area at about 8000 ft., White Mountain Road.

11. **E. hookeri** S. Wats. Rare, desert scrub at ca. 4200 ft. on the west side of the White Mountains near Chalfant.: 18 miles south of Benton, *Peirson 12465* (RSA, UC).

12. **E. inflatum** Torr. & Frem. Common, gravelly basaltic soils, sagebrush and shadscale scrub and pinyon woodlands below 6500 ft.: Westgard Pass Road, 8.5 miles west of White Mountain Road, 4600 ft., *L 2637*; Black Canyon, 6500 ft., *D 1752*. Our plant is var. *inflatum*, a first-year flowering perennial. A strictly annual variant is var. *contiguum* which occurs to the south of the White Mountains but may be found at the lower elevations at the south end of the range in early spring. A closely related species, *E. trichopes* Torr., differs from *E. inflatum* in being strictly annual, with several whorled branchlets at each lower node and with a four-lobed involucre. It is also to be expected at the extreme southern tip of the White Mountians.

13. **E. kearneyi** Tidestr. var. **monoense** (S. Stokes) Reveal. Infrequent, sandy, often pumice soils, sagebrush scrub and pinyon woodland, below 8500 ft.: White Mountains, *Purpus 6426* (UC, US).

14. **E. kennedyi** Porter ex Wats. var. **purpusii** (Bdg.) Reveal. Infrequent but locally common, gravelly and rocky soils, sagebrush scrub and pinyon woodland, below 8000 ft.: Westgard Pass on north side of Cedar Flat, 7350 ft., *Alexander & Kellogg 2502* (UC); White Mountains, 8000 ft., *Menzies s.n.* (CAS). As now defined, the var. *kennedyi* is restricted to the high mountains of southern California.

15. **E. latens** Jeps. (including *E. monticola* S. Stokes). Infrequent, sandy or stony ridges and outcrops, subalpine habitats, 10,000–11,100 ft.: Davis Creek, on pine-clad slopes at ca. 10,500 ft., *D 3108;* Chiatovich Creek, moist grassy area among boulders at 11,100 ft., *M 2268*.

16. **E. maculatum** Heller. Common, sandy and gravelly soils, desert scrub and pinyon woodland, throughout the range, 4500–7000 ft.: west base of Westgard Pass Road, 4500 ft., *HM 792*; Payson Canyon, 6800 ft., *HM 365*; Silver Canyon, 6600 ft., *HM 271*; near Pinyon Hill, Esmeralda Co., 7000 ft., *D M62;* mouth of Pinchot Creek among shrubs in wash, 6500 ft., *D 3270*.

17. **E. microthecum** Nutt.
A. Flowers white .... 17a. var. *laxiflorum*
AA. Flowers yellow .... 17b. var. *ambiguum*

17a. Var. **laxiflorum** Hook. Common, dry open places, pinyon woodland and subalpine forests, in northern half of the range, 8000–11,000 ft.; Chiatovich Flat, 10,300 ft. *D 2557*.

17b. Var. **ambiguum** (M. E. Jones) Reveal. Common in similar places as the above variety: Chiatovich Creek, 8500 ft., *D 3113*; south of Queen Mine, 10,500 ft., *Ferris 6754, 6764* (POM); Middle Creek, 7500 ft., *Jaeger s.n.* (POM).

18. **E. nidularium** Cov. Common, dry slopes and in open washes, desert scrub and pinyon woodland, throughout the range, below 7500 ft.: Westgard Pass, 7.4 miles west of White Mountain Road, 5000 ft., *L 2656*; Payson Canyon, at head of Deep Springs Valley, 5519 ft., *M & L 1739*; Black Canyon, 6000 ft., *D 1755A*; west slope of Silver Canyon, 7400 ft., *HM 208*.

19. **E. ovalifolium** Nutt.
A. Leaf-blades 5–20 mm. long; flowering stems mostly more than 1 dm. long
19a. var. *ovalifolium*
AA. Leaf-blades less than 5 mm. long; flowering stems less than 1 dm. long
19b. var. *nivale*

19a. Var. **ovalifolium.** Open hillsides and flats throughout the range, 6000–13,000 ft.: Westgard Pass, 3.8 miles west of White Mountain Road, 6450 ft., *L 2742*; Silver Canyon, 10,000 ft., *HM 228*; White Mountain Peak, 13,000 ft., *Cook s.n.* (UC); south fork of Chiatovich Creek in moist grassy area, 11,000 ft., *M 2268*; Queen Canyon, 7800 ft., *M 2761*; Trail Canyon, 8000 ft., *D 2744, 2702*; north of Pinyon Hill, Esmeralda Co., 7000 ft., *D 2869*.

19b. Var. **nivale** (Canby) M. E. Jones. High alpine form on rocky slopes and meadows, 9500 to 13,400 ft.: north slope of County Line Hill, 10,800 ft., *M 2137*; Sagehen Flat above Crooked Creek Spring, 10,250 ft., *L 3157*; ridge northwest of Campito Mountain, 11,200 ft., *HM 590*; meadow on north slope of Sheep Mountain, 11,900 ft., *M 2134*; north of Barcroft Laboratory, 12,700 ft., *HM 594*; road to White Mountain Peak, 13,400 ft., *HM 514*; Chiatovich Creek, 10,000 ft., *M 2086*.

20. **E. palmerianum** Reveal. Infrequent on the lower slopes of the White Mountains, sagebrush scrub, below 6000 ft.: observed south of Benton.

21. **E. panamintense** Mort. Infrequent, pinyon woodland below 9000 ft. Known only from the upper part of Marble Canyon, 7000 ft., *D 2891*.

22. **E. pusillum** Torr. & Gray. Infrequent but locally common, dry washes and hillsides, desert scrub and pinyon woodland, below 6500 ft.: Payson Canyon, 5913 ft., *L 2966*; north of Pinyon Hill, 6500 ft., *D 2871*; east side of Montgomery Pass, *Eastwood & Howell 9532* (UC).

23. **E. rosense** Nels. & Kenn. Frequent, dry soils on ridges and flats of alpine

fell-fields, 10,000–12,500 ft.: Sheep Mountain, 12,000 ft., *Kamb 1236* (UC); ridge above Cottonwood Creek, 12,000 ft., *D 1679*; McAfee Meadow, 11,500 ft., *D s.n.* (UC); White Mountain Peak, 12,000 ft., *D 2609B*. This species has been confused with *E. anemophilum* Greene of western Nevada.

24. **E. rupinum** Reveal. Rare, desert scrub and pinyon woodland: 10 miles up Wyman Creek on stony slopes in pinyon, *Maguire & Holmgren 26031* (NY, UC, US, UTC).

25. **E. saxatile** S. Wats. Infrequent, pinyon woodland and subalpine rocky ridges, 5000–9500 ft.: White Mountain Road, 9500 ft., *Cook s.n.* (UC); 5 miles south of Benton Station at foot of Marble Creek, 5000 ft., *Robinson & Lindner c37* (UC).

26. **E. spergulinum** Gray var. **reddingianum** (M. E. Jones) J. T. Howell. Known only from the head of Crooked Creek in a sandy wash near the meadow, 10,200 ft., *Maguire & Holmgren 26054* (UC).

27. **E. umbellatum** Torr.

A.   Primary rays of umbel simple, not branched or bracteate in the middle.
  B.   Calyx-segments yellow; leaves glabrous or nearly so above, tomentose below . . . . 27a. var. *umbellatum*
  BB.   Calyx-segments cream-colored or reddish to purple.
    C.   Calyx-segments cream to pale yellow with a tan spot
                                       27b. var. *dicrocephalum*
    CC.   Calyx-segments reddish-brown to pink with a large reddish or purplish spot . . . . 27c. var. *versicolor*
AA.   Primary rays of umbel branched and bracteate in the middle; calyx-segments yellow . . . . 27d. var. *subaridum*

27a. Var. **umbellatum**. Common, slopes and flats, desert scrub and pinyon woodland, 7000–10,200 ft.: Westgard Pass Road, 2.2 miles west of White Mountain Road, 7000 ft., *Bacigalupi et al. 8212* (JEPS); Roberts Ranch, Wyman Creek, 8000 ft., *D 1701*; Crooked Creek Laboratory, 10,150 ft., *Muller 1078* (JEPS); Chiatovich Creek, 8000 ft., *D 2567*; Trail Canyon, 8530 ft., *D 3087*.

27b. Var. **dicrocephalum** Gand. Rare and locally abundant, pinyon woodland and subalpine habitats, 9000–12,000 ft.: north of Schulman Grove on White Mountain Road, 10,000 ft., *HM 379*; head of Wyman Creek, 9750 ft., *HM 317*; northwest corner of Sagehen Flat, Crooked Creek, 10,250 ft., *L 3165*; 2 miles south of Barcroft Laboratory on White Mountain Road, 12,000 ft., *Cook s.n.* (UC).

27c. Var. **versicolor** S. Stokes. Rare and infrequent, gravelly soils, dry slopes and ridges, pinyon woodland and subalpine exposures, 10,000–11,000 ft.: Silver Canyon, 10,000 ft., *D 1520*; 1.5 miles south of the county line at head of Old Silver Canyon, 10,700 ft., *HM 826*; ridge west of County Line Hill, 10,400 ft., *HM 530*; southwest of Sheep Mountain, *HM 589*.

27d. Var. **subaridum** S. Stokes. Frequent, desert scrub and pinyon woodland, 5000–9000 ft.: Cedar Flat, 7250 ft., *Alexander & Kellogg 2488* (UC); Mollie Gibson Canyon, 2 miles north of Payson Canyon, *L 2946*; Crooked Creek Ranger Station, 9500 ft., *D 1553*.

28. **E. wrightii** Torr. ex Benth. var. **subscaposum** S. Wats. Common, rocky soils, at higher elevations from 7000–11,200 ft.: Cedar Flat, 7000 ft., *D 2841*; Piute Creek, 11,150 ft., *HM 887*.

The following species are to be expected in the White Mountains, but are not yet known from collections:

E. elatum Dougl. ex Benth. Expected on the northern flank in the pinyon belt below 7500 ft.

E. nudum Dougl. ex Benth. var. **pubiflorum** Benth, in DC. Expected on the northern or eastern flank in the pinyon belt below 7500 ft.

E. shockleyi S. Wats. Expected on the eastern flank in the sagebrush scrub on clay slopes and exposed hills mostly below 7000 ft.

3. Oxyria

1. **O. digyna** (L.) Hill. Infrequent, meadows and around rocks, 11,500–13,000 ft.: McAfee Creek, 11,500 ft., *L 3314*; Pellisier Flats, under rocks on the east slope at 12,800 ft., *M 2218*.

4. Oxytheca

A. Bracts of upper nodes connate-perfoliate into a disk 1–2 cm. broad; involucres more or less sessile; leaves glabrous . . . . 2. *O. perfoliata*
AA. Bracts not united as above; involucres peduncled; leaves hirsute
1. *O. dendroidea*

1. **O. dendroidea** Nutt. Dry stony slopes and washes, pinyon woodland, 7000–8000 ft.: Cedar Flat, 7000 ft., *D s.n.*; 6 miles up Wyman Creek in sandy soil of canyon bottom, *Maguire & Holmgren 26063* (UC); Post Meadow, Indian Creek, 7500 ft., *Archer 7233* (UC).

2. **O. perfoliata** Torr. & Gray. Sandy and gravelly alluvia and washes, desert scrub and pinyon woodland, 4500–6000 ft.: below Toll House Springs on Westgard Pass Road, *Eastwood & Howell 9574* (CAS); mouth of Black Canyon, 4500 ft., *D 2630*; Silver Canyon, *Heller 8305* (UC); Birch Creek (Mono Co.), 5800 ft., *D 3478*.

5. Polygonum

A. Stems terete; leaves 0.5–2 cm. long, lanceolate to oblong; plants prostrate to ascending . . . . 1. *P. aviculare*
AA. Stems angled; leaves 1–4 cm. long, linear to lance-oblong; plants erect
2. *P. douglasii*

1. **P. aviculare** L. Sporadic as a weed, meadows and roadsides, 4500–8500 ft.: Roberts Ranch, Wyman Creek, 8000 ft., *D 3167*; Trail Canyon, 8300 ft., *D 2519*.

2. **P. douglasii** Greene var. **johnstonii** Munz. Occasional on dry hillsides and

meadows, subalpine, 9000–10,600 ft.: head of Silver Canyon, 10,450 ft., *HM 855*; Campito Mountain, 10,600 ft., *L 3174*.

6. Rumex

A.   Plants ± dioecious; leaves mostly basal, 4–10 cm. long, entire
2. *R. paucifolius*
AA. Plants monoecious.
  B.   Stems ascending; outer sepals 1.2–1.5 mm. long; valves in fruit 2–3 mm. long, one with a callosity; leaves flat, not crisped, 6–12 cm. long
3. *R. salicifolius*
  BB. Stems erect; outer sepals 1 mm. long or less; valves in fruit 4–6 mm. long with 3 callosities; basal leaves 10–30 mm. long, margins often crisped
1. *R. crispus*

1. **R. crispus** L. Sporadic weed, moist places below 6000 ft.: Toll House Spring, 5971 ft., *L 2691, L 2697*; Silver Canyon, 6000 ft., *HM 125*; Birch Creek (Mono Co.), 5800 ft., *D 3480*; Marble Canyon, Nevada, 5500 ft., *Lankester 827* (BM).

2. **R. paucifolius** Nutt. ex Wats.

A.   Stems few, erect, 1.5–7 dm. high; basal leaves broadly lanceolate
2a. ssp. *paucifolius*
AA. Stems numerous, low, 0.5–2 dm. high; basal leaves linear to linear-lanceolate .... 2b. ssp. *gracilescens*

2a. Ssp. **paucifolius.** Moist meadows, 9000–10,100 ft.: Crooked Creek Ranger Station, 9500 ft., *D 1579*; south fork of Crooked Creek, 10,100 ft., *M 2234*.
2b. Ssp. **gracilescens** (Rech.f.) Rech.f. Very common, alpine washes, slopes, and meadows, 9800–13,500 ft.: Crooked Creek Canyon at end of road north of Old Ranger Station, 9800 ft., *L 2877*; 12,000 ft., headwaters of Cottonwood Creek, *D 1666*; McAfee Meadow, 11,700 ft., *D 2830*; White Mountain Road, 13,500 ft., *L 3251*; Pellisier Flats, 1 mile south of Jump-Off, 13,300 ft., *M 2183*.
3. **R. salicifolius** Weinm. Occasional, variable habitats from riparian areas to rocky slopes, throughout the range, 5600–11,500 ft.: upper part of Marble Canyon, 7000 ft., *D M73*; Antelope Springs, 5600 ft., *L 3017*; McAfee Creek, 11,500 ft., *L 3308*; Chiatovich Creek, 8000 ft., *D M74*; Trail Canyon, 10,000 ft., *D 3351*.

FAMILY 22. MALVACEAE

A.   Petals pale lilac or white; annual or biennial; petioles 5–20 cm. long
1. *Malva*
AA. Petals grenadine; perennial; petioles 1–5 cm. long ...... 2. *Sphaeralcea*

1. Malva

1. **M. neglecta** Wallr. Weed, moist places about Montenegro Springs, 7000 ft., *M 2144*.

2. Sphaeralcea

A. Carpels 12–16; reticulate part of carpel rugose or muricate on back; petals 15–35 mm. long . . . . 1. *S. ambigua*

AA. Carpels 9–12; reticulate part of carpel ± smooth on back, petals 8–18 mm. long . . . . 2. *S. parvifolia*

1. **S. ambigua** Gray. Frequent, washes, dry slopes and flats, desert scrub to pinyon woodland, throughout the range, below 8500 ft.: 5.4 miles west of White Mountain Road on Westgard Pass Road, 5900 ft., *L 2685*; Black Canyon, 4500 ft., *D 2623* (in part); Silver Canyon, 6500 ft., *L 2839*; Wyman Creek, 8500 ft., *D 1681*; near Pinyon Hill, 6500 ft., *D s.n.*; Old Davis Ranch, Chiatovich Creek, 7500 ft., *D 2526*.

2. **S. parvifolia** A. Nels. Sporadic on alluvium and slopes, southern canyons, below 5000 ft.: Black Canyon, 4500 ft., *D 2623* (in part); first canyon south of Silver Canyon, 5000 ft., *HM 694*; Fish Lake Valley, 4900 ft., *Lankester & Edwards 794* (BM).

FAMILY 23. VIOLACEAE
1. Viola

1. **V. nephrophylla** Greene. Sporadic, in moist, shaded places, throughout the range: Marble Fork of Black Canyon, 5800 ft., *D 2722*; Indian Creek (Nevada), 6000 ft., *Lankester 740* (BM).

FAMILY 24. LOASACEAE

A. Stamens many; style entire to 3-cleft . . . . 1. *Mentzelia*

AA. Stamens 5; style entire . . . . 2. *Petalonyx*

1. Mentzelia

A. Petals 5–8 cm. long; capsule turbinate or broadly obconic; plants 4–20 dm. tall . . . . 3. *M. laevicaulis*

AA. Petals 0.2–2 cm. long; capsule clavate or cylindric; plants 1–4 dm. tall.

  B. Floral bracts broadly ovate, partly concealing flowers; petals 4–5 mm. long; capsule 8–10 mm. long . . . . 2. *M. congesta*

  BB. Floral bracts lance-linear or wider, not concealing flowers; petals 2–20 mm. long.

    C. Petals 2–6 mm. long; leaves dentate to entire.

      D. Seeds irregularly angled, tuberculate; upper leaves linear to lanceolate; capsule 10–16 mm. long; petals yellow . . 1. *M. albicaulis*

      DD. Seeds cubic-rhomboid, regularly angled, smooth or granular; upper leaves ovate; capsule 15–25 mm. long; petals yellow with orange spot at base . . . . 4. *M. montana*

    CC. Petals 7–20 mm. long; leaves pinnatifid.

      D. Petals 7–12 mm. long . . . . 6. *M. veatchiana*

      DD. Petals 12–20 mm. long . . . . 5. *M. nitens*

1. **M. albicaulis** Dougl. ex Hook. Frequent dry slopes and flats, desert scrub to pinyon woodland, throughout the range, 5000–8000 ft.: 7.4 miles west of White Mountain Road on Westgard Pass Road, 5000 ft. *L 2650*; Silver Canyon, 7350 ft., *HM 111*; Roberts Ranch, Wyman Creek, 8000 ft., *D 1727*; side canyon off Cottonwood Creek, 7800 ft., *M 2061*; Old Davis Ranch, Chiatovich Creek, 7500 ft., *D 2564*; Queen Canyon, 7800 ft., *M 2758*.

2. **M. congesta** (Nutt.) Torr. & Gray. Sporadic, on dry slopes and flats, desert scrub to pinyon woodland, throughout the range, 7500–9200 ft.: ca. 1 mile south of Studebaker Flat on White Mountain Road, 8600 ft., *HM 803;* Chiatovich Creek, 9200 ft., *D M89* Trail Canyon, 7500 ft., *D 2864.*

3. **M. laevicaulis** (Dougl.) Torr. & Gray. Infrequent, dry washes, southern canyons, below 7000 ft.: Black Canyon, 7000 ft., *D 2848;* 2.9 miles north of Deep Springs Valley Road in Birch Creek, 5500 ft., *L 2980;* mouth of Birch Creek in Deep Springs Valley, 6000 ft., *M & L 1738;* also reported from Wyman Creek.

4. **M. montana** A. Davids. Known only from Westgard Pass, *Zavortink 2644* (LA.)

5. **M. nitens** Greene. Desert scrub to pinyon woodland, below 7300 ft.: 2.9 miles east of Big Pine on Westgard Pass Road, *HM 17;* 5 miles west of Deep Springs Valley, *Kerr 639* (CAS); first canyon south of Silver Canyon, *HM 150;* Silver Canyon, *Brandegee 1913* (UC); slopes above Benton, 6000 ft., *J. & H. Grinnell 1054* (JEPS).

6. **M. veatchiana** Kell. Uncommon, pinyon woodland, 5700 to 7500 ft.: Black Canyon at Marble Canyon, 5700 ft., *D 2669;* 2 miles north of Cedar Flat, 7500 ft., *Cook s.n.* (UC).

2. Petalonyx

1. **P. nitidus** Wats. Sporadic and apparently not common, dry hillsides and washes, desert scrub and pinyon woodland, restricted to western canyons below 5700 ft.: Black Canyon at Marble Canyon, 5700 ft., *M 2112;* Silver Canyon: 4600 ft., *Alexander & Kellogg 4278* (UC); first canyon north of Silver Canyon, 5100 ft., *HM 206.*

FAMILY 25. SALICACEAE

A. Leaves broadly lanceolate, ovate-lanceolate, to deltoid; stamens 6–many
1. *Populus*
AA. Leaves elliptic, lanceolate, or oblanceolate; stamens 2–6 . . . . . . 2. *Salix*

1. Populus

A. Stamens 6–12; leaves 2–4 (6) cm. long, round-ovate to deltoid; stigma-lobes filiform . . . . 2. *P. tremuloides*
AA. Stamens 12–60; leaves 3–8 cm. long, ovate to lanceolate; stigma-lobes deltoid.
  B. Leaves dark green above, ovate . . . . 3. *P. trichocarpa*
  BB. Leaves light green above, mostly lanceolate . . . . . . 1. *P. angustifolia*
1. **P. angustifolia** James. Rare, known only from two canyons, 7000–8300 ft.:

Wyman Creek, 7000 ft., *HM 863*; Queen Canyon, 8300 ft., below mining area, *M 2765*.

2. **P. tremuloides** Michx. Rocky areas and moist slopes and meadows, 6000–11,000 ft.; dwarfed and procumbent on exposed sites at upper elevations: Silver Canyon, 10,400 ft. dwarfed trees, *L 2830*; McClouds Camp, Cottonwood Creek, 9500 ft., *D 1610*; Cottonwood Creek, south fork at 9200 ft., *L 2920*.

3. **P. trichocarpa** Torr. & Gray. Frequent, in canyons at springs and riparian areas, 4500–8500 ft.: Toll House Springs, Westgard Pass Road, 5971 ft., *L 2689*; Silver Canyon, 7000 ft., *M 2327*; Wyman Creek, 2 miles below Roberts Ranch, 7500 ft., *D 3039*; Chiatovich Creek, 1½ miles above Davis Ranch, 7500 ft., *D 3062*.

2. Salix

A.   Leaf-blades entire or subserrulate.
   B.   Mature leaves glabrous beneath.
     C.   Leaf-blades 1.5–4 cm. wide, lanceolate .... 6. *S. lutea*
     CC.   Leaf-blades 1–2 cm. wide, oblanceolate .... 5 *S. lasiolepis*
   BB.   Mature leaves pubescent beneath.
     C.   Leaves linear to lance-linear, less than 1 cm. wide .... 1. *S. exigua*
     CC.   Leaves oblanceolate to elliptic-oblong, 0.6–2 cm. wide.
       D.   Capsule 4.5–5 mm. long, glabrous .... 5. *S. lasiolepis*
       DD.   Capsule 5–7 mm. long, silky .... 2. *S. geyeriana*
AA.   Leaf-blades serrulate to serrate-crenate.
   B.   Mature leaves pubescent beneath .... 1. *S. exigua*
   BB.   Mature leaves glabrous or glaucous beneath.
     C.   Catkin-scales dark brown; leaves pale green beneath
                                     7. *S. pseudocordata*
     CC.   Catkin-scales yellow, deciduous; leaves glaucous beneath.
       D.   Stamens 2, glabrous; twigs yellowish or brownish; shrub 2–5 m. tall .... 6. *S. lutea*
       DD.   Stamens 4–6, pubescent at base; twigs reddish to yellowish; trees 5–15 m. tall
         E.   Leaves dark green above; petals glandular at upper end; capsule 5–7 mm. long .... 4. *S. lasiandra*
         EE.   Leaves light green above; petals not glandular; capsule 3.5–5 mm. long .... 3. *S. laevigata*

1. **S. exigua** Nutt. Common, riparian areas throughout the range, 4500–9500 ft.: Toll House Springs, Westgard Pass Road, 5971 ft., *L 2693*; Silver Canyon, 4600 ft., *D M80*; Roberts Ranch, Wyman Creek, 8300 ft., *L 2787*; McCloud Camp, Cottonwood Creek, single shrub in canyon, 9500 ft., *D 1614*; Milner Creek, *D 3236*; Chiatovich Creek, 8000 ft., *D 2568a*.

2. **S. geyeriana** Anderss. Riparian areas of creeks, 10,000–11,000 ft.: Mono Co., White Mountains, 11,000 ft., *Shockley 470* (JEPS); Chiatovich Creek, 10,500 ft., *D 3058, M2081*.

3. **S. laevigata** Bebb. Sporadic, middle and lower elevation riparian areas,

6000–7000 ft.; Silver Canyon: *Setchell & Duran 3a* (UC); 6000 ft., *HM 241*.

4. **S. lasiandra** Benth. Not common, scattered in canyons on alluvia and streambanks, below 8500 ft.: Wyman Creek, 2 miles below Roberts Ranch, *D 1731.*

5. **S. lasiolepis** Benth. Along streambanks and riparian areas, throughout the range, 4500–7500 ft.: Toll House Springs, Westgard Pass Road, 5971 ft., *L 2719*; Marble Canyon, about ¼ mile above Black Canyon, 5700 ft., *D 3000*; Silver Canyon, 4500 ft. *L 2852*; Wyman Creek, 7100 ft., *L 2777.*

6. **S. lutea** Nutt.

A.   Leaves 4–10 cm. long; twigs yellowish to brownish . . . . . . 6a. var. *lutea*
AA. Leaves 4–6 cm. long; twigs yellowish-white . . . . 6b. var. *watsonii*

6a. Var. **lutea.** Common, streambeds and riparian areas, throughout the range, 5600–10,000 ft.: Antelope Springs, 5600 ft., *Raven 7043* (CAS); Crooked Creek, 9950 ft., *L 3198*; McCloud Camp, Cottonwood Creek, 9500 ft., *D 1618*; Trail Canyon, 8200 ft., *D 2509*; also collected by Lankester in Indian Creek at 6000 ft.

6b. Var. **watsonii** (Bebb) Jepson. Meadows and streambanks, upper elevations in eastern canyons, 8000–9500 ft.: Wyman Creek, 1 mile below Roberts Ranch, 8000 ft., *D 1734*; intersection of Cottonwood and Poison Creeks, 9400 ft., *L 2918, M & L 1712.*

7. **S. pseudocordata** Anderss. Known only in riparian areas of Crooked Creek, 9000–9800 ft.: Old Ranger Station, 9800 ft., *L 2888*; 9000 ft., *L 2872.*

FAMILY 26. CAPPARIDACEAE

A.   Capsule 15–25 mm. long; petals 6–8 mm. long . . . . 1. *Cleome*
AA. Capsule ca. 4 mm. long; petals 1.5–2 mm. long . . . . 2. *Cleomella*

1. Cleome

1. **C. lutea** Hook. Scattered, slopes and flats, pinyon woodland and desert scrub, 4500–7500 ft.: west base of Westgard Pass, 4500–5000 ft., *HM 789*; Antelope Springs, 5600 ft., *L 3023*; Black Canyon at Marble Canyon, 5700 ft., *D 2856*; 3 miles below Roberts Ranch, Wyman Creek, 7500 ft., *D 1708.*

2. Cleomella

1. **C. parviflora** Gray. Scattered, alkali flats, valleys surrounding the range, below 6000 ft.: Antelope Springs, *D 1942A.*

FAMILY 27. CRUCIFERAE

A.   Fruit a silique, several times longer than wide.
  B.   Siliques long-stipitate, these 1–2 cm. long; anthers twisted
                                                17. *Stanleya*
  BB. Siliques sessile or with short stipes; anthers usually not twisted.
    C.   Stigma-lobes situated over the valves; anthers sagittate at base.
      D.   Calyx urn- or flask-shaped at anthesis.
        E.   Siliques conspicuously beaked, pendant, strongly compressed
                                                18. *Streptanthella*

EE. Siliques inconspicuously or not beaked, erect to deflexed.
    F.   Siliques flattened; seeds usually winged .... 19. *Streptanthus*
    FF. Siliques terete or 4-sided; seeds ± wingless .. 5. *Caulanthus*
DD. Calyx open at anthesis, not urn-shaped ...... 20. *Thelypodium*
CC. Stigma-lobes situated over the placentae; anthers usually not sagittate at base.
    D.   Basal leaves in definite rosettes.
        E.   Flowers yellow; stem ± angled .... 2. *Barbarea*
        EE. Flowers white; stems terete.
            F.   Stems leafy; siliques linear .... 1. *Arabis*
            FF. Stems scapose; siliques ovate to lanceolate .. 13. *Phoenicaulis*
    DD. Basal leaves not in definite rosettes.
        E.   Beaks of fruit indehiscent .... 3. *Brassica*
        EE. Beaks of fruit dehiscent to tip.
            F.   Pubescence lacking or of simple hairs.
                G.   Siliques strongly flattened.
                    H.   Leaves usually pinnate; silique valves unnerved
                                                        4. *Cardamine*
                    HH. Leaves simple; silique valves nerved ...... 1. *Arabis*
                GG. Siliques 4-angled or terete.
                    H.   Plants not creeping from base; seeds uniseriate (except *Rorippa*).
                        I.   Pods ± 4-angled; biennial or perennial .. 2. *Barbarea*
                        II. Pods terete; annual.
                            J.   Siliques 2–10 cm. long, closely appressed
                                        16. *Sisymbrium*
                          JJ. Siliques 0.4–1.2 cm. long, divaricate .. 15. *Rorippa*
                    HH. Plants creeping from base; seeds biseriate .. 15. *Rorippa*
            FF. Pubescence of compound hairs, forked or stellate.
                G.   Leaves pinnatifid to pinnate.
                    H.   Plants annual; leaves finely dissected to bipinnatifid
                                        6. *Descurainia*
                    HH. Plants perennial with heavy caudex; leaves subentire to dentate or lobed .... 9. *Halimolobus*
                GG. Leaves ± entire.
                    H.   Flowers yellow to orange .... 8. *Erysimum*
                    HH. Flowers white to rose or purple .... 1. *Arabis*
AA. Fruit a silicle, 1–3 times longer than wide.
    B.   Silicles flattened.
        C.   Silicles flattened parallel to the partition .... 7. *Draba*
        CC. Silicles flattened perpendicular to the partition.
            D.   Cells of the silicle 1-seeded .... 11. *Lepidium*
            DD. Cells of the silicle 2- many-seeded .... 10. *Hutchinsia*
    BB. Silicles not flattened, but turgid or inflated.
        C.   Plants with mostly basal leaves.
            D.   Silicles 10–15 mm. long, didymous .... 14. *Physaria*

DD. Silicles 3–6 mm. long, not didymous.
 E. Leaves 20–50 mm. long .... 12. *Lesquerella*
 EE. Leaves 2–12 mm. long .... 7. *Draba*
CC. Plants with leafy stems.
 D. Leaves pinnatifid; wet habitats .... 15. *Rorippa*
 DD. Leaves entire; dry habitats .... 12. *Lesquerella*

1. Arabis

A. Siliques 3–8 mm. wide; seeds 2.5–5 mm. long.
 B. Siliques and pedicels reflexed .... 5. *A. glaucovalvula*
 BB. Siliques and pedicels erect or ascending .... 2. *A. dispar*
AA. Siliques mostly 1–3 mm. wide; seeds less than 2 mm. long.
 B. Basal leaves obovate to broadly oblanceolate, obtuse or rounded at apex; outer sepals saccate .... 6. *A. hirsuta*
 BB. Basal leaves linear to linear-oblanceolate (or, if broader, minutely pubescent or with reflexed siliques), acute to obtuse; outer sepals not saccate.
  C. Plants hoary with a minute pubescence.
   D. Siliques and pedicels reflexed to pendulous.
    E. Seeds biseriate; cauline leaves linear, petals 10–20 mm. long
     14. *A. pulchra*
    EE. Seeds uniseriate; cauline leaves oblong to broadly lanceolate; petals 7–11 mm. long .... 13. *A. puberula*
   DD. Siliques and pedicels erect to widely spreading.
    E. Seed-wing more than 0.5 mm. wide; siliques 2.5–3.5 mm. wide
     2. *A. dispar*
    EE. Seed-wing less than 0.5 mm. wide; siliques ± 2 mm. wide
     8. *A. inyoensis*
  CC. Plants not hoary but greenish.
   D. Siliques and pedicels erect to ascending.
    E. Lower leaves densely pubescent, gray to felty.
     F. Petals 4–6 mm. long.
      G. Pedicels 2–5 mm. long; cauline leaves auricled
       9. *A. lemmonii*
      GG. Pedicels 5–10 mm. long; cauline leaves not auricled
       4. *A. fernaldiana*
     FF. Petals 7–14 mm. long .... 8. *A. inyoensis*
    EE. Lower leaves pubescent to glabrous, greenish.
     F. Seeds biseriate; flowers white .... 3. *A. drummondii*
     FF. Seeds mostly uniseriate; flowers rose to purple .. 10. *A. lyallii*
   DD. Siliques and pedicels diverging, perpendicular to stem, pendulous or reflexed.
    E. Basal leaves ciliate and hirsute; siliques pendulous or reflexed
     11. *A. pendulina*
    EE. Basal leaves not ciliate.
     F. Seeds biseriate; cauline leaves linear ...... 14. *A. pulchra*
     FF. Seeds uniseriate; cauline leaves lanceolate to ovate.
      G. Basal leaves linear .... 1. *A. cobrensis*

The shadscale-covered lower slopes of the White Mountains at the Owens Valley base of the Westgard Pass Road; 4,500 ft.

Toll House Springs, a perennial water source in the high elevation desert near 6,000 ft. on the Westgard Pass Road.

The pinyon woodland. Note the presence of trees of all age classes. Sagebrush is the shrubby vegetation; 7,800 ft.

Elevation of 10,000 ft., looking northwest from County Line Hill in the lower subalpine zone. See text for a description of the vegetation variability present.

Sharp patterning of the vegetation near Poison Creek due to geological diversity. The sagebrush vegetation in the foreground is on quartzitic sandstone of the Campito Formation. The well-developed bristlecone-limber pine forest in the background is on Reed Dolomite. The light dolomite areas in the far background are above timberline.

A local aspen forest near 9,500 ft. elevation along Crooked Creek.

The timberline region on the east flanks of Sheep Mountain just above the Patriarch area. Some of the trees in the foreground died as long as 2,000 years ago.

A well-developed alpine fell-field at 12,700 ft. Mt. Barcroft is in the background.

GG. Basal leaves spatulate to oblanceolate.
H.   Pedicels 2–6 mm. long; cauline leaves glabrous
9. *A. lemmonii*
HH. Pedicels 6–20 mm. long; cauline leaves usually pubescent.
I.   Siliques pendulous to closely appressed
7. *A. holboellii*
II. Siliques perpendicular to stem, arcuate or ± pendulous.
J.   Basal leaves entire, finely pubescent, 2–5 mm. wide
8. *A. inyoensis*
JJ. Basal leaves in part dentate, coarsely pubescent, 4–20 mm. wide . . . . 12. *A. perennans*

1. **A. cobrensis** Jones. Known only from Chiatovich Creek under cottonwoods and sagebrush at 8000 ft., *D 3065*.

2. **A. dispar** Jones. Known only from Cedar Flat, 7300 ft., not uncommon on rocky slopes, *D 3291*.

3. **A. drummondii** Gray. Known only from around rocks, Crooked Creek Ranger Station, 9500 ft., *D 1536*.

4. **A. fernaldiana** Rollins var. **stylosa** (Wats.) Rollins. Uncommon, riparian creek banks, 8900–9600 ft.: Cottonwood Creek, 8900 ft., *M 2019*; Chiatovich Creek, 9600 ft., *M 2087*.
Plants from Cottonwood Creek are often sterile and appear to be of hybrid origin with this species and an unknown second parent.

5. **A. glaucovalvula** Jones. Rare, known only from Black Canyon at Marble Canyon, 5700 ft., *D 2859*.

6. **A. hirsuta** (L.) Scop. var. **glabrata** Torr. & Gray. Known only from Roberts Ranch, Wyman Creek, 8100 ft., *M 2151*.

6a. **A. hirsuta** (L.) Scop. var. **pycnocarpa** (Hopkins) Rollins. Washes and meadows, middle and northern canyons, 8000–10,000 ft.: Roberts Ranch, Wyman Creek, 7.3 miles east of White Mountain Road, 8000 ft., *L 3039*; Lone Tree Creek, 9700 ft., *M 2253*; Chiatovich Creek at Big Meadow, 8800 ft., *D 3329*.

7. **A. holboellii** Hornem. var. **pendulocarpa** (A. Nels.) Rollins. Known only from Sheep Mountain on stable soils among talus at 12,100 ft., *M 2223*.

7a. **A. holboellii** Hornem. var. **retrofracta** (Grah.) Rydb. Sporadic, rocky slopes, 5900–9500 ft.: Toll House Springs, 5971 ft., *Eastwood & Howell 9608* (CAS); Crooked Creek Ranger Station, 9500 ft., *D 1578*; Montgomery Pass, 7200 ft, *Ripley & Barneby 3706* (CAS); east side of Montgomery Pass, *Eastwood & Howell 9541* (CAS).

8. **A. inyoensis** Rollins. Uncommon, of sporadic distribution in rocky places, 7000–12,500 ft.: Silver Canyon, 7000 ft., *M 2290*; ½ mile north of Barcroft Lab, 12,500 ft., *Bacigalupi et al. 8114* (JEPS).

9. **A. lemmonii** Wats.

A.   Basal leaves spatulate; siliques horizontal or descending; raceme ± secund
9a. var. *lemmonii*

AA. Basal leaves narrowly oblanceolate; siliques ascending; raceme not secund
9b. var. *depauperata*

9a. Var. **lemmonii.** Rocky slopes and washes, subalpine and alpine, throughout the range, 10,300–13,800 ft.: junction of White Mountain Road and Crooked Creek Road, 10,300 ft., *Cook s.n.* (UC); McAfee Meadow, *D 2831*; ¼ mile south of Barcroft Lab, *Tucker 2261* (UC); east slope of White Mountain Peak, 13,600 ft., *J. & L. Roos 5144* (RSA); Pellisier Flats, south slope of ridge below Mt. Dubois, 12,900 ft., *M 2188*.

9b. Var. **depauperata** (Nels. & Kenn.) Rollins. Known only from the ridge south of White Mountain Peak on slopes and flats at 12,000 ft., *D 1636*.

10. **A. lyallii** Wats. var. **nubigena** (Macbr. & Pays.) Rollins. Stony slopes and roadsides, subalpine to alpine, 10,000–12,500 ft.: Crooked Creek at entrance to cave, 10,000 ft., *L 3082*; just south of Barcroft Lab, 12,450 ft., *Bacigalupi et al. 8162* (JEPS).

11. **A. pendulina** Greene. Known only from Cottonwood Creek, 10,000 ft., *D 1647A*.

12. **A. perennans** Wats. Rare, pinyon woodland, 5000–8000 ft.: 4 miles north of Cedar Flat on White Mountain Road, 8000 ft., *Cook s.n.* (UC); Black Canyon at 5700 ? ft., *D s.n.*

13. **A. puberula** Nutt. Flats and hillsides, pinyon woodland about 8000 ft.: Chiatovich Creek, 8000 ft., *D s.n.*; Trail Canyon, 7800 ft., *D 2746*.

14. **A. pulchra** Jones var. **gracilis** Jones. Common, especially abundant in wetter years, washes and dry slopes, pinyon woodland and upper desert scrub, 5500–8600 ft.; Westgard Pass Road, below Toll House Springs, *D 3551*; 1 mile east of summit of Westgard Pass, 7000 ft., *Munz 13522* (CAS); Mollie Gibson Canyon, 3 miles above Payson Canyon, 7950 ft., *L 2942*; Black Canyon at Marble Canyon, 5600 ft., *D 2628*; White Mountain Road, 8600 ft., *M 2391*; Silver Canyon, 7500 ft., *Munz 13551* (CAS).

2. Barbarea
1. **B. orthoceras** Ledeb.

A. Siliques erect and appressed, 2.5–3.5 cm. long . . . . . . 1a. var. *orthoceras*
AA. Siliques spreading or ascending, 2.5–5 cm. long . . . . 1b. var. *dolichocarpa*

1a. Var. **orthoceras.** Along streams and wet places, 8000–10,000 ft.: Crooked Creek, 9900 ft., *L 3281*; Crooked Creek Ranger Station, 9500 ft., *D 1538*; Chiatovich Creek, 8000 ft., *D 3070*.

1b. Var. **dolichocarpa** Fern. Uncommon, wet places, 9800–11,500 ft.: Poison Creek, 9800 ft., *Tucker 3417* (DAV); McAfee Creek, 11,500 ft., *L 3311*.

3. Brassica
1. **B. campestris** L. Sporadic weed. Collected only at Montenegro Springs, head of Marble Canyon, 7000 ft., *L 3122*.

4. Cardamine

1. **C. pensylvanica** Muhl. ex Willd. Infrequent, moist places and washes: Silver Canyon, 6000 ft., *HM 134*; Chiatovich Creek, 8500 ft., *D 3068*.

5. Caulanthus

A.   Cauline leaves auriculate at base, sessile .... 1. *C. cooperi*
AA. Cauline leaves not auriculate at base, sessile or petioled.
B.   Plants pilose to hirsute .... 4. *C. pilosus*
BB. Plants glabrous.
C.   Sepals pubescent; stems ± inflated .... 2. *C. crassicaulis*
CC. Sepals glabrous; stems ± not inflated .... 3. *C. glaucus*

1. **C. cooperi** (Wats.) Pays. Desert scrub, below 7000 ft. Not uncommon on the east side of Owens Valley: near Laws, *Heller 8184* (DS); Toll House Springs, *Eastwood & Howell 9606* (CAS); Black Canyon, 5600 ft., *Duran 2720* (DS).
2. **C. crassicaulis** (Torr.) Wats. Dry slopes and washes of eastern portion of the range, 6500–8000 ft.: east side of Westgard Pass, 7000 ft., *Hovanitz s.n.* (UC); Wyman Creek: 7500 ft., *D 3047*; 8.7 miles west of White Mountain Road, Wyman Creek, *L 3032*.
3. **C. glaucus** Wats. Rocky slopes and washes, southern end of range, below 8000 ft.: Toll House Springs, *Eastwood & Howell 9609* (CAS); Black Canyon, 5600 ft., *D 2627*; Silver Canyon, 7000 ft., *M 2504*.
4. **C. pilosus** Wats. Washes, flats and hillsides, desert scrub and pinyon woodland, 4000–8500 ft.: Indian Creek, 8500 ft., *Lankester 801* (BM); near Trail Canyon, 7000 ft., *D 2749* (CAS); east side of Montgomery Pass, *Eastwood & Howell 9540* (CAS); also reported near Bishop.

6. Descurainia

A.   Upper leaves at least twice pinnate; siliques 10–30 mm. long
                                                                         4. *D. sophia*
AA. Upper leaves once pinnate; siliques 3–15 mm. long.
B.   Seeds uniseriate in each locule; style prominent.
C.   Siliques 9–15 mm. long; stems ± glandular-pubescent above
                                                           3. *D. richardsonii*
CC. Siliques 3–7 mm. long; stems not glandular-pubescent above
                                                   1. *D. californica*
BB. Seeds biseriate in each locule; style minute .... 2. *D. pinnata*

1. **D. californica** (Gray) O. E. Schulz. Sporadic, dry slopes and washes, pinyon scrub to subalpine forest, throughout the range, 6000–10,200 ft.: Westgard Pass, 7400 ft., *L 2899*; mouth of Wyman Creek, *Ferris 1360* (DS); Crooked Creek, 10,000 ft., *L 3282*; Indian Creek, 6000 ft., *Lankester 735* (BM).

2. **D. pinnata** (Walt.) Britt.

A. Segment of upper leaves narrowly oblong to linear; raceme ± glandular
pubescent; seeds 2–4 per locule .... 2b. ssp. *paradisa*

AA. Segments of upper leaves ovate to oblanceolate; raceme glabrous; seeds
8–12 per locule .... 2a. ssp. *glabra*

2a. Ssp. **glabra** (Woot. & Standl.) Detl. Disturbed habitats throughout the
range, below 8500 ft.: Antelope Springs, 4900 ft., *Raven 7039* (CAS); Black
Canyon, 5700 ft., *D s.n.* (RSA), *D 2653*; Silver Canyon, 7100 ft., *L 2857*;
Wyman Creek, near mouth, *Ferris & Bacigalupi 8050* (RSA); Wyman Creek,
7.3 miles east of White Mountain Road, 8000 ft., at Roberts Ranch, *L 3041*;
Trail Canyon, 8300 ft., *D 2520*.

2b. Ssp. **paradisa** (Nels. & Kenn.) Detl. Upper desert scrub to lower subalpine forest: Silver Canyon, 5800 ft., *L 2865*; Wyman Creek, near line-cabin
at 9700 ft., *L 2821*; Crooked Creek Ranger Station, 9500 ft., *D 1573*.

3. **D. richardsonii** (Sweet) O. E. Schulz.

A. Plants glandular-pubescent; petals 2–3.5 mm. long; seeds 1–1.2 mm. long
3b. ssp. *viscosa*

AA. Plants not glandular-pubescent; petals 1.5–2 mm. long; seeds ca. 0.8 mm.
long .... 3a. ssp. *incisa*

3a. Ssp. **incisa** (Englem.) Detl. Disturbed and rocky places, 8000–9000 ft.:
Silver Canyon, 8700 ft., *L 2846*; Cottonwood Creek, 8800 ft., *M 2034*.

3b. Ssp. **viscosa** (Rydb.) Detl. Dry slopes and meadows, 8000–12,000 ft.:
McAfee Meadows, 12,000 ft., *Maguire & Holmgren 26081* (UC); Chiatovich
Creek, 8000 ft., *D 3097*; *D s.n.*

4. **D. sophia** (L.) Webb. Occasional weed, roadsides, washes, and disturbed
habitats, 5000–8000 ft.: 7.4 miles west of White Mountain Road on Westgard
Pass, 5000 ft., *L 2666a*; 1 mile east of top of Westgard Pass, 7000 ft., *Munz
13523* (CAS); Wyman Creek, Roberts Ranch, 8000 ft., *D 1730, L 3040*.

7. Draba

A. Plants annual; styles minute.
  B. Flowers white; pedicels ± shorter than silicles.
    C. Pedicels usually pubescent; hairs dentate .... 2. *D. cuneifolia*
    CC. Pedicals glabrous; leaves entire .... 6. *D. reptans*
  BB. Flowers yellow; pedicels as long as or longer than silicles
8. *D. stenoloba*
AA. Plants perennial; style usually well developed.
  B. Leaves glabous or with simple hairs .... 3. *D. crassifolia*
  BB. Leaves pubescent, some hairs compound.
    C. Flowering stems with one or more leaves; seeds wingless.
      D. Flowers white.
        E. Flowering stems glabrous except at base; silicles mostly glabrous
4. *D. fladnizensis*

EE. Flowering stems pubescent; silicles pubescent .. 1. *D. breweri*
DD. Flowers yellow .... 3. *D. crassifolia*
CC. Flowering stems leafless, or, if with 1–2 leaves then with winged
seeds.
  D.   Scapes densely stellate-pubescent, 1–3 cm. tall; leaves 2–6 mm.
long, 1 mm. wide; pedicels 1–4 mm. long .... 7. *D. sierrae*
  DD. Scapes glabrous above, 1–10 cm. tall; leaves 3–11 mm. long,
1–1.7 mm. wide; pedicels 3–10 mm. long .... 5. *D. oligosperma*

1. **D. breweri** Wats. Meadows, dry washes, and rocky slopes, subalpine to
alpine, throughout the range, 10,000–13,500 ft.: near Crooked Creek Lab,
10,200 ft., *Tucker 3425* (UC); McAfee Meadow, 12,000 ft., *J. & L. Roos
5136* (CAS); just below Barcroft Lab, 12,500 ft., *Tucker 2263* (UC); ridge
south of White Mountain Peak, 12,000 ft., *D 1642*; meadow, Pellisier Flats,
13,100 ft., *M 2207*.
  2. **D. cuneifolia** Nutt.

A.   Style nearly lacking; pubescence simple on lower part of stems; silicles
glabrous or with simple hairs .... 2a. var. *cuneifolia*
AA. Style evident; pubescence nearly all compound; silicles glabrous or with
stellate hairs .... 2b. var. *integrifolia*

2a. Var. **cuneifolia**. Known only from Marble Canyon, 5700 ft., *D 2727*.
2b. Var. **integrifolia** Wats. Known only from Black Canyon at Marble Canyon, 5700 ft., *D M35*.
3. **D. crassifolia** Grah. var. **nevadensis**. Hitchc. Uncommon, meadows at
higher elevations: at snow marker, White Mountain Road, 11,650 ft., northeast of Piute Mountain, *L 3290*; McAfee Meadow, 11,700 ft., *L 3304, D 2820*.
4. **D. fladnizensis** Wulf. Rare, slopes and talus, alpine habitats, 11,700–
14,000 ft.: McAfee Meadow, 11,700 ft., *L 3306*; White Mountain Road,
13,500 ft., *L 3255*; White Mountain Road, 13,950, near White Mountain Peak,
L 3244.
  5. **D. oligosperma** Hook.

A.   Petals 0.5–2.0 mm. longer than sepals; styles 0.1–1 mm. long
                                            5a. var. *oligosperma*
AA. Petals and sepals nearly the same length; styles 0.1–0.4 mm. long; plants
dwarf .... 5b. var. *subsessilis*

5a. Var. **oligosperma**. Very common, rocky slopes and flats, subalpine and
alpine, throughout the range, 9800–14,000 ft.: Crooked Creek cave, 1 mile east
of lab at 9900 ft., *L 2887*; Patriarch Grove, 12,000 ft., *L 2825*; Cottonwood
Creek, 11,000 ft., *D 1631*; above Barcroft Lab on White Mountain Road,
13,950 ft., *L 3242*.
5b. Var. **subsessilis** (Wats.) O. E. Schulz. Rocky slopes, subalpine to alpine,
10,000–14,230 ft.: Crooked Creek Lab, 10,250 ft., *Bacigalupi et al. 8061*

(JEPS); east slope of White Mountain Peak, 13,000–14,230 ft., *Maguire & Holmgren 26077* (UC); Type: *Shockley 455*, White mountains, Mono Co.

6. **D. sierrae** C. W. Sharsm. Common, slopes and flats, alpine, 11,000–14,000 ft.: Barcroft Lab, 12,500 ft., *Cook s.n.* (UC); road to White Mountain Peak, 13,950 ft., *L 3242*; throughout Pellisier Flats.

8. **D. stenoloba** Ledeb. var. **nana** (O. E. Schulz) C. L. Hitchc. Meadows and sandy spots, throughout the range, 8000–13,000 ft.: below pond, Crooked Creek Lab, 10,140 ft., *L 2634*; McAfee Meadow, *D 2819*; Chiatovich Creek, 8000 ft., *D s.n.*

Rollins reports that two collections of cushion *Draba* may be undescribed species. These include *Duran 2821A* from flats near White Mountain Peak, and *Mitchell 2193* from Pellisier Flats at 13,300 ft.

8. Erysimum

1. **E. argillosum** (Green) Rydb. A complex and variable species found from the upper desert scrub to the subalpine forest, 6400–10,400 ft.: 4 miles west of White Mountain Road on Westgard Pass Road, 6400 ft., *L 2711*; above "The Narrows," Westgard Pass Road, 6800 ft., *L 2756*; Wyman Creek, 9500 ft., *L 2816*; hill northwest of Crooked Creek Lab, 10,400 ft., *Tucker 3412* (UC); Cottonwood Creek, 9700 ft., *L 2912*; first creek north of Poison Creek, 9800 ft., *HM 450*.

9. Halimolobus

A. Cauline leaves sessile, auriculate and clasping the stem; siliques 2–4 cm. long, glabrous . . . . 2. *H. virgata*
AA. Cauline leaves petiolate or sessile, not auriculate; siliques 1.5–2.5 cm. long, densely pubescent . . . . 1. *H. diffusus*

1. **H. diffusus** (Gray) O. E. Schulz var. **jaegeri** (Munz) Rollins. Rocky places, frequently throughout the southern half of the range, 5700–8700 ft.: 3.8 miles west of summit of Westgard Pass Road, 6450 ft., *L 2749*; east side of Westgard Pass, 6000 ft., *Raven s.n.* (UC); mouth of Mollie Gibson Canyon, 6800 ft., *M & L 1729*; Black Canyon, 5700 ft., *D s.n.*; Silver Canyon, 8000 ft., *Applegate 6943* (UC); Wyman Creek, 4 miles from highway, *Maguire & Holmgren 26023* (UC); Cottonwood Creek, 8700 ft., *D 2579*.

2. **H. virgata** (Nutt.) O. E. Schulz. Meadows, subalpine forest, 8800–10,000 ft.: Crooked Creek, 9850 ft., *L 2878*; Chiatovich Creek at Big Meadows, 8800 ft., *D 3059, D 3329*.

10. Hutchinsia

1. **H. procumbens** (L.) Desv. Alkaline places and edge of meadows, up to 9500 ft.: Wyman Creek, 2 miles below Roberts Ranch, 7500 ft., *D 3042*; Crooked Creek Ranger Station, 9500 ft., *D M84*; Chiatovich Creek, 7500 ft., *D 2766*.

11. Lepidium

A. Styles nearly lacking.
 B. Pedicels terete or only slightly flattened; basal leaves 5–15 cm. long
4. *L. virginicum*
 BB. Pedicels strongly flattened; basal leaves 1–6 cm. long
3. *L. lasiocarpum*
AA. Styles well developed, 0.4–2 mm. long.
 B. Style 1.5–2 mm. long; pedicels 2–3 mm. long; petals sulphur-yellow; silicles 2–3 mm. long . . . . 1. *L. flavum*
 BB. Styles 0.4–0.8 mm. long; pedicels 5–8 mm. long; petals white; silicles 4–7 mm. long . . . . 2. *L. fremontii*

1. **L. flavum** Torr. Locally frequent, washes and canyons, desert scrub to lower pinyon woodland, 4000–5700 ft.: west side of Westgard Pass, 4200 ft., *HM 23*; Black Canyon at Marble Canyon, 5700 ft., *D M35*; also collected at Benton Station, and near Laws at 4000 ft.

2. **L. fremontii** Wats. Common, slopes and flats, desert scrub, below 6000 ft.: 5.4 miles west of White Mountain Road on Westgard Pass Road, 5900 ft., *L 2764*; Black Canyon, 4500 ft., *D 2622*; second ridge south of Silver Canyon, 5500 ft., *HM 149*; also reported from Indian Creek at 6000 ft.

3. **L. lasiocarpum** Nutt. Rocky slopes and washes, below 7000 ft.: 7.4 miles west of White Mountain Road on Westgard Pass Road, 5000 ft., *L 2661, 2662*; Antelope Springs, *Raven 7053* (CAS); Black Canyon, 5700 ft., *D 2644*; Silver Canyon, 7000 ft., *M 2292*; mouth of Wyman Creek, *Ferris & Bacigalupi 8052* (UC).

4. **L. virginicum** L. var. **pubescens** (Greene) C. L. Hitchc. Introduced, waste and disturbed places, below 7050 ft.: Black Canyon, 5700 ft., *D s.n.*; Montenegro Springs, 7050 ft., *L 3123*; Indian Creek, ca. 5800 ft., *Lankester 816* (BM).

12. Lesquerella

1. **L. kingii** Wats.
A. Leaves ovate to suborbicular to oblanceolate . . . . la. var. *kingii*
AA. Leaves often narrow-spatulate . . . . lb. var. *cordiformis*

1a. Var. **kingii.** Scattered, rocky slopes, throughout, 7500–10,150 ft.: Mollie Gibson Canyon, ca. 3 miles north of Payson Canyon, 7950 ft., *L 2941*; Wyman Creek, ½ mile south of mine shacks at 8000 ft., *L 2817*; Crooked Creek Lab, 10,150 ft., *L 3104*.

1b. Var. **cordiformis** (Rollins) Maguire & Holmgren. Common, rocky slopes and flats and dry creek banks, subalpine forest and alpine: broad saddle at head of Wyman Creek, ca. 9500 ft., *Maguire & Holmgren 26052* (UC); head of Crooked Creek, 10,200 ft., vicinity of lab, *Tucker 2227* (UC); southeast of Campito Meadow, 10,800 ft., *Maguire & Holmgren 26120* (UC); north spur of Sheep Mountain, 12,000 ft., *Kamb s.n.* (UC).

94

13. Phoenicaulis

1. **P. eurycarpa** (Gray) Abrams. Loose stony slopes and flats, alpine, 13,000–14,230 ft.: White Mountain Peak: 13,100 ft., *D 2618*; 13,900 ft., *Jepson 7385* (JEPS); east slope of White Mountain Peak, 13,000–14,230 ft., *Maguire & Holmgren 26071* (UC); also from higher elevations in Trail Canyon and Montgomery Creek.

14. Physaria

1. **P. chambersii** Rollins. Known only on dry limestone talus slope at 8500 ft., Trail Canyon, *D 3349*.

15. Rorippa

A. Stems rooting freely from nodes; flowers white or yellow; siliques 7–18 mm. long .... 3. *R. nasturtium-aquaticum*
AA. Stems from underground rhizomes; flowers yellow; siliques 3–10 mm. long.
  B. Stems diffusely branched from base; pedicels 2–4 mm. long.
    C. Siliques strongly curved; style 0.5 mm. long or less; leaf-segments linear to oblong, acute .... 1. *R. curvisiliqua*
    CC. Siliques not curved; style 1–2 mm. long; leaf-segments obovate or rounded .... 4. *R. obtusa*
  BB. Stems erect, branched above; pedicels 3–8 mm. long .. 3. *R. islandica*

1. **R. curvisiliqua** (Hook.) Bessey. Wet areas of creeks, known only from Crooked Creek area, 10,000–10,200 ft.: Crooked Creek Lab, 10,150 ft., *Breedlove 1027* (DS), *Jepson 7344* (JEPS).
2. **R. islandica** (Oeder) Borb. var. **fernaldiana** Butters & Abbe. Known only from Birch Creek, Mono Co., in water at 5800 ft., *D 3479*.
3. **R. nasturtium-aquaticum** (L.) Hayek. Introduced, springs and creeks, throughout the range, below 8000 ft.: Toll House Springs, 5970 ft., *L 2702*; Silver Canyon, 7000 ft., *M 2313*; Wyman Creek, Roberts Ranch, 8000 ft., *D 1725, 3140*; Chiatovich Creek, 8000 ft., *D 3099*; also known from Indian Creek at 6000 ft.
4. **R. obtusa** (Nutt.) Britt. Wet meadows and streamsides, 8000–11,000 ft.: Silver Canyon near Big Prospector Meadow, 9700 ft., *Jepson 7354* (JEPS); Roberts Ranch, Wyman Creek, 8000 ft., *L 3042*; head of Crooked Creek, 10,150 ft., *Maguire & Holmgren 26143* (UC); south slope of Sheep Mountain, 11,000 ft., *M 2135*.

16. Sisymbrium

1. **S. altissimum** L. Introduced weed, below 6000 ft.: Westgard Pass, 7.4 miles west of White Mountain Road, 5000 ft., *L 2666*; Antelope Springs, 5600 ft., *L 3016, Raven 7040* (CAS); Black Canyon at Marble Canyon, 5700 ft., *D 2728*; Indian Creek, 6000 ft., *Lankester 734* (BM).

17. Stanleya

A. Lower leaves pinnate; inner surface of petal-claw villous .... 2. *S. pinnata*
AA. Lower leaves entire or runcinate; inner surface of petal-claw glabrous
                          1. *S. elata*

1. **S. elata** Jones. Desert slopes and washes, throughout the range, below 8000 ft.: 7.4 miles west of White Mountain Road on Westgard Pass Road, 5000 ft., *L 2665*; Black Canyon, 5700 ft., *D 2693*; Wyman Creek, Roberts Ranch, 8000 ft., *D 1693*; Indian Creek, 6000 ft., *Lankester 841* (BM).

2. **S. pinnata** (Pursh) Britt. Canyons and on slopes, below 6000 ft.; Antelope Springs, *Raven 7054* (CAS); Silver Canyon: 4500 ft., *L 2853*; 5700 ft., *M 2000*.

18. Streptanthella

1. **S. longirostris** (Wats.) Rydb. Sporadically abundant on slopes amongst desert scrubs, below 6200 ft.: near Queen, 6200 ft., *D 3255*; observed near Laws.

19. Streptanthus

1. **S. cordatus** Nutt. Frequent on slopes, pinyon woodland and subalpine forest, 7000–10,000 ft.: Westgard Pass Road, 7100 ft., *L 2762*; Mollie Gibson Canyon, 7400 ft., *M 2073*; White Mountain Road, 8600 ft., *HM 346*; Silver Canyon, 8600 ft., *HM 220*; Wyman Creek, 8.7 miles east of White Mountain Road, 7900 ft., *L 3034*; summit trail to Big Prospector Meadow, 10,000 ft., *Jepson 7259* (JEPS); Cottonwood Creek, 10,000 ft., *D 1647* (JEPS).

The Duran collection from Cottonwood Creek (*D 1647*) is the type of *S. cordatus* var. *duranii* Jeps.

20. Thelypodium

A.   Cauline leaves linear-sagittate, sessile; plants 3–7 dm. tall; basal leaves 2–5 cm. long . . . . 1. *T. crispum*

AA. Cauline leaves linear to oblanceolate, not sagittate, subsessile; plant 10–20 dm. high; basal leaves 10–30 cm. long . . . . 2. *T. integrifolium*

1. **T. crispum** Greene. Meadows and flats, northern canyons, 7500–8500 ft.: Chiatovich Creek: 7500 ft., *D 2767*; 8100 ft., *M 2088*; 8500 ft., *D 2533*.

2. **T. integrifolium** (Nutt.) Endl. Near springs and moist areas, southern canyons, 7000–8000 ft.: Marble Canyon, 7000 ft., *D 2850*; Black Canyon, 7000 ft., *D s.n.*; Roberts Ranch, Wyman Creek, 8000 ft., *D 1688* (JEPS).

FAMILY 28. PRIMULACEAE

A.   Leaves linear-lanceolate; scapes 0.1–0.3 dm. tall; calyx lobes 1–1.5 mm. long . . . . 1. *Androsace*

AA. Leaves oblanceolate; scapes 2.5–6 dm. tall; calyx lobes 5–8 mm. long 2. *Dodecatheon*

1. Androsace

1. **A. septentrionalis** L. ssp. **subumbellata** (A. Nels.) Robbins. Dry rocky slopes and flats, alpine fell-fields, throughout the range, 11,000–14,100 ft.: meadow just northeast of Piute Trail Pass, White Mountain Road, 11,800 ft., *L 3285*; White Mountain Road, 13,400 ft., *HM 501*; Pellisier Flats, 1 mile south of Jump-Off, 13,300 ft., *M 2181*.

2. Dodecatheon

1. **D. redolens** (Hall) H. J. Thomp. Damp grasslands, meadows and stream-sides, 9000–11,800 ft.: Crooked Creek Ranger Station, 9500 ft., *D 1565;* Cottonwood Creek at Poison Creek, 9450 ft., *L 2915;* head of Cottonwood Creek, 11,700 ft., *D 2592;* McAfee Creek, 11,500 ft., *L 3319.*

FAMILY 29. CRASSULACEAE
1. Sedum

1. **S. rosea** (L.) Scop. ssp. **integrifolium** (Raf.) Hult. Frequent wet meadows and sandy soils, alpine, above 11,500 ft.: meadow below White Mountain Peak on road, 12,300 ft., *L 3305;* Pellisier Flats, 13,200 ft., *M 2190.*

FAMILY 30. SAXIFRAGACEAE
A. Plants herbaceous.
    B. Petals 5–7 mm. long; fertile stamens alternating with sterile staminodia
                                                                       2. *Parnassia*
    BB. Petals 1.5–4 mm. long; fertile stamens not alternating with staminodia
                                                                       1. *Heuchera*
AA. Plants shrubby.
    B. Leaves opposite; fruit a capsule . . . . 3. *Philadelphus*
    BB. Leaves alternate; fruit a berry . . . . 4. Ribes

1. Heuchera

A. Style more than 1 mm. long; flowers 3–6 mm. long; petals 3–4 mm. long; stamens slightly exceeding sepals . . . . 2. *H. rubescens*
AA. Styles not more than 1 mm. long; flowers 2–2.5 mm. long; petals ca. 1.5 mm. long; stamens not exceeding sepals . . . . 1. *H. duranii*

1. **H. duranii** Bacig. Common, slopes, canyons, rock crevices, and occasionally on flats, thoughout the range, (6000) 8500–12,000 ft.: Silver Canyon, 8600 ft., *HM 224;* Wyman Creek, 8750 ft., *L 2803;* flat above spring at head of Crooked Creek, 10,300 ft., *L 3166;* head of Cottonwood Creek, 11,700 ft., *D 2584;* first creek south of McAfee Creek, 11,950 ft., *HM 620;* McAfee Meadow, *D 2817;* Indian Creek, 6000 ft., *Lankester 750* (BM); Chiatovich Creek, 10,800 ft., *M 2101.*

2. **H. rubescens** Torr. var. **alpicola** Jeps. Rock crevices and wet places, 5800–10,000 ft.: Mollie Gibson Canyon, ½ mile north of Payson Canyon road, 7100 ft., *L 2948;* Black Canyon, 5800 ft., *D s.n.;* Wyman Creek, 7650 ft., *L 2810;* Cottonwood Creek, 8700 ft., *D 2577;* south fork of Cottonwood Creek, 9800 ft., *HM 454.*

The Duran collection from Black Canyon is the type for var. *pachypoda* (Greene) Rosend., Butt. & Lak. f. *ambigua* Rosend., Butt. & Lak.

2. Parnassia

1. **P. parviflora** DC. Wet meadows and hummocks. Known only from Chiatovich Creek, 8700 ft., *D 3115.*

This plant has petals 5–7 mm. long with an affinity to *P. parviflora*. Plants of *P. palustris* L. var. *californica* Gray, the common species in California, have petals 10–18 mm. in length.

3. Philadelphus

1. **P. microphyllus** Gray ssp. **stramineus** (Rydb.) C. L. Hitchc. Dry rocky places, pinyon woodland, 5500–9000 ft.: Black Canyon at Marble Canyon, 5700 ft., *D 2685*; Wyman Creek, 2 miles below Roberts Ranch, *D 1721*; between ranger station meadow and Roster Meadow, Cottonwood Creek, 8500 ft., *D M82*.

4. Ribes

A. Nodal spines absent.
    B. Flowers yellow; leaves glabrous .... 1. *R. aureum*
    BB. Flowers white to pink; leaves glandular pubescent .... 2. *R. cereum*
AA. Nodal spines present.
    B. Ovary and berry glabrous, leaves ± glabrous ...... 3. *R. divaricatum*
    BB. Ovary and berry soft-pubescent or glandular, leaves soft or glandular-puberulent .... 4. *R. velutinum*

1. **R. aureum** Pursh. Uncommon, stream edges and marshes, 8000–8500 ft.; known only from Wyman Creek: Wyman Creek, 8000 ft., *M 2044*; Roberts Ranch, Wyman Creek, 8300 ft., *L 2785, D 1689*.

2. **R. cereum** Dougl. Dry rocky slopes and cliffs, throughout the range, pinyon woodland to alpine, 7000–12,500 ft.: slopes south of Black Canyon Spring, 8500 ft., *D 3016*; Silver Canyon, 7,200 ft., *HM 593*; head of Silver Canyon, 10,500 ft., *HM 246*; Wyman Creek, 9700 ft., *L 2824*; Crooked Creek, ca. 2 miles east of lab, 10,000 ft., *Tucker 3410* (DAV); Patriarch Grove, 11,100 ft., *Blakley 3605* (JEPS); Pellisier Flats on east-facing cliffs, 12,500 ft., *M 2206*; Chiatovich Flats, 10,300 ft., *D 2562*.

3. **R. divaricatum** Dougl. var. **inerme** (Rydb.) McMinn. Moist places, pinyon woodland to subalpine forest of northeastern canyons: Chiatovich Creek, 8200 ft., *D 3064* (RSA).

4. **R. velutinum** Greene

A. Leaves soft-pubescent, without glands; berry velvety-pubescent
                                            4a. Var. *velutinum*
AA. Leaves glandular-pubescent; berry stipitate-glandular
                                          4b. Var. *glanduliferum*

4a. Var. **velutinum**. Dry slopes and washes. Known only from Silver Canyon, *Heller 8264* (UC).

4b. Var. **glanduliferum** (Heller) Jeps. The common variety, slopes and canyons in dry places, upper desert to pinyon woodland, 6500–10,000 ft.: Westgard Pass Road, 6750 ft., *HM 397*; Black Mountain Road, 8100 ft., *HM 388*; slopes south of Black Canyon Spring, 8500 ft., *D 3017*; Wyman Creek, 8750 ft., *L 2802*; Cottonwood Creek, 8800 ft., *M 2033*.

FAMILY 31. ROSACEAE

A. Ovary superior; fruit a follicle, achene, or drupe.
  B. Fruit of 1–5 dehiscent follicles.
    C. Foliage stellate-pubescent; petals 3–5 mm. long.
      D. Leaves simple, 3–7 lobed; carpels inflated .... 11. *Physocarpus*
      DD. Leaves twice-pinnate; carpels coriaceous .... 3. *Chamaebatiaria*
    CC. Foliage not stellate-pubescent; petals 1.5–2.0 mm. long; leaves entire;
      woody cespitose plant forming dense mats ...... 10. *Petrophytum*
  BB. Fruit of indehiscent achenes or drupes.
    C. Fruit of dry achenes.
      D. Leaves simple or 3-lobed; plants woody.
        E. Petals present.
          F. Flowers solitary, cream to yellow; leaves cuneate, 3-lobed;
          plants 1–3 (5) m. tall .... 14. *Purshia*
          FF. Flowers paniculate, whitish to pinkish; leaves not lobed; plants
          0.2–2 m. tall .... 6. *Holodiscus*
        EE. Petals absent; flowers solitary or fasciculate; leaves entire; plants
        1–9 m. high .... 2. *Cercocarpus*
      DD. Leaves compound or pinnately dissected.
        E. Plants shrubby.
          F. Stems not prickly.
            G. Leaves pinnate; flowers yellow .... 12. *Potentilla*
            GG. Leaves ± 5-lobed; flowers whitish .... 4. *Cowania*
          FF. Stems prickly .... 15. *Rosa*
        EE. Plants herbaceous.
          F. Styles jointed with ovary, deciduous.
            G. Stamens 5.
              H. Leaves with more than 3 leaflets .... 8. *Ivesia*
              HH. Leaves with 3 leaflets .... 16. *Sibbaldia*
            GG. Stamens 10 or more.
              H. Filaments 10, dilated; flower tube deep .. 7. *Horkelia*
              HH. Filaments 20 or more, filiform or narrow; flower tube
              shallow or none .... 12. *Potentilla*
          FF. Styles not jointed with ovary, persistent .... 5. *Geum*
    CC. Fruit of drupes .... 13. *Prunus*
AA. Ovary inferior; fruit a pome.
  B. Leaves oblanceolate; styles 2; flowers 1–3 in a sessile umbel; fruit bitter
  to taste .... 9. *Peraphyllum*
  BB. Leaves oval to elliptical, rounded or obovate; styles 2–5; flowers in a
  raceme .... 1. *Amelanchier*

1. Amelanchier

1. **A. pallida** Greene. Infrequent, pinyon woodland, eastern canyons, 7500–8500 ft.: Wyman Creek, 7700 ft., *M 2036*; Indian Creek, ca. 8500 ft., *Lankester & Edwards 807* (BM); Chiatovich Creek, 7500 ft., *D 2791* (DS).

2. Cercocarpus

A.   Leaves 1.2–3 cm. long, elliptic .... 2. *C. ledifolius*
AA. Leaves mostly less than 1 cm. long, linear .... 1. *C. intricatus*

1. **C. intricatus** Wats. Limestone outcrops and canyon walls, southern canyons, pinyon woodland, 5800–10,000 ft.: Black Canyon Spring, 8500 ft., *D 3015*; Silver Canyon, 6000 ft.. *D 3457.*

This species occasionally hybridizes with the following. (See R. Brayton & H. Mooney, 1966. Evolution 20: 383–391).

2. **C. ledifolius** Nutt. Dry slopes, upper pinyon woodland and subalpine, throughout the range, 8500–10,500 ft.: Black Canyon Spring, 8500 ft., *D 3014*; Wyman Creek, 8750 ft., *L 2801*; Crooked Creek Lab, 10,200 ft., *HM 51.*

3. Chamaebatiaria

1. **C. millefolium** (Torr.) Maxim. Dry slopes, pinyon woodland and subalpine forest, throughout the range, 6900–10,500 ft.: Mouth of Mollie Gibson Canyon, 6950 ft., *L 2955*; Crooked Creek Lab, 10,200 ft., *Tucker 2222* (DAV); Cottonwood Creek, 9500 ft., *D 1603*; Chiatovich Creek, 8500 ft., *D 3103.*

4. Cowania

1. **C. mexicana** Don var. **stansburiana** (Torr.) Jeps. Dry slopes and canyons, desert scrub and pinyon woodland, in southern half of range, 6500–8200 ft.: 10 miles northeast of Big Pine on Westgard Pass Road, 6500 ft., *Keck 524* (POM); 3 miles north of Westgard Pass on White Mountain Road, 8200 ft., *Nord 1-A* (UC); Silver Canyon, 7500 ft., *Grinnell s.n.* (JEPS), *Jepson 7222* (JEPS).

5. Geum

1. **G. macrophyllum** Willd. Moist places, edges of springs and creeks, meadows, northern canyons, 7500–9200 ft.: moist islands in Lone Tree Creek, 9200 ft., *M 2249*; Chiatovich Creek, 8000 ft., *D 3095.*

6. Holodiscus

1. **H. microphyllus** Rydb. Rocky outcrops, slopes and canyons, pinyon woodland and subalpine forest, throughout the range, 6900–10,500 ft: mouth of Mollie Gibson Canyon, 6960 ft., *L 2956*; canyon off Black Canyon below Grandview Mine, 7700 ft., *M 2122*; White Mountain Road at Mexican Mine, 10,000 ft., *Cook s.n.* (UC); Crooked Creek Lab, 10,200 ft., *Tucker 2221* (DAV); near McCloud Camp, Cottonwood Creek, 9500 ft., *D 1613*; Chiatovich Creek, 8500 ft., *D 3104.*

7. Horkelia

1. **H. hispidula** Rydb. Slopes and flats south of White Mountain Peak, subalpine forest, 10,000–11,000 ft.: 1½ mile south of county line at head of old Silver Canyon Road, 10,700 ft., *HM 829*; south fork, Crooked Creek, 10,300

ft., *M 2238*; northwest corner of Sagehen Flat, 10,250 ft., *L 3158*; Cottonwood Creek, 11,000 ft., *D 1627*.

8. Ivesia

A.   Leaflets 10–40 pairs.
   B.   Leaflets 1–2 mm. long; pistils 8–18; receptacle short-hairy; petals obovate to rounded .... 2. *I. lycopodioides*
   BB.   Leaflets 2–8 mm. long; pistils 1–8; receptacle white-hirsute; petals linear or spatulate .... 1. *I. gordonii*
AA.   Leaflets 5–10 pairs; leaflets 1.5–3 mm. long; pistils usually 3; petals oblanceolate to oval .... 3. *I. shockleyi*

1. **I. gordonii** (Hook.) Torr. & Gray. Rare, dry rocky slopes in alpine. Known only from south fork of Perry Aiken Creek, 13,000 ft., *HM 637*.

2. **I. lycopodioides** Gray ssp. **scandularis** (Rydb.) Keck. Seepage banks, springs and meadows throughout the alpine, 11,000–13,500 ft.: north side of Sheep Mountain, 11,900 ft., *M 2132*; ridge above Cottonwood Creek, 12,000 ft., *D 1678*; McAfee Meadow, 11,700 ft., *D M55*; White Mountain Road, 13,500 ft., *L 3248*; south of Mt. Dubois, Pellisier Flats, 13,200 ft., *M 2196*.

3. **I. shockleyi** Wats. Open rocky slopes, subalpine and alpine, throughout the range, 10,500–13,000 ft.: Cottonwood Creek, 11,000 ft., *D 1634*; above Eva Bell Mine, 10,600 ft., *HM 849*; McAfee Canyon, 11,500 ft., *L 3326*; Pellisier Flats, 13,000 ft., *M 2185*.

9. Peraphyllum

1. **P. ramosissimum** Nutt. Dry slopes and washes, rarely by springs, pinyon woodland, 5500–8000 ft.: northwest of Cedar Flat, 8000 ft., *DeDecker 5880* (RSA); Montenegro Springs, 7050 ft., *L 3126*; Black Canyon, 5800 ft., *D 2646a*.

10. Petrophytum

1. **P. caespitosum** (Nutt.) Rydb. Forming mats on limestone and dolomite rocks, ledges and canyon walls, pinyon woodland to subalpine forest, 5700–10,000 ft.: Black Canyon at Marble Canyon, 5700 ft., *D 2886*; Schulman Grove, 9600 ft., *Blakley 4651* (JEPS); Crooked Creek Cave, 10,000 ft., *L 3267*; also reported from Wyman Creek, at 9500 ft.

11. Physocarpus

1. **P. alternans** (Jones) J. T. Howell. Infrequent, southern canyons, 5900–9000 ft.: Marble Canyon of Black Canyon, 5900 ft., *D 2675* (RSA); Wyman Creek, 8800 ft., *J. & L. Roos 5842* (RSA).

12. Potentilla

A.   Plants woody shrubs .... 6. *P. fruticosa*
AA.   Plants herbaceous.
   B.   Styles fusiform and glandular.

C.   Basal leaves with 3 leaflets . . . . 1. *P. biennis*
CC. Basal leaves with 5 or more leaflets.
    D.   Leaflets greenish above; leaves pinnate . . . . . 9. *P. pennsylvanica*
    DD. Leaflets grayish-silver above; leaves subpalmate
                                                  10. *P. pseudosericea*
BB. Styles filiform, not glandular.
    C.   Basal leaves pinnate with 5 or more leaflets.
        D.   Petals acute or acuminate at apex . . . . 11. *P. saxosa*
        DD. Petals rounded or emarginate at apex.
            E.   Leaves white, with dense tomentum; leaflets 4–6 pairs; leaf blades lance-oblong in outline . . . . 2. *P. breweri*
            EE. Leaves gray-green, densely villous or pilose; leaflets 2–4 pairs; leaf blades round-ovate in outline . . . . 4. *P. drummondii*
    CC. Basal leaves palmate or, if pinnate, 3-foliate.
        D.   Anthers round to oval, 0.5 mm. long; leaves sometimes subpinnate
                                                 3. *P. diversifolia*
        DD. Anthers ovate to lance-cordate, usually 1 mm. long.
            E.   Leaflets divided more than halfway to midrib, segments linear, digitate.
                F.   Leaflets densely tomentose beneath, dark green above
                                          5. *P. flabelliformis*
                FF. Leaflets densely silky on both sides or tomentose beneath
                                      8. *P. pectinisecta*
            EE. Leaflets crenate or serrate or variously dissected and segments broader . . . . 7. *P. gracilis*

1. **P. biennis** Greene. Damp meadows, streambanks, and wet road sides, throughout the range, 7500–10,000 ft.; Black Canyon Spring, 8400 ft., *D 1749*; Silver Canyon, *Jepson 7229* (JEPS); Wyman Creek, 7800 ft., *L 2773, M 2038*; Crooked Creek, 10,000 ft., *Cook s.n.* (UC); Lone Tree Creek, 9700 ft., *M 2248*; Chiatovich Creek, 7500 ft., *D 2790*; Trail Canyon, 8300 ft., *D 2518*.

2. **P. breweri** Wats. Open slopes and washes, alpine, 11,000–13,000 ft.: east slope of Sheep Mountain, 11,500 ft., *Cook s.n.* (UC); Cottonwood Creek, 11,000 ft., *D 1635;* Barcroft Lab, 12,500 ft., *Cook s.n.* (UC); Estey Plateau, White Mountain Peak, 13,000 ft., *Cook s.n.* (UC).

3. **P. diversifolia** Lehm. Known only from the Old Ranger Station, road north of Crooked Creek, 9800 ft., common here, *L 2891.*

4. **P. drummondii** Lehm. ssp. **bruceae** (Rydb.) Keck. Open slopes and fell-fields, alpine, 10,000–13,000 ft.: Crooked Creek Lab, 10,200 ft., *Cook s.n.* (UC); above Barcroft Lab, 13,000 ft., *Muller 1064* (JEPS).

This taxon is nearly indistinct from *P. breweri* and perhaps should be referred to the same species.

5. **P. flabelliformis** Lehm. Moist soil around the base of the range, below 8300 ft.: Trail Canyon, 8300 ft., *D 2503*; also collected near Bishop by Heller.

6. **P. fruticosa** L. Meadows and moist creeks and canyon walls, alpine and subalpine, 8500–12,000 ft.: slope south of cave, Crooked Creek, 10,000 ft., *L*

102

3208; McAfee Creek, 11,800 ft., *HM 608*; upper end of Big Meadows, Chiato-vich Creek, 8900 ft., *D 2532*.

7. **P. gracilis** Dougl. ex. Hook ssp. **nuttallii** (Lehm.) Keck. Meadows and moist rocky places, pinyon woodland and subalpine forest, throughout the range, 7500–10,200 ft.: Roberts Ranch, Wyman Creek, 8000 ft., *D 1707*; south fork, Crooked Creek, 10,200 ft., *M 2232*; Poison Creek at Cottonwood Creek, 9300 ft., *M & L 1716*; Chiatovich Creek, 7500 ft., *D 2777*.

8. **P. pectinisecta** Rydb. Meadows and moist slopes, throughout the range, 6000–11,500 ft.: near cave, Crooked Creek, 10,000 ft., *L 3221*; meadow of Poison and Cottonwood creeks, 9450 ft., *L 3130*; McAfee Creek, 11,500 ft., *L 3309*; Chiatovich Creek, 7500 ft., *D 2777*.

9. **P. pennsylvanica** L. var. **strigosa** Pursh. Frequent, meadows and moist slopes, throughout the range, 9500–14,050 ft.: Crooked Creek Lab, 10,100 ft., *L 3115*; Cottonwood Creek, 9700 ft., *HM 253*; McAfee Meadow, 11,700 ft., *D M52*; road to White Mountain Peak, 13,200 ft., *HM 521*; south slope of Mt. DuBois, Pellisier Flats, 13,000 ft., *M 2191*; Chiatovich Creek, 11,200 ft., *D 3332*.

The Jepson collection from Sheep Mountain, 11,400 ft., is the type var. *ovium* Jepson (*Jepson* 7307, JEPS).

10. **P. pseudosericea** Rydb. Frequent, moist places, meadows and slopes, sub-alpine and alpine; restricted to dolomite in the subalpine forest; 9800–13,500 ft.: Sheep Meadow, 11,400 ft., *HM 840*; McAfee Meadow, 11,700 ft., *D M56*; road to White Mountain Peak, 13,400 ft., *HM 505*; south end of Pellisier Flats, 12,400 ft., *M 2290*; Trail Canyon at head of stream, 9800 ft., *D 3357*.

11. **P. saxosa** Lem. ex Greene ssp. **sierrae** Munz. Rock crevices and cliffs, throughout the range, 7000–10,800 ft.: 1 mile below Roberts Ranch, Wyman Creek, 8000 ft., *D 1695*; Cottonwood Creek, ca. 8500 ft., *D M53*; Lone Tree Creek, 10,800 ft., *M 2250*.

13. Prunus
A.   Shrub 1–2 m. tall; branchlets spinose; leaves 1–2 cm. long; sepals ca. 3 mm. long; petals ± rose-colored . . . . 1. *P. andersonii*
AA. Shrub or small tree 1–5 m. tall; branchlets not spinose; leaves 3–8 cm. long; sepals ca. 1 mm. long; petals white . . . . 2. *P. virginiana*

1. **P. andersonii** Gray. Dry slopes and washes, throughout the range, 5700–8500 ft.: Westgard Pass, 7100 ft., *M 2006*; Marble Canyon just above Black Canyon, 5700 ft., *D 3003*; White Mountain Road, 8500 ft., *HM 768-B*; Silver Canyon, *Heller 8186* (UC); road between Wyman Creek and Crooked Creek, 7900 ft., *M 2107*; mouth of Queen Canyon, 7100 ft., *D 3252*.

2. **P. virginiana** L. var. **demissa** (Nutt.) Sarg. Dry washes. Known only from Indian Creek, 7000–7800 ft.: Indian Creek (in Nevada), 7000 ft., *Lankester 857* (BM); Indian Creek, in Mono Co., California, above Post Meadow at 7800 ft., *D 2574*.

14. Purshia
A. Leaves pubescent above, without punctations of sunken glands
2. *P. tridentata*
AA. Leaves glabrous above, punctate with sunken glands .... 1. *P. glandulosa*
1. **P. glandulosa** Curran. Common, dry slopes and canyons, pinyon woodland and subalpine forest, throughout the range, 5000–10,000 ft.: 5.4 miles west of White Mountain Road on Westgard Pass, 5900 ft., *L 2678*; Silver Canyon, 10,000 ft., *D 1518*; 2 miles below Roberts Ranch, Wyman Creek, 7500 ft., *D 1724*; mouth of Queen Canyon, 7100 ft., *D 3253*.
2. **P. tridentata** (Pursh) DC. Dry slopes and canyons, pinyon woodland, 7000–9500 ft.: White Mountain Road, 9300 ft., *HM 331*; Silver Canyon: 7300 ft., *HM 802*; 9200 ft., *HM 799*.

15. Rosa
1. **R. woodsia** Lindl. var. **ultramontana** (Wats.) Jeps. Moist canyons, streamsides, springs, throughout the range, 5000–10,000 ft.: Toll House Springs, 5970 ft., *L 2703*; Silver Canyon, 6000 ft., *HM 130*; south fork, Cottonwood Creek, 9800 ft., *HM 451*; Trail Canyon, 8300 ft., *D 2506*.

16. Sibbaldia
1. **S. procumbens** L. Meadows and fell-fields. Known only from McAfee Meadow and Creek: McAfee Creek, 11,800 ft., *HM 609*; McAfee Meadow, 11,700 ft., *D 2808*.

FAMILY 32. LEGUMINOSAE
A. Leaves palmate, or, if pinnate, 1- 3-foliate.
B. Leaflets 4–many, palmate .... 4. *Lupinus*
BB. Leaflets 3 (4–6 in *Trifolium monoense*) and palmate or pinnate.
C. Leaves palmately 3-foliate .... 9. *Trifolium*
CC. Leaves pinnately 3-foliate.
D. Pods curved or spirally coiled; flowers blue to purple . 5. *Medicago*
DD. Pods ovoid, straight; flowers white or yellow .... 6. *Melilotus*
AA. Leaves pinnate, leaflets more than 3.
B. Leaf-rachis prolonged into a tendril .... 10. *Vicia*
BB. Leaf-rachis not prolonged into a tendril.
C. Plants dotted with glands; pods indehiscent.
D. Pods prickly; flowers yellow to white .... 3. *Glycyrrhiza*
DD. Pods not prickly; flowers rose to purplish or blue ...... 2. *Dalea*
CC. Plant not dotted with glands; pods mostly dehiscent.
D. Trees .... 8. *Robinia*
DD. Herbs.
E. Keel petals narrowed into cuspidate or mucronate apex
7. *Oxytropis*
EE. Keel petals muticous, not narrowed into a point or beak
1. *Astragalus*

104

1. **Astragalus**

A. Plants annual .... 1. *A. acutirostris*
AA. Plants perennial.
  B. Stipules of the lower nodes connate into a sheath opposite the petals.
    C. Flowers small; keel 3.5–5.5 mm. long .... 6. *A. kentrophyta*
    CC. Flowers larger; keels 6–14 mm. long .... 13. *A. whitneyi*
  BB. Stipules not connate into a sheath opposite the petiole.
    C. Pubescence well developed, hairs curly or incumbent or spreading at right angles.
      D. Flowers small, the banner up to 8 mm. long, the keel up to 6.5 mm. long.
        E. Densely tufted or matted plant with cottony-tomentose pubescence .... 11. *A. purshii*
        EE. Stems developed; plants without cottony-tomentose pubescence 7. *A. lentiginosus*
      DD. Flowers larger, the banner 10 mm. or more long, keel 8 mm. or more long.
        E. Plants tufted or matted; stems short.
          F. Petals 3.5–4 cm. long, scarlet .... 4. *A. coccineus*
          FF. Petals less than 3 cm. long, purple or white.
            G. Leaflets silvery-pilose, hairs appressed .. 9. *A. newberryi*
            GG. Leaflets silky- or cottony-tomentose, hairs entangled 11. *A. purshii*
        EE. Plants matted or caulescent; stems developed.
          F. Calyx bracteolate at base; plant hirsute throughout; pods short-stipitate .... 8. *A. malacus*
          FF. Calyx ebracteolate; plants glabrous, villosulous, strigulose or white-silky; pods sessile .... 7. *A. lentiginosus*
    CC. Pubescence appressed or nearly so, hairs straight.
      D. Calyx-tube 6–13.5 mm. long, ± pubescent.
        E. Plants acaulescent; pod densely cottony-tomentose 9. *A. newberryi*
        EE. Plants caulescent; pod glabrous or strigulose.
          F. Pod erect, 1.7–3 cm. long; leaflets mostly acute 12. *A. serenoi*
          FF. Pod ± deflexed, 2–5.5 cm. long; leaflets obtuse 3. *A. casei*
      DD. Calyx-tube less than 6 mm. long ,or, if longer, then glabrous.
        E. Plants ± acaulescent; silvery strigulose; petals whitish or pink-tipped .... 2. *A. calycosus*
        EE. Plants caulescent; nearly glabrous throughout; petals purple with white wing-tips, or pink-purple.
          F. Pod stipitate.
            G. Pod leathery; leaves 1.5–5 cm. long......5. *A. inyoensis*

GG. Pod papery; leaves 5–15 cm. long ...... 10. *A. oophorus*
FF. Pod sessile, papery-membraneous, glabrous
7. *A. lentiginosus*

1. **A. acutirostris** Wats. Uncommon, sandy or gravelly slopes, south and west sides of the range, below 5800 ft.: near mouth of Payson Canyon, *Wiggins 8801* (DS); Birch Creek (Mono Co.), 5800 ft., *D 3482*.

2. **A. calycosus** Torr. Frequent, moist sandy areas, slopes, or rarely along streams, pinyon woodland to lower alpine, throughout the range, 6000–11,500 ft.: Wyman Creek, 0.1 mile east of White Mountain Road, 10,000 ft., *L 3053*; ridge west of County Line Hill, 10,400 ft., *HM 533*; meadow ½ mile westsouthwest of Crooked Creek Lab, 10,200 ft., *L 3147*; Cottonwood Creek, 9000 ft., *D 1599*; southeast slope of Sheep Mountain, 11,450 ft., *L 3177*; mouth of Queen Canyon, 7100 ft., *D 3245*.

3. **A. casei** Gray. Dry flats and slopes, north and east side of range, 7000–8000 ft.: near Pinyon Hill, 7000 ft., *D 2861*; northeast slope of Boundary Peak in Trail Canyon, 8000 ft., *Train 3950* (UC); mouth of Queen Canyon, 7100 ft., *D 3247*; east side of Montgomery Pass, *Eastwood & Howell 9539* (CAS).

4. **A. coccineus** Bdg. Uncommon, hillsides and flats, south end of range above Owens Valley, desert scrub to lower pinyon woodland, 5000–7000 ft.: 5.4 miles west of White Mountain Road on Westgard Pass, 5000 ft., *L 2679*; Black Canyon, 5500 ft., *D s.n.*; east of Laws in Silver Canyon, *Heller 8190* (UC).

5. **A. inyoensis** Sheld. Rocky flats and hillsides, upper desert to lower subalpine forest, southern end of range, 6400–10,000 ft.: 3.8 miles west of White Mountain Road on Westgard Pass, 6450 ft., *L 2728*; White Mountain Road, 9800 ft., *HM 337*; Silver Canyon, 9200 ft., *HM 755*; also reported from Mollie Gibson Canyon at 8400 ft.

6. **A. kentrophyta** Gray.

A. Leaves 3–5-foliate; petals whitish with purple keel-tip . . 6a. var. *danaus*
AA. Leaflets 5–9; petals pink-purple with pale or white wing-tips
6b. var. *implexus*

6a. Var. **danaus** Barneby. Sporadically frequent, dry open flats and ridges, subalpine and alpine, 10,000–11,800 ft.: north of Schulman Grove, ca. 10,000 ft., *HM 393*; ridge west of Blanco Mountain, 10,500 ft., *D 3314*; south of Sheep Meadow, 11,800 ft., *HM 576*; Cottonwood Creek, 10,500 ft., *D 1628*.

6b. Var. **implexus** (Canby) Barneby. Frequent, hillsides in sandy or rocky soil, subalpine to lower alpine, 9500–11,400 ft.: Schulman Grove, 10,200 ft., *Smith 1255* (JEPS); near Patriarch Grove, 11,000 ft., *Bacigalupi et al. 8170* (JEPS); Wyman Creek, 9500 ft., *D 1741*; southeast slope of Sheep Mountain on White Mountain Road, 11,450 ft., *L 3186*; slope east of Piute Mountain, 11,400 ft., *Bacigalupi et al. 8151* (JEPS).

7. **A. lentiginosus** Dougl.

A. Racemes loose, 5 cm. or more in fruit . . . . 7a. var. *fremontii*
AA. Racemes compact, up to 4 cm. long in fruit . . . . 7b. var. *semotus*

7a. Var. **fremontii** (Gray) Wats. Dry open slopes and flats, pinyon woodland to subalpine forest, 7000–10,300 ft.: Westgard Pass, 7100 ft., *L 2764*; Silver Canyon, 8000 ft., *D 1516*; head of Wyman Creek, 9750 ft., *HM 321*; ½ mile south of Crooked Creek Lab on White Mountain Road, 10,300 ft., *HM 882*.

7b. Var. **semotus** Jeps. Sandy and gravelly soils, slopes, flats, roadbeds, pinyon woodland to subalpine forest throughout the range, 6000–10,300 ft.: Wyman Creek, 1.5 miles east of White Mountain Road, 9350 ft., *L 3050*; 5.3 miles east of Crooked Creek Lab in canyon, 9400 ft., *Bacigalupi et al. 8085* (JEPS); meadow ½ mile westsouthwest of Crooked Creek Lab, 10,200 ft., *L 3146*; Chiatovich Creek, 8500 ft., *D 2539*.

8. **A. malacus** Gray. Dry slopes, northern end of the range, 7000–8000 ft.: Benton Station, *Jones s.n.* (POM); mouth of Queen Canyon, 7000 ft., *D 3244*; Queen Canyon, 7800 ft., *M 2755*; Montgomery Pass, 7200 ft., *Ripley & Barneby 3704* (CAS).

9. **A. newberryi** Gray. Dry slopes, pinyon woodland, below 8000 ft.: Westgard Pass, *Jones s.n.* (POM); Mollie Gibson Canyon, 3 miles north of Payson Canyon, 7950 ft., *L 2944*; Black Canyon at Marble Canyon, 5900 ft., *D 2723*.

10. **A. oophorus** Wats. Dry slopes and creeks, pinyon woodland to subalpine forest, throughout the range, 6500–10,200 ft.: Mollie Gibson Canyon, 7950 ft., *L 2943*; head of Wyman Creek, 9750 ft., *HM 310*; White Mountain Road, 9800 ft., *HM 339*; Crooked Creek, 9300 ft., *HM 92*; Chiatovich Creek, 8700 ft., *M 2098*; near Trail Canyon, 7000 ft., *D M47*.

11. **A. purshii** Dougl. var. **tinctus** Jones. Dry hillside and sandy places, pinyon woodland to subalpine forest in the northern end of the range, 6000–10,300 ft.: Chiatovich Creek: 7500 ft., *D 2748-A*; 9700 ft., *M 2099*; Chiatovich Flats, 10,300 ft., *D 2560*; Trail Canyon, 8000 ft., *D 2748*; mouth of Queen Canyon, 7000 ft., *D 3246*; also reported from Indian Creek at 6000 ft.

12. **A. serenoi** (Kuntze) Sheld. Slopes and canyons, desert scrub and pinyon woodland, below 7400 ft.: Deep Springs Valley, 6300 ft., *HM 685*; Black Canyon at Marble Canyon, 5700 ft., *D 2658* (JEPS); Silver Canyon, 7350 ft., *HM 120*.

13. **A. whitneyi** Gray. Dry ridges, flats and hillsides, pinyon woodland and subalpine forest of northern canyons, 6000–10,500 ft.: Indian Creek (Nev.), 6000 ft., *Lankester 753* (BM); Chiatovich Creek, 10,300 ft., *D 3124*; Queen Canyon, 8300 ft., *M 2764*; ridge south of Queen Mine, 10,500 ft., *Ferris 6725* (DS).

2. Dalea

A. Corolla 5–6 mm. long; leaflets 2–4 mm. long; branches spine-tipped with amber glands . . . . 2. *D. polyadenia*
AA. Corolla 8–12 mm. long; leaflets 6–8 mm. long . . . . 1. *D. fremontii*

1. **D. fremontii** Torr.
A. Pubescence closely appressed; leaves canescent . . . . . . la. var. *fremontii*
AA. Pubescence spreading; leaves greener . . . . lb. var. *saundersii*

la. Var. **fremontii.** Rare. Known only on open hillsides and washes of Black Canyon at 4500 ft., *D 2625.*

lb. Var. **saundersii** (Parish) Munz. Dry desert washes and slopes, in southern end of range, below 6000 ft.: 2.9 miles east of Big Pine on Westgard Pass Road, 4200 ft., *HM 4;* 7.4 miles west of White Mountain Road on Westgard Pass, 5000 ft., *L 2641;* Silver Canyon, 5700 ft., *M 2001.*

2. **D. polyadenia** Torr. ex Wats. Dry alluvial slopes and flats, desert scrub below 5500 ft.: Deep Springs Valley, 5000 ft., *HM 859;* mouth of Birch Creek at Westgard Pass Road, 5050 ft., *L 2975;* first canyon north of Silver Canyon, 5200 ft., *HM 205.*

3. Glycyrrhiza

1. **G. lepidota** Pursh. Uncommon, waste places, roadsides, moist streamsides: Silver Canyon, 5300 ft., in area grazed by cattle, *M 2067.*

4. Lupinus

A.   Plants annual.
B.   Racemes 1–2.5 cm. long; seeds smooth, brownish .... 2. *L. brevicaulis*
BB.   Racemes 2–8 cm. long; seeds ± wrinkled, pinkish .. 7. *L. flavoculatus*
AA.   Plants perennial.
B.   Banner glabrous on back.
C.   Leaves in dense basal clusters; plant cespitose; racemes shorter than leaves .... 4. *L. caespitosus*
CC.   Leaves distributed along stem or in basal clusters; plants cespitose or caulescent; racemes exceeding leaves in length.
D.   Keel ciliate on upper edge toward tip; flowers 11–14 mm. long; racemes 5–30 cm. long .... 6. *L. confertus*
DD.   Keel glabrous on upper edge; flowers 4–9 mm. long; racemes 3–5 cm. long .... 3. *L. breweri*
BB.   Banner pubescent on back.
C.   Flowers 10–13 mm. long; racemes 5–15 cm. long.
D.   Seeds 2–4; bracts ca. 2 mm. long .... 1. *L. argenteus*
DD.   Seeds 5–6; bracts 3.5–5 mm. long .... 5. *L. caudatus*
CC.   Flowers 8–10 mm. long; racemes 10–20 cm. long .... 8. *L. palmeri*

1. **L. argenteus** Pursh var. **tenellus** (Dougl. ex Don) D. Dunn. Frequent, pinyon woodland to subalpine forest, throughout the range, 6400–10,250 ft.: Westgard Pass Road, 6400 ft., *L 2713;* north of Schulman Grove, 10,000 ft., *HM 391;* Silver Canyon, 9200 ft., *HM 756;* head of Wyman Creek, 9750 ft., *HM 322;* northwest corner of Sagehen Flat, 10,250 ft., *L 3161;* Cottonwood Creek, 8900 ft., *L 2931.*

2. **L. brevicaulis** Wats. Uncommon, flats and hillsides, pinyon woodland, throughout the range, below 7500 ft.: above Toll House Springs, *Eastwood & Howell 9619* (CAS); White Mountain Road, 7300 ft., *L 2908;* north of Pinyon Hill, 6500 ft., *D 2893;* mouth of Pinchot Creek, 6800 ft., *D 3265.*

3. **L. breweri** Gray var. **bryoides** C. P. Sm. Dry sandy areas among sage and

meadows, Inyo and Mono counties, 9500–10,500 ft.: head of Wyman Creek, ca. 9500 ft., *Maguire & Holmgren 26049* (UC); Crooked Creek Lab, 10,150 ft., *L 3103*; Adamson's Camp, Mono Co., 10,500 ft., *D 1683*.

4. **L. caespitosus** Nutt. ex Torr. & Gray. Dry, open areas of alluvia, meadows, or washes, subalpine to alpine, 9900–12,500 ft.: intersection of north and south fork, Crooked Creek, 9900 ft., *M 2017*; Cottonwood Creek, 10,500 ft., *D 1646*; roadside just south of Barcroft Lab, 12,450 ft., *Bacigalupi et al. 8137* (JEPS).

5. **L. caudatus** Kell. Dry slopes and flats, throughout the range, below 9500 ft.: 1 mile below Roberts Ranch, Wyman Creek, 8000 ft., *D 1729*; Crooked Creek Ranger Station, 9500 ft., *D 1557*; Chiatovich Creek, 7500 ft., *D 2778*; Trail Canyon, 7200 ft., *D 2530*.

6. **L. confertus** Kell. Meadows and damp areas, 8000–9700 ft.: Chiatovich Creek: 8000 ft., *D 3101* (RSA); 9700 ft., *M 2094*.

7. **L. flavoculatus** Heller. Desert scrub and pinyon woodland, southern end of the range, below 7000 ft.: Westgard Pass Road: 4500–5000 ft., *HM 786*; Cedar Flat, 7000 ft., *D 3296*.

8. **L. palmeri** Wats. Dry flats and washes, desert scrub and pinyon woodland, southern end of the range, 5900–8300 ft.: Toll House Springs, 6000 ft., *Straw 934* (RSA); 1 mile east of summit of Westgard Pass, 7000 ft., *Munz 13,500* (RSA); 5.1 miles north of Westgard Pass on White Mountain Road, 8300 ft., *Balls 22395* (RSA).

5. Medicago
A. Flowers yellow; stems prostrate to decumbent; leaflets 6–15 mm. long; fruit subreniform .... 1. *M. lupulina*
AA. Flowers blue-violet or purple; stems ascending to erect; leaflets 10–25 long; fruit coiled .... 2. *M. sativa*

1. **M. lupulina** L. Locally frequent, naturalized in waste places: Indian Creek, Nevada, meadow, *Lankester 819* (BM).

2. **M. sativa** L. Naturalized in waste places: Toll House Springs, *L 2722*; Montenegro Springs, Marble Canyon, 7050 ft., *L 3120*; Silver Canyon, 7000 ft., *M 2329*.

6. Melilotus
A. Flowers white; plants 1–2 m. tall .... 1. *M. albus*
AA. Flowers yellow; plants 0.2–1.3 m. tall.
B. Flowers 2–3 mm. long; pods 1.5–2 mm. long .... 2. *M. indicus*
BB. Flowers 5–7 mm. long; pods 2–3 mm. long .... 3. *M. officinalis*

1. **M. albus** Desr. Naturalized in waste places throughout the range, lower and mid-elevations: Antelope Springs, Deep Springs Valley, 5600 ft., *L 2995*; Silver Canyon, 4600 ft., *D M43*; also in Silver Canyon at 7000 ft.

2. **M. indicus** (L.) All. Naturalized in waste places: Antelope Springs, Deep Springs Valley, 5600 ft., *L 3021*.

109

3. **M. officinalis** (L.) Lam. Infrequently naturalized: Marble Creek (Nevada), 5500 ft., *Lankester 824* (BM).

7. Oxytropis
A. Pods pendulous, stipitate; stipules nearly free, adnate to petiole at base only
1. *O. deflexa*
AA. Pods spreading or erect, sessile; stipules adnate to half their width.
B. Plants glandular and resinous-odoriferous, green; dorsal side of bracts
glabrous . . . . 4. *O. viscida*
BB. Plants glandular, silvery; dorsal side of bracts pilose.
C. Pods spreading, 8–13 mm. long; valves papery-membraneous
2. *O. oreophila*
CC. Pods erect, 13–20 mm. long; valves leathery . . . . 3. *O. parryi*

1. **O. deflexa** (Pall.) DC. var. **sericea** Torr. & Gray. Known only from Cottonwood Creek in grassy meadows about 9500 ft.: 9500 ft., *D 1650*; 9700 ft., *HM 255*.
2. **O. oreophila** Gray. Uncommon, rocky slopes, subalpine and alpine, 10,200–12,000 ft.: Crooked Creek Lab, 10,200 ft., *Cook s.n.* (UC); 1 mile north of Sheep Mountain, 11,900 ft., *J. & L. Roos 5160* (UC).
3. **O. parryi** Gray. Rocky slopes and flats, alpine regions, 11,000–12,000 ft.: Sheep Mountain, 12,000 ft., *D 2597*; McAfee Meadow, ca. 11,700 ft., *D s.n.*
4. **O. viscida** Nutt. Uncommon, alpine fell-fields ca. 12,000 ft.: northeast slope of Sheep Mountain, next to elevation marker at 12,200 ft., *L 3303*.

8. Robinia
1. **R. pseudo-acacia** L. Introduced at Toll House Springs, Westgard Pass Road, 5971 ft., *L 2704*.

9. Trifolium
A. Heads without an involucre at base of flowers.
B. Peduncles axillary; corolla white to pale pink . . . . 6. *T. repens*
BB. Peduncles terminal or subterminal.
C. Calyx glabrous . . . . 5. *T. productum*
CC. Calyx pubescent.
D. Leaflets 4–6 . . . . 3. *T. monoense*
DD. Leaflets 3.
E. Heads on long peduncles; corolla whitish . . . . . . 1. *T. longipes*
EE. Heads sessile; corolla reddish . . . . 4. *T. pratense*
AA. Heads with an involucre at base of flowers.
B. Corolla cream with purple-tipped keel; flowers 1–4 per head
2. *T. monanthum*
BB. Corolla white to light purple; flowers many . . . . . . 7. *T. wormskjoldii*

1. **T. longipes** Nutt. Rare. Known only from streambanks and meadows in Crooked Creek: 9000 ft., *L 2871*; 9700 ft., *M 2259*.

110

2. **T. monanthum** Gray. Frequent in meadows, throughout the range, 8000–12,500 ft.: Crooked Creek Lab, 10,200 ft., *Tucker 3424* (DAV); south slope of Sheep Mountain, 11,100 ft., *M 2130*; Cottonwood Creek, 11,000 ft., *D 1629*; Barcroft Lab, 12,500 ft., *Cook s.n.* (UC); Chiatovich Creek, 8500 ft., *D 2536*.

3. **T. monoense** Greene. Common, meadows, flats, and slopes, subalpine and alpine, throughout the range, 10,000–13,500 ft.: north fork of Crooked Creek, 10,000 ft., *D 1526*; southeast slope, Sheep Mountain, *L 3178*; head of Cottonwood Creek, 12,000 ft., *D 2601*; McAfee Meadow, 11,700 ft., *D 2826*; White Mountain Road, 13,500 ft., *L 3253*; south of Mt. DuBois, Pellisier Flats, 13,000 ft., *M 2173*; Chiatovich Creek, 10,300 ft., *D 2563*.

4. **T. pratense** L. Naturalized in moist places: Marble Canyon, ½ mile above Black Canyon, 5800 ft., *D 2857*; Montenegro Springs, 7050 ft., *L 3119*.

5. **T. productum** Greene. Known only from rock crevices, 3 miles below Roberts Ranch, Wyman Creek, ca. 7000–7500 ft., *D 3026*.

6. **T. repens** L. Naturalized in wet places, infrequent in the range: Montenegro Springs, 7050 ft., *L 3118*; Indian Creek, Nevada, 6000 ft., *Lankester 702* (BM).

7. **T. wormskjoldii** Lehm. Meadows and wet places, throughout the range, 5000–10,000 ft.: Antelope Springs, Deep Springs Valley, 5600 ft., *L 3000*; Wyman Creek, 7200 ft., *M 2046*; east end of road, Crooked Creek, 9000 ft., *HM 95*; Trail Canyon, 8300 ft., *D 2524*.

10. Vicia

1. **V. americana** Muh. ssp. **oregana** (Nutt.) Abrams. Uncommon, dry places among sage: Chiatovich Creek, 8000 ft., *D 2545*.

FAMILY 33. ONAGRACEAE

A. Seeds with coma at one end .... 2. *Epilobium*
AA. Seeds without coma.
   B. Ovary 4-celled.
      C. Stigma capitate .... 1. *Camissonia*
      CC. Stigma deeply 4-lobed .... 4. *Oenothera*
   BB. Ovary 2-celled; flowers minute .... 3. *Gayophytum*

1. Camissonia
Key to species by Peter H. Raven

A. Petals purple; the flowers opening in the morning.
   B. Stems heavily glandular-pubescent .... 4a. *C. heterochroma* ssp. *heterochroma*
   BB. Stems glaucous, not glandular .... 4b. *C. heterochroma* ssp. *monoensis*
AA. Petals not purple; the flowers opening in the morning or evening.
   B. Petals entirely yellow.
      C. Plants with a conspicuous basal rosette of large pinnately divided

leaves . . . . 7. *C. walkeri* ssp. *tortilis*
CC. Plants with an inconspicuous basal rosette of small entire leaves
6. *C. pusilla*
BB. Petals white or white with yellow base.
   C.   Petals yellow at the base, 1.5–2.5 mm. long; seeds with a thick wing
      around the concave face . . . . 5. *C. pterosperma*
   CC. Petals not yellow at the base, often larger; seeds not winged.
     D.   Leaves pinnately divided; capsules prominently pedicellate, the
        pedicel 1–4 cm. long.
       E.   Lateral leaflets reduced in number; leaves often nearly simple
           3b. *C. claviformis* ssp. *integrior*
       EE. Lateral leaflets well developed and numerous
           3a. *C. claviformis* ssp. *claviformis*
     DD. Leaves not pinnately divided; capsules sessile or nearly so.
       E.   Petals 1.8–2.9 mm. long; capsule cylindrical, not especially en-
         larged near base . . . . 2. *C. chamaenerioides*
       EE. Petals 4–8 mm. long; capsule markedly enlarged near the base.
        F.   Plants heavily glandular-pubescent
           1b. *C. boothii* ssp. *intermedia*
        FF. Plants not glandular-pubescent
           1a. *C. boothii* ssp. *desertorum*

1. **C. boothii** (Dougl.) Raven
1a. Ssp. **desertorum** (Munz) Raven. Frequent, open sandy areas on alluvium or slopes, flats, or washes, desert scrub to pinyon woodland, throughout the range, below 8000 ft.: 7.4 miles west of White Mountain Road on Westgard Pass, 5000 ft., *L 2643*; Black Canyon, 7000 ft., *D 1747*; first canyon south of Silver Canyon, 5000 ft., *HM 705*; road between Dead Horse Creek and Cottonwood Creek, 7900 ft., *M 2106*; below old Devernois Ranch at mouth of Willow Creek, 4800 ft., *Peirson 12459* (UC); near Pinyon Hill, 7000 ft., *D 2865*; above Chiatovich Ranch, 6000 ft., *Purpus s.n.* (UC).
1b. Ssp. **intermedia** (Munz) Raven. Infrequent, sandy places, flats, washes, at lower elevations: White Mountains, *Purpus 6425* (UC); Deep Springs Valley, 4000 ft., *Ferris 1357* (DS).
2. **C. chamaenerioides** (Gray) Raven. Desert scrub to lower pinyon woodland, southern end of the range, below 6000 ft.: Black Canyon, 5700 ft., *D 2672*.
3. **C. claviformis** (Torr. & Frem.) Raven.
3a. Ssp. **claviformis.** Known only from 3 miles east of Westgard Pass, *Linsley & MacSwain 59–76* (UC).
3b. Ssp. **integrior** (Raven) Raven. Sandy soil, desert scrub along lower flanks of the range, below 6500 ft.: Westgard Pass, 14.8 miles northeast of Zurich, *Everett & Balls 21904* (RSA); 7.6 miles northeast of Deep Springs, *Raven 12835* (RSA); Fish Lake Valley, 4900 ft., *Lankester 775* (BM); mouth of Pinchot Creek, 6500 ft., *D 3275*.

112

4. **C. heterochroma** (Wats) Raven.

4a. Ssp. **heterochroma.** Dry soils. Known only from 2 miles west of Westgard Pass, 7000 ft., *Raven 6251* (CAS).

4b. Ssp. **monoensis** (Munz) Raven. Dry soils, below 8000 ft.: Silver Canyon, 7.7 miles east of Laws, 8000 ft., *Munz 12693*. (RSA).

5. **C. pterosperma** (Wats.) Raven. Rare, southern end of range, below 7000 ft.: west side of Westgard Pass, *Eastwood & Howell 9622* (CAS); Cedar Flat, 7000 ft., *D s.n.*

6. **C. pusilla** Raven. Dry slopes and flats and roadways, primarily on eastern and southern flank, 6000–8000 ft.: Westgard Pass, 7300 ft., *D s.n.*; Cottonwood Creek, 8000 ft., *D s.n.*; near Pinyon Hill, 6500 ft., *D 2860*; Indian Creek, 6000 ft., *Lankester 813* (BM); Chiatovich Creek, *D. s.n.*

7. **C. walkeri** (A. Nels.) Raven ssp. **tortilis** (Jeps.) Raven. Dry washes and slopes below 6000 ft.: Black Canyon at Marble Canyon, 5700 ft., *D 2655*.

2. Epilobium

A. Hypanthium not prolonged above the ovary; petals 8–20 mm. long
3. *E. angustifolium*
AA. Hypanthium prolonged above the ovary; petals 3–8 mm. long.
  B. Plants annual, 3–20 dm. tall; lower portion of stem with exfoliating epidermis; capsules 2–2.5 cm. long . . . . 6. *E. paniculatum*
  BB. Plants perennial, 0.3–10 dm. tall; epidermis not exfoliating; capsules 2–6 cm. long.
    C. Scaly buds or shoots (turios) present on rootstocks; petals 3–5 mm. long; plants 2–6 dm. tall . . . . 4. *E. brevistylum*
    CC. Turios not present on rootstocks; petals 4–8 mm. long; plants 0.3–10 dm. tall.
      D. Stems 0.3–4 dm. tall, simple above with opposite leaves.
        E. Plants 0.3–1.5 dm. tall; sepals 2 mm. long; petals 4–5 mm. long; leaves 0.8–2 cm. long . . . . 2. *E. anagallidifolium*
        EE. Plants 1–4 dm. tall; sepals 3–4 mm. long; petals 5–8 mm. long
5. *E. hornemannii*
      DD. Stems 3–10 dm. tall, branched freely above with alternate leaves; sepals ca. 2 mm. long; petals 5–6 mm. long . . 1. *E. adenocaulon*

1. **E. adenocaulon** Hausskn. var. **occidentale** Trel. Streamsides throughout the range, 5700–10,000 ft.: Marble Canyon, 5700 ft., *D.s.n.*; Silver Canyon, 6500 ft., *Jepson 7412* (JEPS); spring on Piute Trail, Sacramento Canyon, 10,000 ft., *D 2880*; Cottonwood Creek, 9000 ft., *D 1596*.

2. **E. anagallidifolium** Lam. Moist soil and streambanks, subalpine to alpine: Chiatovich Creek, 10,300 ft., *D 3120*.

3. **E. angustifolium** L. ssp. **circumvagum** Mosquin. Moist places and streambanks, pinyon woodland to alpine, throughout the range 7000–11,500 ft.: Wyman Creek, 7500 ft., *HM 867*; McAfee Creek, 11,500 ft., *L 3316*; Old Davis Ranch, Davis Creek, ca. 7000 ft., *Shockley 516* (JEPS); Chiatovich Creek, 8000 ft., *D 2568*.

4. **E. brevistylum** Barb. Wet places, pinyon woodland to subalpine forest, throughout the range, 5900–10,000 ft.: Wyman Creek, 5900 ft., *M 2154*; White Mountain, 10,000 ft., *Shockley 484* (JEPS); Lone Tree Creek, 10,000 ft., *M 2252*; Chiatovich Creek, 8500 ft., *D 3116*.

5. **E. hornemannii** Rchb. Rare, known only from McAfee Creek, 11,500 ft., *L 3312*.

6. **E. paniculatum** Nutt. ex Torr. & Gray. Sporadic, found around places of habitation in disturbed areas: Toll House Springs, 5971 ft., *L 3332*; Old Davis Ranch, Davis Creek, ca. 7000 ft., *Shockley 600* (JEPS).

3. Gayophytum

A. Plants flowering from near the base, the first flower 1–5 (10) nodes from the cotyledons.
- B. Branches separated by 2–8 nodes; seeds not staggered; capsules not torulose; pollen 55–68 microns in diameter . . . . 1. *G. decipiens*
- BB. Branches separated by 1–2 nodes; seeds often staggered; capsules often torulose; pollen 70–98 microns in diameter . . . . 2. *G. diffusum*

AA. Plants not flowering near the base, the first flower 5–20 nodes from the cotyledons.
- B. Petals 0.7–1.5 mm. long; capsules 3–9 mm. long; style ca. 0.3 mm. long; pollen 48–58 microns in diameter . . . . 3. *G. ramosissimum*
- BB. Petals 1.2–3 mm. long; capsules 3–15 mm. long; style 0.7–1.5 mm. long; pollen 70–98 microns in diameter . . . . 2. *G. diffusum*

1. **G. decipiens** Lewis & Szweyk. Sporadically frequent, washes and meadows in sandy soils, subalpine forest, 9500–10,500 ft.: Black Canyon, 9600 ft., *Coville & Funston 1797* (JEPS); Silver Canyon, near Big Prospector Meadow, 9700 ft., *Jepson 7355* (JEPS); head of Wyman Creek, *Munz 21042* (LA); Crooked Creek Lab, 10,200 ft., *Tucker 2243* (UC).

2. **G. diffusum** Torr. & Gray ssp. **parviflorum** Lewis & Szweyk. Common, hillsides and flats, subalpine forest, 9500–10,500 ft.: Wyman Creek, 9500 ft., *D 1745b*; Sagehen Flat, 10,250 ft., above Crooked Creek Spring, *L 3163*.

3. **G. ramosissimum** Torr. & Gray. Frequent, hillsides and flats, throughout the range, 7500–10,500 ft.: north rim of Reed Flat, 10,400 ft., *J. & L. Roos 5127* (RSA); Wyman Creek, 9500 ft., *D 1745a*; Crooked Creek Lab, 10,150 ft., *Lewis 1351* (LA); northwest corner of Sagehen Flat, 10,300 ft., *L 3163*; Chiatovich Creek, 7500 ft., *D 2786*.

4. Oenothera

A. Plants 3–12 dm. tall, erect; petals yellow, aging orange-red; basal leaves 10–18 cm. long . . . . 3. *Oe. hookeri*
AA. Plants 1–4 dm. tall, erect or cespitose; petals white to cream, aging red; basal leaves 2–10 cm. long.
- B. Plants erect; sepals 1.7–2.2 cm. long; petals 2.5–3.5 cm. long
1. *Oe. avita*

BB. Plants ± cespitose; sepals 2.5–3.5 cm. long; petals 2.5–5 cm. long
2. *Oe. caespitosa*

1. **Oe. avita** (Klein) Klein. Dry places among rocks, on slopes and roadbeds, throughout the range but primarily on the eastern and northern flank, below 8000 ft.: Wyman Creek, 8000 ft., *L 2815*; Fish Lake Valley, 4900 ft., *Lankester 820* (BM); Queen Canyon, 7700 ft., *M 2745*; near Pinchot Creek, 7000 ft., *D 2753*. Also observed near the school in Deep Springs Valley, 4800 ft.

2. **Oe. caespitosa** Nutt. ssp. **marginata** (Nutt.) Munz. Frequent, dry, sandy or rocky open places, slopes, washes, and roadsides, pinyon woodland to subalpine forest, 5200–10,300 ft.: Toll House Springs, 5971 ft., *L 2723*; 5 miles east of Westgard Pass, *Linsley & MacSwain 59–77* (UC); Black Canyon, 5700 ft., *D s.n.*; Silver Canyon, *Brandegee s.n.* (UC); Coldwater Canyon, *Brandegee s.n.* (UC); ½ mile north of Crooked Creek Lab, 10,300 ft., *HM 547*; Cottonwood Creek, 9500 ft., *D 1648*; intersection of north and south forks, Chiatovich Creek, 8500 ft., *M 2079*.

3. **Oe. hookeri** Torr. & Gray ssp. **angustifolia** (Gates) Munz. Frequent, moist places, washes, meadows, springs, below 8500 ft.: Toll House Springs, 5971 ft., *L 3333a*; Antelope Springs, Deep Springs Valley, 5600 ft., *L 3015*; Birch Creek, 4.8 miles north of Deep Springs Valley Road, 6000 ft., *L 2982*; Roberts Ranch, Wyman Creek, 8000 ft., *D 1728*.

FAMILY 34. ELAEAGNACEAE
1. Shepherdia

1. **S. argentea** Nutt. Moist streambanks in northeastern canyons, 5000–8300 ft.: Indian Creek, 7400 ft., *Archer 7222* (UC); Middle Creek, 5000 ft., *Jaeger s.n.* (POM); Trail Canyon, 8300 ft., *D 2507*.

FAMILY 35. CORNACEAE
1. Cornus

1. **C. aff. stolonifera** Michx. Growing in matted willows on steep slope at 9000 ft., north fork of McAfee Creek, *M 2136-A* (specimens lost).

FAMILY 36. LORANTHACEAE
1. Phoradendron

A. Leaves reduced, 1–2 mm. long, scalelike . . . . 2. *P. juniperinum*
AA. Leaves oblanceolate, 1–1.5 cm. long, green . . 1. *P. bolleanum* ssp. *densum*

1. **P. bolleanum** (Seem.) Eichl. ssp. **densum** (Torr.) Wiens. Known only from Black Canyon at Marble Canyon, 5700 ft., growing on *Juniperus osteosperma*, *D 2885*.

2. **P. juniperinum** Engelm. ex Gray. Known only from White Mountain Road, 8100 ft., 50 meters north of Grandview Mine, on *Juniperus osteosperma*, *L 3026*.

FAMILY 37. CELASTRACEAE
1. Forsellesia

A. Leaves pubescent; petals 4–7 mm. long; stipules less than 1 mm. long;

young branches ca. 1 mm. in diameter . . . . 1. *F. nevadensis*
AA. Leaves glabrous; petals 6–9 mm. long; stipules mostly more than 1 mm.
long; young branches ca. 0.5 mm. in diameter . . . . 2. *F. stipulifera*

1. **F. nevadensis** (Gray) Greene. Rare, 6000–7000 ft.: White Mountains, in
rocks, *Purpus 5794* (UC).
2. **F. stipulifera** (St. John) Ensign. Rare. Known only from Black Canyon
at 5700 ft., *D 2645*.

FAMILY 38. EUPHORBIACEAE
1. **Euphorbia**
A. Stipules united into a conspicuous white scale . . . . . . 1. *E. albomarginata*
AA. Stipules distinct, linear . . . . 2. *E. fendleri*

1. **E. albomarginata** Torr. & Gray. Known only from Payson Canyon Road,
5720 ft., *HM s.n.*
2. **E. fendleri** Torr. & Gray. Frequent, dry slopes, pinyon woodland, 6500–
8500 ft.: Westgard Pass just above "The Narrows," 6950 ft., *L 2760*; Mollie
Gibson Canyon, 7400 ft., *M 2072*; Black Canyon, 6500 ft., *D 1748*; White
Mountain Road, ¾ mile north of Studebaker Flat, 8500 ft., *HM 758*.

FAMILY 39. ACERACEAE
1. **Acer**
A. Leaves simple; shrub or small tree 2–6 m. tall . . . . 1. *A. glabrum*
AA. Leaves pinnate; tree 6–20 m. tall . . . . 2. *A. negundo*

1. **A. glabrum** Torr. var. **diffusum** (Greene) Smiley. Infrequent, rocky slopes
in canyons, 8000–9000 ft.: Birch Creek, 8400 ft., *D 3032* (RSA); Wyman
Creek, 8600 ft., *M 2263*; Cottonwood Creek, 8700 ft., *D 2576*.
2. **A. negundo** L. ssp. **californicum** (Torr. & Gray) Wesmael. Around dwel-
ling in Cottonwood Creek, 5800 ft., *M 2159*.

FAMILY 40. SIMAROUBACEAE
1. **Ailanthus**
1. **A. altissima** (Mill.) Swingle. Cultivated at Toll House Springs, 5971 ft.,
L 3335A.

FAMILY 41. ZYGOPHYLLACEAE
1. **Tribulus**
1. **T. terrestris** L. Naturalized in waste places and along roadsides: Toll House
Springs, 5971 ft., *L 3334A*.

FAMILY 42. GERANIACEAE
1. **Erodium**
1. **E. cicutarium** (L.) L'Hér. Frequent, waste places and dry slopes, weedy,

116

below 7000 ft.: Westgard Pass, 7.4 miles west of White Mountain Road, 5000 ft., *L 2659*; Black Canyon near mine, 5700 ft., *D 3006*; Antelope Springs, Deep Springs Valley, 5600 ft., *L 3001*; Silver Canyon, 5600 ft., *M & L 1997*.

FAMILY 43. LINACEAE
1. Linum

1. **L. lewisii** Pursh. Frequent, dry slopes, pinyon woodland to subalpine forest, 7400–11,500 ft.: Westgard Pass, 7400 ft., *L 2896*; north of Schulman Grove on White Mountain Road, 10,000 ft., *HM 384*; Sagehen Flat, 10,300 ft., *Cook s.n.* (UC); east slope of Sheep Mountain, 11,500 ft., *Cook s.n.* (UC); Cottonwood Creek; McClouds Camp, 9500 ft., *D 1623*; 11,000 ft., *D 1633*.

FAMILY 44. POLYGALACEAE
1. Polygala

1. **P. acanthoclada** Gray. Rare, dry slopes and flats, northern end of range: Chiatovich Creek, 7500 ft., *D s.n.*

FAMILY 45. UMBELLIFERAE

A. Fruit terete or somewhat compressed laterally, the ribs not prominently winged .... 2. *Berula*
AA. Fruit compressed dorsally, at least some of the ribs winged.
  B. Lateral ribs winged, dorsal ribs filiform.
    C. Leaves simply pinnate, divisions ovate; aquatic ...... 5. *Oxypolis*
    CC. Leaves pinnately or ternate-pinnately divided; divisions linear or filiform .... 4. *Lomatium*
  BB. Lateral, intermediate and dorsal ribs winged or prominent.
    C. Stems tall, leafy.
      D. Umbellets not capitate .... 1. *Angelica*
      DD. Umbellets capitate .... 7. *Sphenosciadium*
    CC. Stems poorly developed.
      D. Sepals prominent .... 6. *Pteryxia*
      DD. Sepals not prominent .... 3. *Cymopterus*

1. Angelica

A. Leaf-divisions linear to linear-oblong, 0.2–0.8 cm. broad; rays 20–40
    2. *A. lineariloba*
AA. Leaf-divisions lanceolate to lance-ovate, 1–3.5 cm. broad; rays 7–14
    1. *A. kingii*

1. **A. kingii** (Wats.) Coult. & Rose. Moist soils near streamsides, marshes, meadows, etc., pinyon woodland, throughout the range, 6000–9500 ft.: Marble Canyon fork of Black Canyon, 7000 ft., *D 2851*; Wyman Creek, 6000 ft., *HM 861*; Cottonwood Creek, 9500 ft., *D 1652*; Trail Canyon, 8300 ft., *D 2500*; Queen Canyon, 8000 ft., *Ferris 6692* (DS).
2. **A. lineariloba** Gray. Moist areas, streamsides, etc., throughout the range,

117

7500–9500 ft.: Wyman Creek, ca. 1 mile below Roberts Ranch, 7500 ft., *D 3152*; Crooked Creek, 9400 ft., *Bacigalupi et al. 8097* (JEPS); Chiatovich Creek, 9500 ft., *D 3119*.

2. Berula

1. **B. erecta** (Huds.) Cov. Marshes. Known only from Antelope Springs, Deep Springs Valley, 5600 ft., *L 3002*.

3. Cymopterus

A. Leaves hirtellous to scaberulous.
  B. Leaf-blades 1.5–2.5 cm. long; umbels congested and globose; involucres of conspicuous united bracts . . . . 2. *C. cinerarius*
  BB. Leaf-blades 3–10 cm. long; umbels not globose; involucre wanting or of few linear bracts . . . . 1. *C. aboriginum*
AA. Leaves glabrous.
  B. Flowers greenish-yellow; fruit 6–10 mm. long; leaf-blades 3–12 cm. long; involucre wanting . . . . 3. *C. panamintensis*
  BB. Flowers purplish; fruit 8–18 mm. long; leaf-blades 1.5–5 cm. long; involucral bracts white . . . . 4. *C. purpurascens*

1. **C. aboriginum** Jones. Pinyon woodland, 5700–8000 ft.: Westgard Pass, 7000 ft., *Alexander & Kellogg 2493* (UC); Marble Canyon of Black Canyon, 5750 ft., *D 2733*; Silver Canyon, *Brandegee s.n.* (UC).
2. **C. cinerarius** Gray. Common, dry rocky slopes and flats, subalpine forest and alpine fell-fields, 10,000–13,100 ft.: head of old Silver Canyon, 10,600 ft., *HM 823*; east of Piute Mountain, along road, 11,000 ft., *Bacigalupi et al. 8158* (JEPS); head of Poison Creek, 10,800 ft., *HM 834*; Sheep Mountain, north of Campito Meadow, 11,500 ft., *Maguire & Holmgren 26116* (UC); Cottonwood Creek, 10,500 ft., *D 1645*; road above Barcroft Lab, 13,100 ft., *HM 629*; also on Chiatovich Flats.
3. **C. panamintensis** Coult. & Rose. Rocky slopes, desert scrub and lower pinyon woodland at southern end of range, 5500–7000 ft.: Toll House Springs, 5971 ft., *L 2717*; Westgard Pass, 6850 ft., *Everett & Balls 21944* (DS); second ridge south of Silver Canyon, 5500 ft., *HM 147*.
4. **C. purpurascens** (Gray) Jones. Known only along the east slope of Montgomery Pass, *Eastwood & Howell 9544* (CAS) and Westgard Pass Road, 9.5 miles northwest of intersection with Saline Valley Road. Rocky slopes near old mine, north of road at summit, *Mathias 3201* (LA).

4. Lomatium

A. Flowers purple, rarely yellow; plants hoary-pubescent . . 2. *L. mohavense*
AA. Flowers white to yellow to yellow and purple.
  B. Rays 8–22; flowers white . . . . 3. *L. nevadense*
  BB. Rays 1–14; flowers cream to yellow to yellow and purple
                                         1. *L. foeniculaceum*

1. **L. foeniculaceum** (Nutt.) Coult. & Rose.
A.   Petals glabrous; umbels with usually only 1 ray . . . . . lb. ssp. *inyoense*
AA. Petals pubescent along margins; rays 2–14 . . . . la. ssp. *fimbriatum*

la. Ssp. **fimbriatum** Theobald. Frequent, open flats and slopes in dry soils, pinyon woodland to subalpine forest, throughout the range, 6000–10,500 ft.: 0.1 miles northwest of summit of Westgard Pass, 7300 ft., *Theobald 708* (LA), TYPE; Deep Springs Valley, 6300 ft., *HM 684*; head of Silver Canyon, 10,450 ft., *HM 856*; Wyman Creek, 10,000 ft., *L 3056*; Trail Canyon, 8000 ft., *D 2701*; mouth of Queen Canyon, 7100 ft., *D 3251*.

lb. Ssp. **inyoense** (Math. & Const.) Theobald. Dry slopes and flats, subalpine forest, 10,000–11,000 ft.: White Mountain Road between Crooked Creek and Sheep Mountain, 10,800 ft., *Pawek 58–9* (UC).

2. **L. mohavense** (Coult. & Rose) Coult. & Rose. Dry places, upper desert scrub to lower pinyon woodland, below 8500 ft.: Westgard Pass between "The Narrows" and the summit, *Eastwood & Howell 9626* (CAS); east side of Montgomery Pass, *Eastwood & Howell 9543* (CAS).; Studebaker Flat, 8500 ft., *Cook s.n.* (UC).

3. **L. nevadense** (Wats.) Coult. & Rose. Dry slopes and flats, desert scrub to pinyon woodland below 7500 ft.: north side of Cedar Flat, 7350 ft., *Alexander & Kellogg 2493a* (UC); Benton Station, *D 3552*; mouth of Queen Canyon, 7100 ft., *D 3248*.

5. Oxypolis

1. **O. occidentalis** Coult. & Rose. Streams and wet places. Known only from Silver Canyon at 7000 ft., *M & L 2474*.

6. Pteryxia

1. **P. petraea** (Jones) Coult. & Rose. Rocky slopes and canyon walls, pinyon woodland, throughout the range, 6000–8800 ft.: Westgard Pass, 6650 ft., *Alexander & Kellogg 2498* (UC); Black Canyon, 6000 ft., *D 3008*; Silver Canyon, 7500 ft., *Alexander & Kellogg 4270* (UC); Wyman Creek, 8750 ft., *L 2806*; observed in Indian Creek.

7. Sphenosciadium

1. **S. capitellatum** Gray. Streams and meadows, throughout the range, below 10,000 ft.: Roberts Ranch, Wyman Creek, 8000 ft., *D 3145*; meadow of Poison and Cottonwood creeks, 9450 ft., *L 3136*; Poison Creek, 10,000 ft., *Jepson 7373* (JEPS); Cottonwood Creek, 9200 ft., *L 3294*.

FAMILY 46. GENTIANACEAE

A.   Corolla rotate with fringed gland on upper surface, greenish-white with purple dots; leaves 5–12 cm. long . . . . 1. *Frasera*
AA. Corolla campanulate to funnelform, white to greenish to bluish; if with greenish dots then with dark bands without; leaves 1–6 cm. long
2. *Gentiana*

1. Frasera

1. **F. puberulenta** A. Davids. Dry slopes and sandy soils, subalpine forest, primarily south of the peak, 8000–10,500 ft.: secondary canyon of Black Canyon, 8000 ft., *M 2140*; edge of Reed Flat, 10,300 ft., *Munz 21019* (UC); near Schulman Grove, 10,200 ft., *Smith 1257* (JEPS); Old Silver Canyon Road, 9600 ft., *HM 278*; Wyman Creek, 9500 ft., *D 1736*; ½ mile south of Crooked Creek Lab, 10,400 ft., *HM 550*.

2. Gentiana

A. Plants perennial; flowers white with greenish to purplish spots within and dark bands without, the tube 2–3 cm. long . . . . 2. *G. newberryi*
AA. Plants annual or biennial; corolla 0.7–2.0 cm. long.
  B. Leaves white-margined; corolla lobes without a basal fimbriate crown; corolla blue, 12–15 mm. long . . . . 3. *G. prostrata*
  BB. Leaves not white-margined; corolla lobes with a basal fimbriate crown; corolla blue to white, 8–20 mm. long.
    C. Plants 5–50 cm. tall; flowers clustered; leaves 1.5–3.5 cm. long; corolla blue to bluish-lavender . . . . 1. *G. amarella*
    CC. Plants 3–8 cm. tall; flowers solitary, corolla white to greenish to bluish; leaves 0.8–1.5 cm. long . . . . 4. *G. tenella*

1. **G. amarella** L. Uncommon. Known only from one canyon: Meadow of Poison and Cottonwood Creek, 9450 ft., *L 3132, D 1616*.

2. **G. newberryi** Gray. Meadows and moist places, alpine fell-fields, 11,000–12,000 ft.: just northeast of Piute Trail Pass, 11,800 ft., *L 3284*; McAfee Creek, 11,800 ft., *HM 614*.

3. **G. prostrata** Haenke. Meadows, primarily in alpine fell-fields, 11,000–12,500 ft., but occasionally lower in elevation: head of Cottonwood Creek, 11,700 ft., *D 2587*; McAfee Meadow, 11,700 ft., *D M124*; ¼ mile below Barcroft Lab, 12,500 ft., *Tucker 2257* (UC).

4. **G. tenella** Rottb. Meadows and wet places, throughout the range, 8500–12,500 ft.: south fork of Cottonwood Creek, 9800 ft., *HM 461*; McAfee Meadow, 11,700 ft., *D 2816*; ¼ mile below Barcroft Lab, 12,500 ft., *Tucker 2255* (UC); Chiatovich Creek, 8500 ft., *D 3105*.

FAMILY 47. APOCYNACEAE
1. Apocynum

A. Corolla 4–6 mm. long; follicles 7–12 cm. long, erect . . . . . . 2. *A. medium*
AA. Corolla 2–3 mm. long; follicles 12–20 cm. long, pendulous
                                    1. *A. cannabinum*

1. **A. cannabinum** L. var. **glaberrimum** A. DC. Uncommon, riparian areas below 6500 ft.: just north of Black Canyon, 4800 ft., *M 2077*; narrows of Wyman Creek, 6300 ft., *M 2152*.

2. **A. medium** Greene var. **floribundum** (Greene) Woodson. Known only from dry flats, 8000 ft., Chiatovich Creek, *D 2569*.

120

FAMILY 48. ASCLEPIADACEAE
1. Asclepias

A.   Leaves oval to oblong, opposite; corolla lobes rose-purple, 8–10 mm. long
                                                        2. *A. speciosa*
AA. Leaves linear to linear-lanceolate, in whorls; corolla greenish-white, often
     tinged purple, lobes 4–5 mm. long . . . . 1. *A. fascicularis*

1. **A. fascicularis** Dcne. Uncommon, dry to somewhat moist areas, southern part of the range below 6000 ft.: Antelope Springs, Deep Springs Valley, 5600 ft., *L 2988*; Black Canyon, ½ mile above Marble Canyon, 5700 ft., *D 3004*; near mouth of Silver Canyon, 4300 ft., *D 3127*; Silver Canyon, 5300 ft., *M 2069*.

2. **A. speciosa** Torr. Uncommon. Known only from recently flooded area beside Cottonwood Creek near Indian dwellings at 5600 ft., *M 2165*.

FAMILY 49. SOLANACEAE

A.   Plants shrubby, 1–3 m. tall . . . . 1. *Lycium*
AA. Plants herbaceous.
   B.   Stems erect, simple or branched; corolla 2.5–3 cm. long; capsule 8–12
        mm. long . . . . 2. *Nicotiana*
   BB. Stems ascending to decumbent; corolla 3–5 mm. in diameter; berry 6–7
        mm. in diameter . . . . 3. *Solanum*

1. Lycium

A.   Leaves 0.3–1.5 cm. long; corolla whitish-lavender, the tube 10–16 mm.
     long; fruit fleshy, red, 4–8 mm. long . . . . 1. *L. andersonii*
AA. Leaves 1–3 cm. long; corolla greenish-white, 8–12 mm. long; fruit dry,
     greenish, 6–10 mm. long . . . . 2. *L. cooperi*

1. **L. andersonii** Gray. Common, but sporadic in distribution, washes, dry slopes and ridges, desert scrub, 5000–6000 ft.: Black Canyon, 5700 ft., *D s.n.*; first canyon south of Silver Canyon, 5000 ft., *HM 700*; ridge north of Silver Canyon, 5800 ft., *HM 195-B*.

2. **L. cooperi** Gray. Rare; reported by Douglas Powell as being present in the range. Known from Candelaria area.

2. Nicotiana

1. **N. attenuata** Torr. Open and disturbed places, throughout the range, 5500–9000 ft.: Payson Canyon, 5913 ft., *L 2969*; Montenegro Springs, 7000 ft., *M 2145*; near mouth of Wyman Creek, *Ferris 6911* (POM); Wyman Creek, 5900 ft., *M 2156*; Trail Canyon, 8000 ft., *D 3090*; also reported from White Mountain Road at 8950 ft.

3. Solanum

1. **S. sarachoides** Sendt. ex Mart. Weed, known only in mud of overflow at Montenegro Springs, 7000 ft., *M 2146*.

FAMILY 50. CONVOLVULACEAE
1. Convolvulus

1. **C. arvensis** L. Weed, waste places and roadsides, below 7000 ft. Observed in Payson Canyon, 6900 ft., at Toll House Springs, and in Fish Lake Valley.

FAMILY 51. CUSCUTACEAE
1. Cuscuta

A. Calyx lobes triangular, acute; corolla lobes triangular-ovate, acuminate; stems slender, pale; scales oblong; styles shorter than ovary; on various hosts . . . . 3. *C. suksdorfii*
AA. Calyx lobes lance-ovate, acute to acuminate; corolla lobes lanceolate to lance-ovate, acute to acuminate; stems very slender or medium, yellow or orange.
   B. Stems very slender, orange; corolla lobes lance-ovate; scales oblong, narrow; styles not longer than ovary; on Chenopodiaceae . . 2. *C. salina*
   BB. Stems medium, yellow; corolla lobes lanceolate; scales lacking; styles longer than ovary; on various hosts . . . . 1. *C. occidentalis*

1. **C. occidentalis** Millsp. Known only from Westgard Pass, 6000 ft., on *Chaenactis. Raven 6988* (CAS).
2. **C. salina** Engelm. On plants inhabiting saline places at lower elevations: Silver Canyon, 4500 ft., on *Atriplex confertifolia*, D 3462.
3. **C. suksdorfii** Yunck. var. **subpedicellata** Yunck. On various shrubs, desert scrub below 5000 ft.: Westgard Pass, 8.5 miles west of White Mountain Road, 4600 ft., common here, *L 2639*.

FAMILY 52. POLEMONIACEAE

A. Calyx not ruptured by maturing capsule.
   B. Plants annual; corolla pink to purplish, 8–15 mm. long; below 13,000 ft.
                                    1. *Collomia*
   BB. Plants perennial; corolla blue and white, 11–13 mm. long; above 13,000 ft. . . . . 11. *Polemonium*
AA. Calyx distended by capsule and usually ruptured by it.
   B. True foliage-leaves absent; annual, 1–5 cm. tall with basal cotyledons
                                    4. *Gymnosteris*
   BB. True foliage-leaves present, cauline or basal.
      C. Leaves mostly opposite near base of plant.
         D. Stamens unequally inserted; leaves entire . . . . 10. *Phlox*
         DD. Stamens equally inserted; leaves ± cleft.
            E. Leaves acerose . . . . 7. *Leptodactylon*
            EE. Leaves not acerose . . . . 8. *Linanthus*
      CC. Leaves mostly alternate.
         D. Calyx regular.
            E. Upper cauline leaves strongly reduced . . . . 3. *Gilia*
            EE. Upper cauline leaves well developed.
               F. Corolla 4–6 mm. long; white . . . . 5. *Ipomopsis*

122

FF. Corolla 7–20 mm. long; lilac or white.
  G.   Leaves palmately cleft into 3–7 lobes .. 7. *Leptodactylon*
  GG. Leaves linear to deltoid, entire and toothed
                                          6. *Langloisia*
DD. Calyx zygomorphic.
  E.   Corolla white, pale blue, to blue; plants cobwebby-pubescent in inflorescence .... 2. *Eriastrum*
  EE. Corolla yellow; plants puberulent .... 9. *Navarretia*

1. Collomia

1. **C. linearis** Nutt. Dry places, 4000–10,300 ft.: Cabin Creek, 10,300 ft., *D 2553*; Chiatovich Creek, 8000 ft., *D 3096*; also observed near Benton.

2. Eriastrum

A.   Corolla 7–8 mm. long.
  B.   Stamens attached at base of throat, 2–2.5 mm. long; stems erect, ± floccose; calyx 5 mm. long with equal lobes .... 2. *E. sparsiflorum*
  BB. Stamens attached at middle of throat, 1–2 mm. long; stems spreading from base, thinly pilose; calyx 5–7 mm. long with unequal lobes
                                        1. *E. diffusum*
AA. Corolla 9–12 mm. long; stamens inserted at base of throat; stems floccose; calyx unequally lobed .... 3. *E. wilcoxii*

1. **E. diffusum** (Gray) Mason. Dry places, desert scrub of western canyons, below 7500 ft.: Black Canyon, 5600 ft., *D 2681*; Silver Canyon, 6600 ft., *HM 273*.

2. **E. sparsiflorum** (Eastw.) Mason. Dry slopes and washes, desert scrub to pinyon woodland, below 6500 ft.: Westgard pass, 4 miles west of White Mountain Road, 6400 ft., *L 2709*; first canyon south of Silver Canyon, 5000 ft., *HM 706*; Wyman Creek, 5900 ft., *M 2157*; Cottonwood Creek, 6100 ft. *M 2162*.

3. **E. wilcoxii** (A. Nels.) Mason. Frequent, rocky slopes and washes, desert scrub to pinyon woodland, throughout the range, 4200 to 8000 ft.: 2.9 miles east of Big Pine on Westgard Pass Road, 4200 ft., *HM 19*; east side of Westgard Pass, 6000 ft., *Raven 7032* (CAS); mouth of Mollie Gibson Canyon, 6960 ft., *L 2959*; Silver Canyon, 7350 ft., *HM 116*; observed in Indian Creek.

3. Gilia

A.   Pollen cream or yellow.
  B.   Corolla funnelform, pink .... 8. *G. latifolia*
  BB. Corolla campanulate to turbinate, white to yellow.
    C.   Corolla white to cream with yellow throat; lower leaves ovate to lance-ovate .... 3. *G. campanulata*
    CC. Corolla yellow; leaves linear-filiform .... 6. *G. filiformis*
AA. Pollen blue or white.
  B.   Lower stems and leaves arachnoid-wooly.

C.　Stems not cobwebby-pubescent at base, but glabrous and glaucous

　　　　　　　　　　　　　　　　　　　　14. *G. sinuata*

CC.　Stems cobwebby-pubescent at base.

　　D.　Upper corolla throat white, violet, or yellow, the throat lacking dark purple.

　　　　E.　Corolla 4–12 mm. long.

　　　　　　F.　Calyx glabrous or lightly cobwebby-pubescent; corolla 4–12 mm. long.

　　　　　　　　G.　Corolla throat broadly expanding; corolla 4–6 mm. long; calyx glabrous .... 11. *G. ochroleuca*

　　　　　　　　GG.　Corolla throat narrowly flaring; corolla 6–12 mm. long; calyx glabrous or cobwebby pubescent . . 1. *G. aliquanta*

　　　　　　FF.　Calyx ± glandular; corolla 7–12 mm. long, the tube light violet .... 12. *G. ophthalmoides*

　　　　EE.　Corolla 8–23 mm. long; calyx lightly glandular; tube purple

　　　　　　　　　　　　　　　　　　　　4. *G. cana*

　　DD.　Upper corolla throat yellow or ± purple; calyx glandular; corolla 7–11 mm. long .... 2. *G. brecciarum*

BB.　Lower stems and leaves not arachnoid-wooly.

　　C.　Plants without a basal rosette, leafy throughout ...... 5. *G. clokeyi*

　　CC.　Plants with well-developed basal rosette; upper leaves reduced.

　　　　D.　Lower leaves strap-shaped, dentate to pinnatifid

　　　　　　　　　　　　　　　　　　　　9. *G. leptomeria*

　　　　DD.　Lowers leaves 1–3-times pinnate.

　　　　　　E.　Corolla with purple spot in throat .... 15. *G. stellata*

　　　　　　EE.　Corolla without purple spot in throat.

　　　　　　　　F.　Plants glandular-villous; corolla 10–14 mm. long, rose-lavender, the throat pale lavender or yellowish

　　　　　　　　　　　　　　　　　　　　13. *G. scopulorum*

　　　　　　FF.　Plants glandular-puberulent.

　　　　　　　　G.　Basal leaves mostly bipinnatifid; cauline leaves 0.5–3.5 cm. long; corolla 8–14 mm. long, the throat yellow or white, the lobes white with violet streaks .... 7. *G. hutchinsifolia*

　　　　　　　　GG.　Basal leaves once-pinnate; cauline leaves smaller; corolla 6–11 mm. long, the throat purple and white, the lobes violet .... 10. *G. malior*

1. **G. aliquanta** A. & V. Grant ssp. **breviloba** A. & V. Grant. Dry rocky slopes, desert scrub to subalpine forest: Chiatovich Creek, 10,500 ft., in Mono Co., Calif., *M 2096*; reported in Munz as below 6200 ft.

2. **G. brecciarum** Jones. Dry slopes, desert scrub to pinyon woodland, throughout the range, 6500–9200 ft.: Black Mountain, 8400 ft., *Powell 1257* (UC); Silver Canyon, 9200 ft., *HM 748*; mouth of Queen Canyon, *D 3249A*.

3. **G. campanulata** Gray. Sandy soils, desert scrub, throughout the range, below 7000 ft.: 5 miles northeast of Benton on Montgomery Pass, *Eastwood &*

Howell 9548 (CAS); Montgomery Pass, Nevada, 6950 ft., *Ripley & Barneby 3717* (CAS); collected by Purpus (5828) in Deep Springs Valley.

4. **G. cana** (Jones) Heller ssp. **triceps** (Brand) A. & V. Grant. Common, especially in southern portion of the range, dry open areas on slopes and washes, alluvia, etc., desert scrub, 4500–6000 ft.: 7.4 miles west of White Mountain Road, on Westgard Pass, 5000 ft., *L 2646*; Black Canyon, 5700 ft., *D M2*; first canyon south of Silver Canyon, 4600 ft., *D 3447*; mouth of Milner Canyon, 5500 ft., *D 3237*.

5. **G. clokeyi** Mason. Known only from Deep Springs, *Grant 9836* (RSA).

6. **G. filiformis** Parry ex Gray. Dry slopes and washes, desert scrub, especially in southern portion of the range, below 6000 ft.: below Toll House Springs, *Eastwood & Howell 9593* (CAS); Black Canyon at Marble Canyon, 5700 ft., *D 2731*; Silver Canyon, 4500 ft., *D 3463*.

7. **G. hutchinsifolia** Rydb. Dry hillsides and flats, Fish Lake Valley and eastern slope of range, below 6500 ft.: north of Pinyon Hill, ca. 6500 ft., *D 2754*.

8. **G. latifolia** Wats. Dry gravelly slopes and canyons, below 7100 ft.: below Toll House Springs, *Eastwood & Howell 9569* (CAS); Black Canyon at Marble Canyon, 5700 ft., *D 2737*; Silver Canyon 4.7 miles east of Laws, 7000 ft., *Munz 12719* (RSA); also Milner Creek at 7100 ft.

9. **G. leptomeria** Gray. Dry open places, desert scrub to pinyon wood'and, throughout the range, 4500–8300 ft.: White Mountain Road, 2 miles north of Cedar Flat, 7800 ft., *Cook s.n.* (UC); directly below Devernois Ranch, 4700 ft., *Peirson 12460* (UC); Hammil Station, west of Birch Creek, *D M3*; Chiatovich Creek, 8300 ft., *D M9*; Trail Canyon, *D M4B*.

10. **G. malior** Day & Grant. Desert scrub to pinyon woodland in southern end of the range, below 8400 ft.: Toll House Springs, 5971 ft., *L 2724*; Black Mountains, 8400 ft., *Powell 1248* (UC).

11. **G. ochroleuca** Jones. Sandy slopes and washes, Deep Springs Valley and Westgard Pass: Deep Springs Valley, 6300 ft., *HM 693*.

12. **G. opthalmoides** Brand. Washes, flats and hillsides, desert scrub to pinyon woodland and subalpine forest, throughout the range, 5000–10,000 ft.: near mouth of Payson Canyon, *Wiggins 8799* (UC); east of summit of Westgard Pass, 7000 ft., *V. & A. Grant 9431* (UC); Black Canyon at Marble Canyon, 5700 ft., *D 2660A*; Cottonwood Creek, 10,000 ft., *D 1581*; near B & B Mine, Trail Canyon, ca. 8000 ft., *D 2711*; 0.5 miles north of mouth of Pinchot Creek, *D 3278*; observed in Silver Canyon at 7400 ft.

13. **G. scopulorum** Jones. Known only from the west side of Westgard Pass, dry slopes and washes, below 6000 ft., *Eastwood & Howell 9596* (CAS).

14. **G. sinuata** Dougl. ex Benth. Dry sandy soils and roadsides, desert scrub to pinyon woodland, below 7200 ft.: Owens Valley, 7 miles south of Bishop, *D 1473*; Wyman Creek, 7200 ft., *M 2042*.

15. **G. stellata** Heller. Slopes and washes in dry places, desert scrub to pinyon woodland, below 6000 ft.: west side of Westgard Pass, *Eastwood & Howell 9596* (RSA); Black Canyon at Marble Canyon, 5700 ft., *D 2660B*.

4. Gymnosteris

1. **G. parvula** (Rydb.) Heller. Meadows and dry slopes, alpine fell-fields, 10,000–11,700 ft.: Reed Flat, 10,000 ft., *D s.n.*; Big Prospector Meadow, 10,300 ft., *Jepson 7309* (JEPS); Campito Meadow, 11,000 ft., *Tucker 3428* (DAV); White Mountain Road, northeast of Piute Mountain, 11,650 ft., *L 3291*; McAfee Meadow, 11,700 ft., *D 2813*.

5. Ipomopsis

A. Plants perennial, densely matted with cushionlike rosettes; basal leaves palmately divided .... 1. *I. congesta*
AA. Plants annual.
  B. Flowers in subcapitate clusters; leaves pinnatifid into mucronulate segments; calyx 3–4 mm. long .... 3. *I. polycladon*
  BB. Lower flowers solitary; leaves entire or toothed; calyx 5–6 mm. long
  2. *I. depressa*

1. **I. congesta** (Hook.) V. Grant ssp. **montana** (Nels. & Kenn.) V. Grant. Slopes and washes in dry soil, common especially above 10,000 ft., pinyon woodland to alpine fell-fields, 7900–12,000 ft.: Mollie Gibson Canyon, 3 miles above Payson Canyon, 7950 ft., *L 2939*; southeast rim of Reed Flat, 10,100 ft., *J. & L. Roos 5115* (RSA); north of Schulman Grove, ca. 10,200 ft., *Smith 1246* (JEPS); Crooked Creek Lab, 10,200 ft., *Tucker 2241* (DAV); Sagehen Flat, 10,500 ft., *HM 540*; McAfee Meadow, 12,000 ft., *D s.n.* (POM).

2. **I. depressa** (Jones) V. Grant. Dry places, desert scrub on western slopes, below 5000 ft.: 3 miles south of Shealy, *D 3234*; directly below Old Devernois Ranch, 4700 ft., *Peirson 12462* (RSA).

3. **I. polycladon** (Torr.) V. Grant. Known only from near Trail Canyon, 7000 ft., *D s.n.* (POM).

6. Langloisia

1. **L. punctata** (Cov.) Goodd. Rocky and gravelly washes and alluvium, 4500–5900 ft.: 8.5 miles west of White Mountain Road on Westgard Pass, 4600 ft., *L 2635*; Black Canyon, 5700 ft., *D s.n.*; Silver Canyon, 5850 ft., *Alexander & Kellogg 4265* (UC).

7. Leptodactylon

1. **L. pungens** (Torr.) Rydb.
A. Middle leaf-segment less than twice as long as the adjacent lateral segments
lb. ssp. *pulchriflorum*
AA. Middle leaf-segment 2–4 times as long as the adjacent lateral segments
la. ssp. *hallii*

1a. Ssp. **hallii** (Parish) Mason. Dry flats and hillsides, pinyon woodland to alpine fell-fields, throughout the range, 7200–12,000 ft.: Westgard Pass, 7200 ft., *D 2780A*; north of Schulman Grove on White Mountain Road, 10,000 ft.,

HM 378; Wyman Creek, 9500 ft., *D 1744*; Silver Canyon, 8700 ft., *L 2848*; Cottonwood Creek, 12,000 ft., *D 2604*; Chiatovich Creek, 7500 ft., *D s.n.*

1b. Ssp. **pulchriflorum** (Brand) Mason. Dry rocky places, throughout the range, 10,000–13,000 ft.: Crooked Creek Lab, 10,500 ft., *Cook s.n.*, (UC); Barcroft Lab, 12,500 ft., *Cook s.n.* (UC); Pellisier Flats, 1 mile south of Mt. DuBois, *M & L 2175*.

8. Linanthus

A.   Plants perennial, woody at base . . . . 1. *L. nuttallii*
AA. Plants annual.
   B.   Flowers borne on pedicels 5 mm. or more long; corolla 2–4 mm. long
                                             3. *L. septentrionalis*
   BB. Flowers ± sessile; corolla 10–15 mm. long . . . . 2. *L. parryae*

1. **L. nuttallii** (Gray) Greene.
A.   Leaves 3–5-cleft into ± filiform lobes . . . . lb. ssp. *floribundus*
AA. Leaves 5–9-cleft into linear-oblanceolate lobes . . . . la. ssp. *nuttallii*

la. Ssp. **nuttallii.** Roadsides, rocky slopes and flats, pinyon woodland to subalpine forest, 7500–10,300 ft.: near Reed Flat, 10,300 ft., *Munz 21034* (UC); Wyman Creek: 7500 ft., *D 3048*; 9450 ft., *L 2813*; east of Crooked Creek Lab, 10,130 ft., *Bacigalupi et al. 8045* (JEPS).

lb. Ssp. **floribundus** (Gray) Munz. Cliffs above south fork of Chiatovich Creek at edge of Pellisier Flats, 12,500 ft., *M 2176*.

2. **L. parryae** (Gray) Greene. Dry desert slopes, below 5500 ft.: two miles south of Benton Station, 5400 ft., *D 3242*.

3. **L. septentrionalis** Mason. Known only from Silver Canyon, 8850 ft., *HM 309*.

9. Navarretia

1. **N. breweri** (Gray) Greene. Dry rocky slopes, 10,000–11,000 ft.: Reed Flat, 10,000 ft., *D 1925A*; head of Silver Canyon, 10,450 ft., *HM 854*; White Mountain Road at Campito Meadow, 10,600 ft., *L 3172*; east slope of Sheep Mountain, 11,000 ft., *J. & L. Roos 5166* (UC).

10. Phlox

A.   Style 2–3 cm. long; corolla tube 2–3 cm. long, rose to whitish
                                                   5. *P. stansburyi*
AA. Style to 1 cm. long; corolla tube 0.8–1.2 cm. long.
   B.   Plants with glandular pubescence.
      C.   Leaves concave above, 3–5 mm. long; styles 2–3 mm. long; calyx
          5–6 mm. long . . . . 2. *P. covillei*
      CC. Leaves flat above, 4–10 mm. long; styles 3–6 mm. long; calyx 7–8
          mm. long . . . . 1. *P. caespitosa*
   BB. Plants without glandular pubescence.

C. Leaves 10–15 mm. long, not greatly pungent; herbage subglabrous to thinly tomentose .... 3. *P. diffusa*
CC. Leaves 5–10 mm. long, pungent; herbage wooly-villous
4. *P. hoodii*

1. **P. caespitosa** Nutt. ssp. **pulvinata** Wherry. Dry rocky soils, subalpine forest to alpine fell-fields, 10,000–13,000 ft.: Reed Flat, 10,300 ft., *Munz 21011* (UC); east slope of Sheep Mountain, 11,500 ft., *Cook s.n.* (UC); head of Cottonwood Creek, 12,000 ft., *D M9*; McAfee Meadow, 12,000 ft., *D 1674*; Estey Plateau, White Mountain Peak, 13,000 ft., *Cook s.n.* (UC).

2. **P. covillei** E. Nels. Common matted plant, on dry slopes and flats, subalpine forest to alpine fell-fields, 9000–13,500 ft.: White Mountain Road, south of McAfee Meadow, 11,700 ft., *L 3027*; White Mountain Road, 13,500 ft., *L 3250*; Mt. Barcroft, 12,700 ft., *Tucker 3432* (UC).

3. **P. diffusa** Benth. ssp. **subcarinata** Wherry. Rare, dry slopes, pinyon woodland to alpine fell-fields; cited by Munz as from 13,500 ft.; known from 1 mile south of Montgomery Pass on road to Tip Top Mine, 7600 ft., *Grant 9617* (RSA).

4. **P. hoodii** Richards ssp. **canescens** (Torr. & Gray) Wherry. Dry rocky places, pinyon woodland to subalpine forest, throughout the range, 8000–10,000 ft.: Crooked Creek, end of road north of Old Ranger Station, 9800 ft., *L 2875*; summit of divide between Crooked and Cottonwood creeks, 10,000 ft., *Tucker 3422* (DAV); Trail Canyon, 8000 ft., *D 2708*.

5. **P. stansburyi** (Torr.) Heller. Common, dry rocky slopes and flats, desert scrub to pinyon woodland, throughout the range, 5000–9000 ft.: 5.4 miles west of White Mountain Road on Westgard Pass, 5900 ft., *L 2681*; Deep Springs Valley, 6300 ft., *HM 686*; Black Canyon, 5000 ft., *D 2631*; Reed Flat, 8500 ft., *J. & L. Roos 5838* (UC); Silver Canyon, 8700 ft., *L 2845*; 2 miles above Roberts Ranch, Wyman Creek, 8500 ft., *D 1685*; Chiatovich Creek, 8500 ft., *D 3060*.

11. Polemonium
1. **P. chartaceum** Mason. Common, rocky slopes, alpine fell-fields, throughout the range, above 13,000 ft.: White Mountain Peak, 14,200 ft., *M 2221*; Pellisier Flats, just south of Jump-Off, 13,500 ft., *M 2197*.

FAMILY 53. HYDROPHYLLACEAE
A. Plants perennial.
 B. Outer calyx lobes enlarged, cordate, inner lobes linear .... 6. *Tricardia*
 BB. Calyx lobes alike.
  C. Flowers in few- to many-flowered cymes; plants caulescent
5. *Phacelia*
  CC. Flowers solitary; leaves in basal rosette; plants acaulescent
3. *Hesperochiron*
AA. Plants annual.

B. Plants viscid, odoriferous . . . . 2. *Eucrypta*
BB. Plants not viscid.
   C. Stamens inserted equally.
      D. Corolla white or bluish . . . . 5. *Phacelia*
      DD. Corolla yellow . . . . 1. *Emmenanthe*
   CC. Stamens inserted unequally; corolla lavendar to bright purple-red
                                                         4. *Nama*

1. Emmenanthe

1. E. penduliflora Benth. Common sporadically, dry places, desert scrub, 5000–6000 ft.: Westgard Pass, 7.4 miles west of White Mountain Road, 5000 ft., *L 2660*; Black Canyon at Marble Canyon, 5700 ft., *D 2653*; first canyon south of Silver Canyon, 5000 ft., *HM 709*; ridge north of Silver Canyon, 5800 ft., *HM 201*.

2. Eucrypta

1. E. micrantha (Torr.) Heller. Occasional in crevices, on hillsides and washes, primarily in southern portion of the range, below 7000 ft.: Toll House Springs, *Eastwood & Howell 9610* (CAS); Black Canyon at Marble Canyon, 5700 ft., *D 2671*; Silver Canyon, 5800 ft., *L 2862*.

3. Hesperochiron

1. H. californicus (Benth.) Wats. Damp open meadows and grassy places; known only from Chiatovich Creek, 7000–9000 ft.: 7500 ft., *D 2769*; 9000 ft., *M 2089*.

4. Nama

A. Style 2-lobed.
   B. Corolla 3–5 mm. long; lavender . . . . 3. *N. densum*
   BB. Corolla 12–16 mm. long, purple to rose-red . . . . 1. *N. aretioides*
AA. Styles divided to near base; corolla 9–12 mm. long; corolla purplish-red
                                                        2. *N. demissum*

1. N. aretiodes (Hook. & Arn.) Brand var. **multiflorum** (Heller) Jeps. Known only from hillsides and flats between Pinchot Creek and Pinyon Hill, 6500 ft., *D 2759*.

2. N. demissum Gray. Dry slopes, flats, and washes, desert scrub, throughout the range, 4500–6600 ft.: Black Canyon at Marble Canyon, 5700 ft., *D 2732*; first canyon south of Silver Canyon, 5000 ft., *HM 721*; Silver Canyon, 5850 ft., *Alexander & Kellogg 4266* (UC); Coldwater Canyon, near Laws, *Brandegee s.n.* (UC); Milner Creek, 5500 ft., *D 3239*.

3. N. densum Lemmon. Open spots, slopes, flats and washes, desert scrub to alpine fell-fields, 4000–11,700 ft.: west base of Westgard Pass, 4500 to 5000 ft., *HM 793A*; Crooked Creek Lab, 10,200 ft., *Tucker 2239* (DAV); McAfee Meadow, 11,700 ft., *D 2803*; near Pinyon Hill, 7000 ft., *D 2751*.

5. Phacelia
Key to species by Lincoln Constance

A. Ovules 2 to each placenta, the seeds 1–4 per capsule.

  B. Leaves entire or few-lobed (or pinnate) with entire divisions.

    C. Perennial; leaves conspicuously white-sericeous; stamens 6–10 mm. long . . . . 9. *P. hastata*

    CC. Annual; leaves not conspicuously sericeous; stamens 2–4 mm. long
1. *P. austromontana*

  BB. Leaves pinnately lobed or pinnately decompound, with toothed or lobed ultimate divisions.

    C. Ill-smelling plants, glandular-viscid throughout; flowers deep violet; seeds cymbiform, excavated on each side of a salient ridge and transversely corrugated . . . . 3. *P. crenulata*

    CC. Plants usually glandular only in inflorescence, if at all, not conspicuously ill-smelling; flowers lavender, blue, or white; seeds neither excavated or corrugated.

      D. Perennial with decumbent branches spreading from a woody crown; flowers dull-white, bluish or purplish . . 12. *P. ramosissima*

      DD. Annual, erect to decumbent from a slender tap-root; flowers conspicuous, white, blue, or lavender.

        E. Calyx-lobes enlarging conspicuously in fruit; inflorescence rather open and few-flowered; stamens included . . 14. *P. vallis-mortae*

        EE. Calyx-lobes enlarging very little in fruit; inflorescence dense and many flowered; stamens usually well-exserted.

          F. Corolla promptly deciduous; calyx-lobes lanceolate to obovate; capsule hairy below middle . . . . 5. *P. distans*

          FF. Corolla tardily deciduous; calyx lobes linear to linear-lanceolate; capsule hairy only at apex . . 13. *P. tanacetifolia*

AA. Ovules more numerous (4–100 per placenta), seeds 5–200 per capsule.

  B. Leaves roundish, crenate, dentate, or shallowly lobed.

    C. Perennial; stamen-filaments glabrous . . . . 11. *P. perityloides*

    CC. Annual; stamen-filaments sparsely hairy at base . . 10. *P. peirsoniana*

  BB. Leaves oblong to ovate, longer than broad, entire to pinnately lobed to bipinnate.

    C. Leaves entire, or occasionally with 1 or 2 lobes; corollas broadly campanulate, pale-colored without any yellow; calyx-lobes conspicuously enlarging in fruit; seeds pitted . . . . 4. *P. curvipes*

    CC. Leaves pinnately lobed (rarely serrate) to bipinnatifid or pinnate; corolla ± tubular funnelform, with a yellow tube; seeds transversely corrugated.

      D. Corolla 5–6.5 mm. long, not longer than calyx, the limb lavender; plants with conspicuous dark-stalked glands throughout
7. *P. glandulifera*

      DD. Corolla 6–16 mm. long, blue to lavender to purplish, at least twice as long as calyx.

E. Seeds 12–20 per capsule; leaves deeply pinnately lobed to bipinnatifid.

    F. Leaves bipinnatifid; stamen-filaments usually pubescent be-
low; calyx-lobes linear to narrowly-oblanceolate
2. *P. bicolor*

    FF. Leaves pinnate or pinnatifid; stamen-filaments glabrous;
calyx-lobes spatulate ....6. *P. fremontii*

EE. Seeds 5–8 per capsule; leaves shallowly pinnately lobed;
stamen-filaments pubescent .... 8. *P. gymnoclada*

1. **P. austromontana** J. T. Howell. Rare, dry stony slopes in Bristlecone forest:
known only from the Ancient Bristlecone area at Schulman Grove, 9500 ft.,
Lankester 874 (BM).

2. **P. bicolor** Torr. ex Wats. Dry open slopes and flats, desert scrub to upper
pinyon woodland, throughout the range, 5000–9000 ft.: Silver Canyon, 7000
ft., *M 2294*; Wyman Creek, 8300 ft., *L 2794*; B & B Mine, *D 3085*; near Pinyon
Hill, 7000 ft., *D 2863*; east slope of Montgomery Pass, *Eastwood & Howell
9531* (CAS).

3. **P. crenulata** Torr. var. **funerea** J. Voss ex Munz. Frequent, dry hillsides
and open washes, desert scrub to pinyon woodland, 5000–9000 ft.: 3.4 miles
west of Westgard Pass, 6250 ft., *HM 65*; east side of Westgard Pass, 7000 ft.,
Hovanitz s.n. (UC); Mollie Gibson Canyon, 7400 ft., *M 2071*; Black Canyon,
5700 ft., *D 2638*; Silver Canyon, 8000 ft., *D 1511*; also Indian Creek, 6000 ft.

4. **P. curvipes** Torr. ex Wats. Dry slopes, desert scrub to pinyon woodland,
4500–8500 ft.: above Toll House Springs, *Eastwood & Howell 9614* (CAS);
Silver Canyon, 8500 ft., *HM 774*; 2 miles below Roberts Ranch, Wyman
Creek, 7500 ft., *D 3040*.

5. **P. distans** Benth. Desert scrub, southern end of range: 3.4 miles west of
Westgard Pass, 6250 ft., *HM 69*.

6. **P. fremontii** Torr. Frequent, dry slopes and washes, desert scrub especially
in southern portion of the range, 4500–8300 ft.: west base of Westgard Pass,
4500–5000 ft., *HM 794*; 4 miles west of White Mountain Road on Westgard
Pass, 6400 ft., *L 2708*; Deep Springs Valley, 6300 ft., *HM 689*; first canyon
south of Silver Canyon, 5000 ft., *HM 718*; Roberts Ranch, Wyman Creek, 8300
ft., *L 2794*.

7. **P. glandulifera** Piper. Dry roadsides, flats and sandy places, northern end
of range, 6000–7500 ft.: Indian Creek, 6000 ft., *Lankester 721* (BM); Chiatovich Creek, 7500 ft., *D 2800*; Trail Canyon, *D M50*.

8. **P. gymnoclada** Torr. ex Wats. Frequent, sandy soil, pinyon woodland,
at northern end of the range, 6500–7500 ft.: mouth of Pinchot Creek, 6500 ft.,
D 3261; Mt. Montgomery Station, *D M88*; east side of Montgomery Pass,
Eastwood & Howell 9537 (CAS).

9. **P. hastata** Dougl. ex Lehm. Frequent, gravelly and rocky places, subalpine
forest to alpine fell-fields, throughout the range, 9500–13,000 ft.: 1½ mile
south of county line at head of Old Silver Canyon, 10,700 ft., *HM 830*; hill west
of head of Wyman Creek, 10,500 ft., *HM 528*; Crooked Creek Lab, 10,150 ft.,

L 3102; east of Campito Mountain, 11,000 ft., *Mason 14562* (UC), east slope of Sheep Mountain, 11,200 ft., *Cook 262* (UC); Cottonwood Creek, 9700 ft., *HM 258*; Cabin Creek, 10,300 ft., *D 2554*; Pellisier Flats, 12,800 ft., *M 2272-A*; Trail Canyon, 10,000 ft., *D 3358*.

Plants from Crooked Creek Laboratory (*L 3102*) are tetraploid. The Mason collection from Campito Mountain is apparently typical *P. hastata* and is also tetraploid. Others have features of indument, corolla shape, and stamen pubescence which indicate an affinity to *P. frigida* Greene ssp. *dasyphylla* (Macbr.) Heckard.

10. **P. peirsoniana** J. T. Howell. Rocky hillsides and canyons, desert scrub to pinyon woodland, southern end of range: 10 miles northeast of Big Pine on Westgard Pass, 6500 ft., *Keck 536* (CAS); northwest of Cedar Flat, 8000 ft., *J. & L. Roos 5878* (CAS); Silver Canyon, 7200 ft., *HM 486-A*.

11. **P. perityloides** Cov. Rock crevices, desert scrub and pinyon woodland: Black Canyon, *Cassel 275* (DS); Black Canyon at Marble Canyon, 5700 ft., *D 2673*.

12. **P. ramosissima** Dougl. ex Lehm. Dry slopes, sandy washes, and moist banks, 6500–8000 ft., pinyon woodland: Westgard Pass, 3.8 miles west of White Mountain Road, 6450 ft., *L 2735*; 2 miles below Roberts Ranch, Wyman Creek, 8000 ft., *D 1715*; Cottonwood Creek, 7400 ft., *M 2057*.

13. **P. tanacetifolia** Benth. Known only from Toll House Springs, *Eastwood & Howell 9602* (CAS).

14. **P. vallis-mortae** J. Voss. Open slopes and washes, desert scrub to pinyon woodland, throughout the range, 4500–8500 ft.: Westgard Pass, 7300 ft., *J. & H. Grinnell 1050-A* (UC); Payson Canyon, 6800 ft., *HM 362*; ¾ mile from Studebaker Flat, 8500 ft., *HM 766*; Black Canyon at Marble Canyon, 5700 ft., *D 2657*; White Mountain Road, 8300 ft., *M 2444*; first canyon south of Silver Canyon, 5000 ft., *HM 715*; near Pinyon Hill in Mono Co., 7000 ft., *D 2862*; also reported from Indian Creek.

6. Tricardia

1. **T. watsonii** Torr. ex Wats. Dry flats and slopes, desert scrub to pinyon woodland, in southern portion of the range, below 7500 ft.: above Toll House Springs, *Eastwood & Howell 9613* (CAS); Westgard Pass, 2.5 miles east of road to Saline Valley, *Raven 13828* (UC); Silver Canyon, 7500 ft., *Munz 13553* (UC).

FAMILY 54. BORAGINACEAE

A. Style deeply 2-cleft or 2-parted; corolla pink or white .... 2. *Coldenia*
AA. Style entire.
  B. Style borne on the summit of an undivided ovary; corolla white with yellow spots in throat and ± purple near the center when aged
                                    5. *Heliotropium*
  BB. Style borne on the receptacle or gynobase, arising between the four-parted ovary.

132

C. Nutlets widely spreading in fruit, the margins armed with hooked prickles ....7. *Pectocarya*
CC. Nutlets erect, the margins not armed except in *Lappula* and *Hackelia.*
  D. Receptacle flat or convex, the nutlets attached ± basally; corolla light blue with yellow-tipped crests in summit of tube
6. *Mertensia*
  DD. Receptacle conical or elongated, the nutlets attached laterally.
    E. Nutlets armed with conspicuous prickles.
      F. Corolla ca. 2 mm. broad; annuals; pedicels erect in fruit
6. *Lappula*
      FF. Corolla 6–10 mm. broad; perennial; pedicels recurved in fruit
4. *Hackelia*
    EE. Nutlets not armed with conspicuous prickles.
      F. Flowers white.
        G. Nutlets keeled on the ventral side, without a distinct ventral groove; lowest leaves in a rosette ...... 8. *Plagiobothrys*
        GG. Nutlets not keeled on the ventral side but grooved above the basal scar; leaves all alternate ...... 3. *Cryptantha*
      FF. Flowers yellow or orange.
        G. Plants perennial; corolla yellowish ...... 3. *Cryptantha*
        GG. Plants annual; corolla orange .... 1. *Amsinckia*

1. Amsinckia

1. **A. tessellata** Gray. Dry sandy or gravelly places, alluvia, slopes, washes, etc., desert scrub, throughout the range, 4500–7500 ft.: Westgard Pass: 7.4 miles west of White Mountain Road, 5000 ft., *L 2647*; White Mountain Road, 7500 ft., *Cook s.n.* (UC); Black Canyon, 5700 ft., *D 2684.*

2. Coldenia

1. **C. nuttallii** Hook. Dry open sandy soil, flats and washes, desert scrub to pinyon woodland, throughout the range, especially the eastern slope: mouth of Birch Creek, at Deep Springs Valley, 5050 ft., *L 2972*; intersection of Wyman Creek Road and road to Dead Horse Creek, 7800 ft., *M 2062*; near Pinchot Creek, 6500 ft., *D M21.*

3. Cryptantha

A. Plants annual.
  B. Calyx circumscissle at maturity; low dense plants 2–10 cm. high; flowers in axils of foliaceous bracts .... 2. *C. circumscissa*
  BB. Calyx not circumscissle.
    C. Gynobase awl-shaped, longer than nutlets; stigma sessile; plants slender, branched dichotomously, 5–15 cm. tall; flowers in axils of foliaceous bracts .... 10. *C. micrantha*
    CC. Gynobase shorter than nutlets; style present; flowers mostly without bracts.

D.   Nutlets verrucose to muricate-papillate or papillate-echinate.
    E.   Margins of nutlets with crenulate or lobulate or knifelike wings.
        F.   Nutlets 1–2 .... 15. *C. utahensis*
        FF.   Nutlets 4 .... 13. *C. pterocarya*
    EE.   Margins of nutlets rounded or obtuse.
        F.   Nutlets 2 (one abortive) .... 14. *C. recurvata*
        FF.   Nutlets 4 in normal fruit.
            G.   Nutlets broadly ovoid, papillate-echinate on back
                    4. *C. echinella*
            GG.   Nutlets lanceolate to lance-ovate, verrucose on back.
                H.   Plants very bristly, hairs spreading .... 1. *C. barbigera*
                HH.   Plants strigose, hairs appressed....11. *C. nevadensis*
DD.   Nutlets smooth.
    E.   Nutlets 1–3.
        F.   Plants 0.3–1 dm. tall, strigose; leaves 0.5–1.5 cm. long;
            nutlets 1 .... 6. *C. glomeriflora*
        FF.   Plants 1–2.5 dm. high, short-hispid; leaves 1–3 cm. long; nut-
            lets 1 or sometimes 2–3 .... 7. *C. gracilis*
    EE.   Nutlets 4 .... 17. *C. watsonii*
AA.   Plants perennial.
    B.   Nutlets smooth.
        C.   Corolla yellowish, 12–14 mm. long; plants 1.5–5 dm. tall
                    3. *C. confertiflora*
        CC.   Corolla white, 3–4 mm. long; plants decumbent to prostrate
                    9. *C. jamesii*
    BB.   Nutlets muricate, tuberculate, or otherwise roughened on back.
        C.   Corolla-tube 7–10 mm. long, longer than calyx .... 5. *C. flavoculata*
        CC.   Corolla-tube 3–4 mm. long, not longer than calyx.
            D.   Stems 0.5–1.5 dm. tall; nutlets lance-linear, inner surface of nutlets
            ± smooth .... 12. *C. nubigena*
            DD.   Stems 1–5 dm. tall; nutlets ovoid, inner surface rugose or tubercled.
                E.   Lower leaves spatulate, 2–3 cm. long .... 8. *C. hoffmannii*
                EE.   Leaves oblanceolate to spatulate, 5–10 cm. long
                      16. *C. virginensis*

1. **C. barbigera** (Gray) Greene. Dry sandy or gravelly places, desert scrub, below 7000 ft.: Black Canyon, 5700 ft., *D M28*; Silver Canyon, *Heller 8270* (UC); Indian Creek, 6000 ft., *Lankester 719* (BM).

2. **C. circumscissa** (Hook. & Arn.) Jtn. Frequent, dry slopes or flats in sandy places, desert scrub to subalpine forest, throughout the range, 500–10,200 ft.: Payson Canyon, 5913 ft., *L 2965;* Black Canyon, 5700 ft., *D M26;* Silver Canyon, 6600 ft., *HM 274;* Wyman Creek, 8300 ft., *L 2797;* Crooked Creek Lab, 10,200 ft., *Tucker 2239-A* (UC); Cottonwood Creek, 9000 ft., *D 1592;* Chiatovich Creek, 8000 ft., *D M24;* mouth of Pinchot Creek, 6500 ft., *D 3263.*

3. **C. confertiflora** (Greene) Pays. Common, dry open slopes, talus slopes

and rocky places, desert scrub to subalpine forest, throughout the range, 4500–9500 ft.: Westgard Pass, 5.4 miles west of White Mountain Road, 5900 ft., *L 2688;* east side of Westgard Pass, 6000 ft., *Raven 7033* (CAS); Silver Canyon, 8000 ft., *D 1512;* Wyman reek, 9500 ft., *L 2818;* between Trail Creek and Pinchot Creek, *D M22;* also Fish Lake Valley at 4900 ft.

4. **C. echinella** Greene. Dry places, stony slopes, and occasionally in very wet places, below 10,200 ft.: 1 mile east of summit of Westgard Pass, 7000 ft., *Munz 13519* (RSA); marsh at head of Crooked Creek, ½ mile westsouthwest of lab, 10,200 ft., *L 3138.*

5. **C. flavoculata** (Nels.) Pays. Frequent, dry slopes, pinyon woodland to subalpine forest, throughout the range, 6000–10,250 ft.: southwest of Westgard Pass, 6250 ft., *HM 70;* Silver Canyon: 7350 ft., *HM 113* Wyman Creek at mouth of Jackass Canyon, 9000 ft., *D 3312;* Crooked Creek Ranger Station, 9500 ft., *D 1551.*

6. **C. glomeriflora** Greene. Rare, but sporadically common, dry slopes and disturbed areas and meadows, 9000–10,500 ft.: Crooked Creek, 9900 ft., *L 3276;* meadow ½ mile westsouthwest of Crooked Creek Lab, 10,200 ft., *L 3140.*

7. **C. gracilis** Osterh. Dry slopes, pinyon woodland, below 7000 ft.: 4 miles west of White Mountain Road on Westgard Pass, 6400 ft., *L 2714;* Black Canyon, 5700 ft., *D s.n.* (RSA); Silver Canyon, 5600 ft., *M 2076.*

8. **C. hoffmannii** Jtn. Dry rocky slopes, stream edges, pinyon woodland to subalpine forest, 6000–10,200 ft.: northwest of Cedar Flat, 7300 ft., *Alexander & Kellogg 2503* (UC); 3.7 miles north of Westgard Pass on White Mountain Road, 7800 ft., *Everett & Balls 21934* (UC); Sierra Viewpoint, White Mountain Road, 9500 ft., *L 2902;* Silver Canyon, 7100 ft., *L 2856;* Indian Creek, 6000 ft., *Lankester 743* (BM).

9. **C. jamesii** (Torr.) Pays. var. **abortiva** (Greene) Pays. Dry sandy slopes and flats, pinyon woodland to alpine fell-fields, throughout the range, 8000–11,700 ft.: Wyman Creek at mouth of Jackass Creek, 9000 ft., *D 3313;* meadow ½ mile westsouthwest of Crooked Creek Lab, 10,200 ft., *L 3145;* McAfee Meadow, 11,700 ft., *D M20;* Chiatovich Creek, ca. 8000 ft., *D M25.*

10. **C. micrantha** (Torr.) Jtn. Known only from open hillsides and flats near Pinyon Hill, 7000 ft., *D 2743.*

11. **C. nevadensis** Nels. & Kenn. Desert scrub, southwestern portion of the range, 4200–6000 ft.: Westgard Pass, 4200 ft., *HM 29;* Westgard Pass, 6000 ft., *Hoffman s.n.* (POM); Black Canyon, 5700 ft., *D 2662;* Silver Canyon, *Brandegee s.n.* (UC).

12. **C. nubigena** (Greene) Pays. Rocky slopes at higher elevations: south of Sheep Mountain, White Mountain Road, 10,800 ft., *Pawek 58–8* (UC).

13. **C. pterocarya** (Torr.) Greene.

A.   Nutlets with broad crenulate or lobulate wing margins
                                                    13a. var. *pterocarya*
AA. Nutlets with narrow, knifelike margins . . . . 13b. var. *purpusii*

13a. Var. **pterocarya.** Dry hillsides, pinyon woodland, throughout the range, 5700–8000 ft.: Black Canyon, 5700 ft., *D 2666*; between B & B Mine and Pinyon Hill, 7500 ft., *D 2866*; Pinchot Creek, 6500 ft., *D M18*.

13b. Var. **purpusii** Jeps. Known only from Payson Canyon at 5270 ft., *HM s.n.* (UC).

14. **C. recurvata** Cov. Dry sandy places, southern portion of the range, below 6500 ft.: Silver Canyon: *Heller s.n.* (UC); *Brandegee s.n.* (UC); Coldwater Canyon, *Brandegee s.n.* (UC).

15. **C. utahensis** (Gray) Greene. Dry washes and rocky places, desert scrub, 4500–7000 ft.: Westgard Pass, 7.4 miles west of White Mountain Road, 5000 ft., *L 2642*; Black Canyon, 5700 ft., *D 2663*; Silver Canyon, 7000 ft., *D 1507*; Coldwater Canyon, *Brandegee s.n.* (UC).

16. **C. virginensis** (Jones) Pays. Pinyon woodland. Known only from 7000 ft., Cedar Flat, *D M19*.

17. **C. watsonii** (Gray) Greene. Dry open places, pinyon woodland to subalpine forest, 7000–10,500 ft.: Silver Canyon: 7400 ft., *HM 211*; Crooked Creek Lab, 10,200 ft., *Tucker 2237* (DAV); Sagehen Flat, 10,500 ft., *HM 439*.

4. Hackelia
A. Plants 5–12 dm. high; corolla blue, 6–7 mm. broad .... 1. *H. floribunda*
AA. Plants 2–4 dm. high; corolla white or tinged pale blue, 6–10 mm. broad
2. *H. patens*

1. **H. floribunda** (Lehm.) Jtn. Occasional, wet open soil or sometimes dry spots, pinyon woodland to lower subalpine forest, 8400–10,000 ft.: Black Canyon Spring, 8400 ft., *M 2127*; Crooked Creek Ranger Station, 9500 ft., *D 1556*; Sacramento Canyon at spring on Piute Trail, 10,000 ft., *D 2881*.

2. **H. patens** (Nutt.) Jtn. Rocky areas and moist slopes, Mono Co. north, 8900–10,250 ft.: foot of basalt ridge on Bucks Peak, 9600 ft., *M 2256*; northwest corner, Sagehen Flat, 10,250 ft., *L 3167*; 4.8 miles east of Crooked Creek Lab, 9500 ft., *Bacigalupi et al. 8082* (JEPS); Cottonwood Creek, 8900 ft., *L 2935*; Munz reports from Poison Canyon also.

5. Heliotropium
1. **H. curassavicum** L. var. **oculatum** (Heller) Jtn. Wet weedy places, sometimes alkaline, at lower elevations in canyons throughout the range: spring near mouth of Black Canyon, 4800 ft., *M 2074*.

6. Lappula
1. **L. redowskii** (Hornem.) Greene.

A. Marginal prickles of nutlets confluent, forming a cupulate margin
1b. var. *desertorum*
AA. Nutlets bordered by a single row of barbed prickles .. 1a. var. *redowskii*

la. Var. **redowskii.** Dry open and disturbed areas, throughout the range, 6000–10,000 ft.: Wyman Creek, 8300 ft., *L 2793*; Crooked Creek, 9900 ft., *L 3273*; Cottonwood Creek, 8900 ft., *L 2923*; Trail Canyon, 8300 ft., *D 2516*.

lb. Var. **desertorum** (Greene) Jtn. Dry slopes and flats, below 7500 ft.: Silver Canyon, 6700 ft., *D 2639*; near B & B Mine, 7500 ft., *D 2709*.

7. Mertensia

1. **M. ciliata** (James) G. Don var. **stomatechoides** (Kell.) Jeps. Moist places, streambanks etc., Mono Co. north, 7500–10,000 ft.: Chiatovich Creek, 9900 ft., *M 2090*; Middle Creek, 7500 ft., *Jaeger s.n.* (POM); also found in Cottonwood and McAfee canyons.

8. Pectocarya

1. **P. setosa** Gray. Dry places, desert scrub to lower pinyon woodland, Inyo Co., usually below 6000 ft.: Marble Canyon off Black Canyon, 5700 ft., *D 2734*; Silver Canyon, *Heller 8187* (CAS).

9. Plagiobothrys

A. Corolla 1–2.5 mm. broad; nutlets tesselate . . . . 1. *P. jonesii*
AA. Corolla 4–7 mm. broad; nutlets rugose . . . . 2. *P. kingii*

1. **P. jonesii** Gray. Gravelly and rocky places, desert scrub to pinyon woodland, 5700–8000 ft.: Westgard Pass, 6000 ft., *Raven 6985* (CAS); Black Canyon, 5700 ft., *D 2665*; Queen Canyon, 7800 ft., *M 2750*.

2. **P. kingii** (Wats.) Gray.

A. Inflorescence elongate, composed of dense, scorpioid cymes; plants 1–4
    dm. tall . . . . 2a. var. *kingii*
AA. Inflorescence glomerate or scarcely elongated; plants 1–2 dm. tall
                                                                    2b. var. *harknessii*

2a. Var. **kingii.** Dry open hillsides, desert scrub to pinyon woodland, through-out the range, 5000–7000 ft.: below Toll House Springs, *Eastwood & Howell 9580* (CAS); near Pinyon Hill, 7000 ft., *D 2741*; mouth of Pinchot Creek, 6500 ft., *D 3259*; east side of Montgomery Pass, *Eastwood & Howell 9545* (CAS).

2b. Var. **harknessii** (Greene) Jeps. Known only from Trail Canyon, ca. 7000 ft., *D M27*.

FAMILY 55. CALLITRICHACEAE
1. Callitriche

1. **C. verna** L. Alpine pools and streams, ca. 11,700 ft.: meadow northeast of Piute Mountain, 11,650 ft., *L 3292*; observed in McAfee Meadow and Canyon at 11,700 ft.

FAMILY 56. LABIATAE

A.   Corolla strongly bilabiate.
    B.   Fertile stamens 4; corolla white or pinkish; plants 3–10 dm. tall
                                                                      4. *Stachys*
    BB.   Fertile stamens 2; corolla blue; plant 1–5 dm. or 3–8 dm. tall and
        shrubby . . . . 3. *Salvia*
AA.   Corolla ± regular.
    B.   Flowers in terminal heads; dry places . . . . 2. *Monardella*
    BB.   Flowers in dense axillary clusters; moist places . . . . 1. *Mentha*

1. Mentha

1. **M. arvensis** L. Wet places below 7000 ft.: Antelope Springs, Deep Springs Valley, 5600 ft., *L 3005*; Wyman Creek, 1 mile above mouth, 6500 ft., *D 3131*.

2. Monardella

A.   Stems silvery with a dense minute puberulance . . . . 1. *M. linoides*
AA.   Stems subglabrous to pubescent, but not silvery-pubescent
                                                  2. *M. odoratissima*

1. **M. linoides** Gray. Dry places, below 8500 ft.: Westgard Pass, 5.4 miles west of White Mountain Road, 5900 ft., *L 2670*; Studebaker Flat, 8500 ft., *Cook s.n.* (UC).

2. **M. odoratissima** Benth.

A.   Leaves ± glaucous, appearing ± glabrous but puberulent under a lens, 1.5–4 cm. long; corolla reddish-purple . . . . 2a. ssp. *glauca*
AA.   Leaves distinctly pubescent, cinereous-puberulent, 1–3 cm. long; corolla rose-lavender to pale, often whitish.
    B.   Leaves 1–2 cm. long, on petioles 1–3 mm. long; heads 1–2 cm. broad; calyx pubescent; corolla rose-lavender . . . . 2c. ssp. *parvifolia*
    BB.   Leaves 2–3 cm. long, on petioles 2–8 mm. long; heads 1.5–2.5 cm. broad; calyx woolly; corolla pale, often whitish . . . . . . 2b. ssp. *pallida*

2a. Ssp. **glauca** (Greene) Epl. Dry open slopes, throughout the range, 6500–10,300 ft.: Black Canyon, 6500 ft., *D 1751*; above Crooked Creek Lab, 10,300 ft., *Cook s.n.* (UC); McCloud Camp, Cottonwood Creek, 9500 ft., *D 1612*; Chiatovich Creek, 9500 ft., *D 3125*.

2b. Ssp. **pallida** (Heller) Epl. Known only from Campito Mountain, 10,700 ft., *Jepson 7286* (JEPS). Cited by Epling (Ann. Miss. Bot. Gard. 12: 1–106).

2c. Ssp. **parvifolia** (Greene) Epl. Dry slopes, ridges, and washes, 9500–10,200 ft.: Wyman Creek, 1.1 miles east of White Mountain Road, 9500 ft., *L 3052*; ridge south of Crooked Creek Lab, 10,175 ft., *Blakley and Muller 3573* (JEPS).

138

3. Salvia

A. Annual, 1–5 dm. tall, herbaceous; leaves oblong-ovate, 2–10 cm. long, 1–2 pinnatifid .... 1. *S. columbariae*

AA. Perennial, 3–8 dm. tall, much-branched shrub; leaves round-obovate to spatulate, 7–15 mm. in diameter, entire .... 2. *S. dorrii*

1. **S. columbariae** Benth. Frequent, dry places, washes, slopes, desert scrub, 4000–6500 ft.: 3.4 miles west of Westgard Pass, 6250 ft., *HM 66*; Black Canyon, 5700 ft., *D s.n.*; first canyon south of Silver Canyon, 5000 ft., *HM 707*.

2. **S. dorrii** (Kell.) Abrams ssp. **argentea** (Rydb.) Munz. Common, dry places, washes, flats, etc., desert scrub to pinyon woodland and lower subalpine forest, throughout the range, 6000–9600 ft.: Mollie Gibson Canyon, 2 miles north of Payson Canyon Road, ca. 7500 ft., *L 2945*; Methuselah Walk, Schulman Grove, 9500 ft., *HM 898*; Old Silver Canyon Road, 9600 ft., *HM 277*; Wyman Creek, ca. 8000 ft., *D 1926*; also Indian Creek at 6000 ft.

4. Stachys

1. **S. albens** Gray. Wet places, streamsides, springs, etc., southern portion of the range, 5000–8000 ft.: Montenegro Springs, 7050 ft., *L 3121*; Silver Canyon, 5000 ft., *D 1504*; Roberts Ranch Meadow, Wyman Creek, 8000 ft., *L 3037*.

FAMILY 57. PLANTAGINACEAE
1. Plantago

1. **P. major** L. Weed, damp places, throughout the range: Antelope Springs, 5600 ft., *L 3022*; Montenegro Springs, 7050 ft., *L 3117, D 2888*; Black Canyon, 6200 ft., *M 2114*; also Silver Canyon at 7000 ft.

FAMILY 58. OLEACEAE
1. Menodora

1. **M. spinescens** Gray. Dry canyons and slopes, desert scrub to pinyon woodland, throughout the range, 4200–7500 ft.: 2.9 miles east of Big Pine on Westgard Pass Road, 4200 ft., *HM 8*; Westgard Pass, 6450 ft., *L 2743*; mouth of Black Canyon, 4500 ft., *D 1931*; Old Davis Ranch, Davis Creek, 7500 ft., *D 2527*.

FAMILY 59. SCROPHULARIACEAE

A. Fertile stamens 5; corolla ± regular, yellow, 20–25 mm. broad
9. *Verbascum*

AA. Fertile stamens 4; corolla bilabiate.
B. Stigmas 2, distinct, flattened .... 5. *Mimulus*
BB. Stigmas wholly united, punctiform or capitate.
C. Corolla gibbous or saccate on lower side of base, white with purple veins, 7–8 mm. long .... 1. *Antirrhinum*
CC. Corolla not gibbous or saccate on lower side of base.
D. Upper lip of corolla flattened with 1 or 2 erect or spreading lobes; leaves opposite.

E.   Corolla 4-lobed, the upper lip of 2 fused lobes, white to blue to lilac .... 10. *Veronica*

EE. Corolla 5-lobed or cleft, the upper lip 2-lobed.

F.   Plants annual; corolla 4–7 mm. long, the upper lip white to violet at top, the lower violet-blue .... 3. *Collinsia*

FF. Plants perennial; corolla 5–7 mm. long, red-brown to maroon or 10–40 mm. long and blue to rose to white or yellow.

G.   Corolla 5–7 mm. long, red-brown to maroon

8. *Scrophularia*

GG. Corolla 10–40 mm. long, blue, lavender, reddish, yellow or white .... 7. *Penstemon*

DD. Upper lip of corolla fused into a beaklike or hooded prolongation (galea); leaves alternate.

E.   Galea arched with the tip prolonged into a conspicuous upturned proboscis; cells of anther of equal size and position; leaves pinnately divided into 12–15 pairs of toothed segments

6. *Pedicularis*

EE. Galea straight; cells of the anther unequal in size and position; leaves entire or with 1–2 pairs of lateral lobes.

F.   Plants annual with yellow roots; calyx tubular only at base extending as a tonguelike structure with bifid apex; bracts green or dull grayish-purple throughout .. 4. *Cordylanthus*

FF. Plants perennial (except *C. exilis*); calyx tubular for over ½ its length with the apex 4-lobed; bract-tips conspicuously colored (yellow, orange, red, or purplish-red) .. 2. *Castilleja*

1. Antirrhinum

1. **A. kingii** Wats. Dry gravelly hillsides and flats, desert scrub to lower pinyon woodland, throughout the range, 5000–8000 ft.: below Toll House Spring, *Eastwood & Howell* 9592 (CAS); Black Canyon at Marble Canyon, 5700 ft., *D 2736*; Silver Canyon, *Brandegee s.n.* (UC); mouth of Pinchot Creek, 6500 ft., *D 3266*; near Pinchot Creek, ca. 6500 ft., *D 2736A*.

2. Castilleja

A.   Plants annual; wet places at lower elevations .... 3. *C. exilis*

AA. Plants perennial.

B.   The upper lip (galea) 5–10 mm. long; corolla 13–16 mm. long; galea ca. 6 mm. long, its margin dark purple proximally, white distally and lower lip ca. 0.5–1 mm. long; inflorescence appearing dull purple to greenish .... 6. *C. nana*

BB. The upper lip (galea) 12–25 mm. or more long.

C.   Leaves linear, ± enrolled, 1–10 cm. long; corolla 30–40 mm. long; calyx 25–35 mm. long, cleft more deeply ventrally (below) than dorsally (above) .... 4. *C. linariaefolia*

CC. Leaves lanceolate, 1–5 cm. long; corolla 20–35 mm. long; calyx 12–27 mm. long, cleft about equally on both sides.

D. Calyx cleft medianly only 1/3 its length, with the apices of the lateral lobes obtuse to rounded; capsule 15–17 mm. long; principal stem leaves with 1 or 2 pairs of widely spreading lobes

2. *C. chromosa*

DD. Calyx cleft medianly about ½ its length with the lateral lobes acute to lance-attenuate; capsule 8–15 mm. long; principal stem leaves entire or occasionally with 1 pair of slender lateral lobes.

E. Plants glandular-pubescent throughout; leaves glandular and wavy-margined; of dry places . . . . 1. *C. applegatei*

EE. Plants glabrous or pubescent but nonglandular in the parts below the inflorescence; leaf margins flat and smooth; of wet places

5. *C. miniata*

1. **C. applegatei** Fern. var. **pinetorum** (Fern.) N. Holmgren. Dry slopes, pinyon woodland to alpine fell-fields, throughout the range, 8500–12,100 ft.: ¾ mile from Studebaker Flat, 8500 ft., *HM 768A*; White Mountain Road, 9300 ft., *HM 335*; Silver Canyon, 10,000 ft., *HM 235*; head of Wyman Creek, 9750 ft., *HM 314*; east of Campito Mountain, *HM 477*; southeast slope of Sheep Mountain, 11,100 ft., *M 2129*.

2. **C. chromosa** A. Nels. Dry slopes and canyons, desert scrub to subalpine forest, throughout the range, 6000–11,100 ft.: Westgard Pass, 4 miles west of White Mountain Road, 6400 ft., *L 2705*; Deep Springs Valley, 6300 ft., *HM 688*; White Mountain Road, 7500 ft., *L 2903*; Silver Canyon, 6600 ft., *Alexander & Kellogg 4277* (UC); Sheep Mountain, 11,100 ft., *M 2129*; near Pinyon Hill, 7500 ft., *D M60*; Chiatovich Creek, 10,500 ft., *M 2095*; east side of Montgomery Pass, *Eastwood & Howell 9538* (CAS).

These plants show an affinity to *C. applegatei* var. *pinetorum* in their glandulosity.

3. **C. exilis** A. Nels. Sporadic in wet places, 4500–7000 ft.: Antelope Springs, Deep Springs Valley, 5650 ft., *Hurd 60–82* (UC); Silver Canyon, 4600 ft., *D M61*; Silver Canyon, 7000 ft., *M 2290*.

4. **C. linariaefolia** Benth. Dry flats and hillsides to moist roadsides and grassy meadows, desert scrub to lower subalpine forest, throughout the range, 6000–9500 ft.: Toll House Spring, 5971 ft., *L 3336-A*; Marble Canyon, 7000 ft., *D 2843*; Wyman Creek: 7000 ft., *HM 866*; Crooked Creek Ranger Station, 9500 ft., *D 1555*; Chiatovich Creek, 8000 ft., *D 2546*.

This species apparently hybridizes with *C. chromosa* (*L 2805*: Wyman Creek, 8750 ft.).

5. **C. miniata** Dougl. ex Hook. Wet places, meadows, streams, etc., pinyon woodland to subalpine forest, Mono Co. north, 7500–10,300 ft.: McCloud Camp, Cottonwood Creek, 9000 ft., *D 1643*; Post Meadow, Indian Creek, 7500 ft., *Archer 7235* (UC); Chiatovich Creek, 10,300 ft., *D 3123*.

This species apparently hybridizes with *C. chromosa* in some parts of its range (*L 2929*: Cottonwood Creek, 8900 ft.).

6. **C. nana** Eastw. Dry slopes and flats, throughout the range, 9500–14,230

ft.: north of Schulman Grove, 10,000 ft., *HM 392*; County Line Hill, 11,100 ft., *M 2138*; Crooked Creek Ranger Station, 9500 ft., *D 1569*; east slope of White Mountain Peak, 13,000–14,230 ft., *Maguire & Holmgren 26075* (UC); Pellisier Flats, south slope of Mt. Dubois, 13,200 ft., *M 2186*.

3. Collinsia

1. **C. parviflora** Dougl. ex Lindl. Moist places, streamsides, sandy open areas, and dry places in meadows, pinyon woodland to subalpine forest, throughout the range, 7500–10,500 ft.: Silver Canyon, near Big Prospector Meadow, 10,200 ft., *Jepson 7360-A* (JEPS); Cottonwood Creek, 10,500 ft., *D 1624*; Chiatovich Creek, 7500 ft., *D s.n.*

4. Cordylanthus

1. **C. helleri** (Ferris) Macbr. Rocky slopes, pinyon woodland, throughout the range, 7000–8000 ft.: summit of Westgard Pass, *Ferris 12537* (RSA); White Mountain Road, 8000 ft., *Lankester 882* (BM); Gilbert Pass, north end of Deep Springs Valley, *Ferris 11594* (RSA); Trail Canyon, 8000 ft., *D 3362*.

5. Mimulus

A. Plants perennial.
    B.   Flowers red .... 2. *M. cardinalis*
    BB. Flowers yellow.
        C.   Plants 0.1–0.5 dm. tall; corolla 8–20 mm. long; mature calyx not
            inflated .... 6. *M. primuloides*
        CC. Plants 0.5–10 dm. tall; corolla 1.5–4 cm. long; mature calyx strongly
            inflated.
           D.   Stems few-flowered; rootstocks yellow; plants 2–4 dm. tall
                    10. *M. tilingii*
           DD. Stems with racemes; rootstocks not yellow; plants 0.5–10 dm. tall
                    5. *M. guttatus*
AA. Plants annual.
    B.   Pedicels longer than calyx; corolla deciduous.
        C.   Corolla 1.5–4 cm. long; calyx strongly inflated ...... 5. *M. guttatus*
        CC. Corolla 0.5–0.9 cm. long; calyx not inflated.
           D.   Corolla 7–9 mm. long; calyx lobes ciliate; pedicel 7–20 mm. long
                    7. *M. rubellus*
           DD. Corolla 5–6 mm. long; calyx lobes not ciliate; pedicel 2–7 mm. long
                    9. *M. suksdorfii*
    BB. Pedicels shorter than calyx; corolla persistent.
        C.   Plant 0.5–2.5 dm. tall; leaves elliptic to obovate, to round, 1–3 cm.
            long; calyx 8–11 mm. long.
           D.   Pedicels 3–8 mm. long; corolla tube usually less than 1¾ times as
              long as calyx .... 1. *M. bigelovii*
           DD. Pedicels 1–2 mm. long; corolla tube more than 1¾ times as long
              as calyx .... 8. *M. spissus*

CC.   Plant 0.1–1.8 dm. tall; leaves lanceolate to oblanceolate to sublinear, 0.6–1.7 cm. long; calyx 4–9 mm. long in fruit.
D.   Leaves 1–1.7 cm. long; calyx 7–9 mm. long in fruit; corolla yellow to red-purple; calyx teeth ca. ¼ as long as tube . . . . 4. *M. densus*
DD.   Leaves 0.6–1 cm. long; calyx 4–8 mm. long in fruit; corolla red-purple; calyx-teeth 1/3 or more as long as tube . . 3. *M. coccineus*

1. **M. bigelovii** (Gray) Gray var. **cuspidatus** Grant. Dry gravelly slopes or flats, 4500–6500 ft.; Westgard Pass, 7.4 miles west of White Mountain Road, 5000 ft., *L 2663*; Payson Canyon, 5913 ft., on coal pile, *L 2964*; Black Canyon, at Marble Canyon, 5700 ft., *D 2691*; Silver Canyon, 4600 ft., *D 3446*; Silver Canyon, 6500 ft., *Alexander & Kellogg 4268* (UC).

2. **M. cardinalis** Dougl. ex Benth. Wet places, streambanks, springs, 5000–7000 ft.: below Montenegro Springs in Marble Canyon, 6800 ft., *L 3124*; Silver Canyon: 5100 ft., *HM 240*; 7000ft., *M 2450*.

3. **M. coccineus** Congd. Rocky places, 9500–10,500 ft.: Crooked Creek, end of road north of Old Ranger Station, 9800 ft., *L 2874*; Crooked Creek, 10,000 ft., *M 2166*; Cottonwood Creek, 9500 ft., *D 1653*.

4. **M. densus** Grant. Dry gravelly or sandy places, upper desert scrub to lower subalpine forest, throughout the range, 6000–10,000 ft.: Westgard Pass, 3.8 miles west of White Mountain Road, 6450 ft., *L 2747*; White Mountain Road, 8800 ft., *M 2007*; Wyman Creek, 9500 ft., *D 1739*; north of Pinyon Hill, 6500 ft., *D 2870*; Chiatovich Creek, 8000 ft., *D 3073*; mouth of Pinchot Creek, 6500 ft., *D 3268*.

5. **M. guttatus** Fisch. ex DC. Common, wet places throughout the range, 4500–9500 ft.; Antelope Springs, 5600 ft., *L 2987*; Silver Canyon, ca. 4600 ft., *D M58*; Wyman Creek, 7500 ft., *M 2039*; intersection of Poison and Cotton-wood creeks, 9450 ft., *L 2914*; Chiatovich Creek, 8000 ft., *D 3092*; Trail Canyon, 8300 ft., *D 2497*.

6. **M. primuloides** Benth.

A.   Leaves nearly glabrous; calyx 6–8 mm. long; corolla 15–20 mm. long
6a. var. *primuloides*
AA.   Leaves with long soft hairs above; calyx mostly ca. 5 mm. long; corolla 8–15 mm. long . . . . 6b. var. *pilosellus*

6a. Var. **primuloides**. Wet places, meadows, springs, etc., pinyon woodland to alpine fell-fields, throughout the range, 6000–12,500 ft.: east end of Crooked Creek Road, 9000 ft., *HM 99*; meadow below Crooked Creek Lab, 10,100 ft., *L 3111*; McAfee Meadow, 12,500 ft., *Tucker 2254* (DAV).

6b. Var **pilosellus** (Greene) Smiley. Wet meadows, Mono Co. north, 8500–10,000 ft.: Crooked Creek Ranger Station, 9500 ft., *D 1581*; behind cave, Crooked Creek, 10,000 ft., *L 3081*; Chiatovich Creek, 8900 ft., *D 2534*.

7. **M. rubellus** Gray. Uncommon, rocky slopes, desert scrub to lower pinyon woodland, 6000–7000 ft.: 1 mile east of Westgard Pass, 7000 ft., *Munz 13527*

(RSA); Silver Canyon, 6500 ft., *L 2836*; mouth of Pinchot Creek, 6500 ft., *D 3276*.

8. **M. spissus** A. L. Grant. Known only from Westgard Pass, 6000–7000 ft.: 3.8 miles west of White Mountain Road, 6450 ft., *L 2726* (JEPS). This is the first published report of this rare species from California. Previous Nevada collections have been from the Silver Peak Range, on the east side of Fish Lake Valley.

9. **M. suksdorfii** Gray. Frequent, wet meadows and slopes, pinyon woodland to alpine fell-fields, throughout the range, 8000–12,300 ft.: Silver Canyon, 8700 ft., *L 2841*; Crooked Creek Lab, 10,200 ft., *Tucker 3423* (DAV), *Jepson 7262* (JEPS); Sheep Mountain, 12,000 ft., *M 2128*; meadow at snow marker, White Mountain Road, 11,650 ft., *L 3289*; Chiatovich Creek, ca. 8000 ft., *D M59*.

10. **M. tilingii** Regel. Uncommon, moist places, 8500–11,400 ft.: lower Mc-Afee Meadow, 11,400 ft., *Shelton s.n.* (UC); Chiatovich Creek, 8500 ft., *D 3106*.

6. Pedicularis

1. **P. attollens** Gray. Meadows and wet places, alpine fell-fields, throughout the range, 11,000–12,500 ft.: Cottonwood Creek, 11,000 ft., *D 1626*; McAfee Canyon, 11,500 ft., *L 3315*; Barcroft Lab, 12,500 ft., *Cook s.n.* (UC); south end of Pellisier Flat, 12,400 ft., *M 2212*.

7. Penstemon

A.   All filaments strongly pubescent at base; shrub 3–6 dm. high; corolla 10–12 mm. long, 3–5 mm. wide, dull yellow . . . . 8. *P. rothrockii*
AA. At least some filaments glabrous at base.
  B.   Anther-sacs dehiscent from the free tips, usually divaricate after dehiscence.
    C.   Inflorescence not glandular-puberulent.
      D.   Flowers 25–35 mm. long, blue-purple; leaves not glaucous
                                                              10. *P. speciosus*
      DD. Flowers 10–20 mm. long, rose-lavender or blue-purple; leaves glaucous or not.
        E.   Corolla 14–20 mm. long, rose-lavender; leaves glaucous
                                                              2. *P. confusus*
        EE. Corolla 10–15 mm. long, blue-purple; herbage bright green
                                                              7. *P. oreocharis*
    CC. Inflorescence glandular-pubescent.
      D.   Flowers blue to blue-purple.
        E.   Leaves glabrous, linear-oblanceolate to spatulate
                                                              4. *P. heterodoxus*
        EE. Leaves puberulent, lanceolate . . . . 5. *P. humilis*
      DD. Flowers rose-pink to rose-purple.
        E.   Corolla 14–20 mm. long; staminode strongly bearded
                                                              6. *P. monoensis*

EE. Corolla 22–30 mm. long; staminode glabrous .... 3. *P. floridus*
BB. Anther-sacs dehiscent across their continuous apices, not divaricate after dehiscence, the free tips remaining saccate.
C. Corolla blue; stems 2–4 dm. high; staminode yellow-pilose below tip
9. *P. scapoides*
CC. Corolla scarlet to vermillion; stem 3–10 dm. high; staminode glabrous
1. *P. bridgesii*

1. **P. bridgesii** Gray. Frequent, dry slopes and sandy washes, pinyon woodland to subalpine forest, throughout the range, 6500–10,000 ft.: 1 mile west of Westgard Pass, 6500 ft., *D 2799*; Mollie Gibson Canyon, 7100 ft., *L 2947*; Black Canyon, 7000 ft., *D s.n.*; Wyman Creek, 9500 ft., *D 1738*; south fork of Cottonwood Creek, 9800 ft., *HM 455*; Post Meadow, Indian Creek, 7500 ft., *D 2572*; east of Benton, 6500 ft., *Jaeger s.n.* (UC).

2. **P. confusus** Jones ssp. **patens** (Jones) Keck. Dry rocky slopes, pinyon woodland, 6800–9500 ft.: Westgard Pass, above "The Narrows," 6800 ft., *L 2757*; Cedar Flat, 7200 ft., *HM 678*; head of Black Canyon, 9500 ft., *HM 328*; Silver Canyon, 8850 ft., *HM 308*.

3. **P. floridus** Bdg.

A. Corolla abruptly inflated, the orifice oblique, the throat 12–15 mm. wide when pressed .... 3a. ssp. *floridus*
AA. Corolla gradually ampliate, the orifice perpendicular, the throat 6–10 mm. wide when pressed .... 3b. ssp. *austinii*

3a. Ssp. **floridus.** Frequent, dry rocky and open flats, washes, desert scrub to pinyon woodland, throughout the range, 5500–8800 ft.: Westgard Pass, 4 miles west of White Mountain Road, 6400 ft., *L 2715*; 14.2 miles northeast of Zurich in Payson Canyon, 6350 ft., *Everett & Balls 21906* (UC); Black Canyon, 5700 ft., *D s.n.*; Silver Canyon, 7000 ft., *M 2343*; Roberts Ranch, Wyman Creek, 8000 ft., *D 1698*; east of Benton, 6500 ft., *Jaeger s.n.* (UC).

3b. Ssp. **austinii** (Eastw.) Keck. Uncommon, dry places, desert scrub to pinyon woodland, 5600–8500 ft.: Birch Creek, 5600 ft., *M 2012*; Silver Canyon, 6000 ft., *HM 127*; Wyman Creek, 8400 ft., *HM 324*.

4. **P. heterodoxus** Gray. Frequent, rocky slopes and meadows, pinyon woodland to alpine fell-fields, throughout the range, (6000) 9500–12,800 ft.: Reed Flat, 10,300 ft., *Munz 21022* (UC); Crooked Creek Ranger Station, 9500 ft., *D 1534*; northeast slope of Sheep Mountain, 11,800 ft., *L 3263*; Grey-Haired Johnny's Corral, north fork, Cottonwood Creek, 12,000 ft., *Maguire & Holmgren 26103* (UC); McAfee Meadow, 12,000 ft., *D 1675*; ¼ mile below Barcroft Lab, 12,500 ft., *Tucker 2259* (UC); Pellisier Flats, east slope, 12,800 ft., *M 2209*.

5. **P. humilis** Nutt. ex Gray. Rocky slopes, Mono Co. north, 6000–7200 ft.: Indian Creek, 6000 ft., *Lankester & Edwards 800* (BM); Montgomery Pass, 7200 ft., *Ripley & Barneby 3705* (CAS); Mt. Montgomery Station, 7000 ft., *D 3280, Jones 1897* (UC).

6. **P. monoensis** Heller. Dry slopes and washes, desert scrub, below 6000 ft.: below Toll House, *Eastwood & Howell 9567* (CAS); Black Canyon at Marble Canyon, 5700 ft., *D 2718*; Silver Canyon, 4600 ft., *D 3445*; Coldwater Canyon, north of Southern Belle Mine, *Brandegee s.n.* (UC); Milner Creek, 5500 ft., *D M79*.

7. **P. oreocharis** Greene. Meadows, 6000–8000 ft.: Mono Co., north: Indian Creek, ca. 6000 ft., *Lankester & Edwards 809* (BM); Chiatovich Creek, 7500 ft., *D s.n.*

8. **P. rothrockii** Gray. Dry slopes and sandy washes, pinyon woodland, throughout the range, 6500–8000 ft.: Westgard Pass, 6850 ft., *Everett & Balls 21945* (UC); White Mountain Road, 7700 ft., *L 3028*; Marble Canyon, 7000 ft., *D s.n.*; Black Canyon, south of Grandview Mine, 7700 ft., *M 2110*; Silver Canyon, 7000 ft., *D 1508*; 11 miles up Wyman Creek, *Maguire & Holmgren 26035* (UC).

9. **P. scapoides** Keck. Dry, rocky open hillsides or flats, pinyon woodland to subalpine forest, south of White Mountain Peak, 6700–10,300 ft.: Westgard Pass, 6700 ft., *D 2798*; White Mountain Road, 8100 ft., *M & L 2443*; Reed Flat, 10,300 ft., *Munz 21038* (UC); Wyman Creek, 9500 ft., *D 1737: Maguire & Holmgren 26160* (UC).

10. **P. speciosus** Dougl ex Lindl.

A. Calyx 4–8 mm. high, the lobes short-tipped . . . . 10a. ssp. *speciosus*
AA. Calyx 8–12 mm. high, the lobes long-tipped . . . . 10b. ssp. *kennedyi*

10a. Ssp. **speciosus.** Dry slopes and rocky areas, desert scrub to lower subalpine forest, 6400–9500 ft.: Westgard Pass, 3.8 miles west of White Mountain Road, 6450 ft., *L 2739*; Wyman Creek, 1.5 miles east of White Mountain Road, 9350 ft., *L 3051*; Crooked Creek Ranger Station, 9500 ft., *D 1571*.

10b. Ssp. **kennedyi** (A. Nels.) Keck. Dry slopes, pinyon woodland to subalpine forest, throughout the range, 6000–10,500 ft.: north of Schulman Grove, 10,000 ft., *HM 375*; northeast of Campito Mountain, 10,800 ft., *HM 479*; White Mountain, 12,000 ft., *Shockley 448* (UC); Davis Canyon, 10,400 ft., *D 3107*; Chiatovich Flats, 10,300 ft., *D 2559*; Trail Canyon, 7500 ft., *D 2755*.

8. Scrophularia

1. **S. californica** Cham. & Schlecht. var. **desertorum** Munz. Dry slopes and rock crevices, desert scrub to pinyon woodland, southern canyons, 6000–8500 ft.: Silver Canyon, 6000 ft., *HM 124*; Wyman Creek: 7000 ft., *HM 864*; 8300 ft., meadow at Roberts Ranch, *L 2786*; Crooked Creek Ranger Station, 9500 ft., *D 1577*.

9. Verbascum

1. **V. thapsus** L. Weed in waste places. Observed in Black Canyon, 5900 ft.

10. Veronica

A. Corolla white, 2–2.5 mm. wide; plants annual; leaves linear-oblong to

spatulate .... 2. *V. peregrina*
AA. Corolla lilac to bright blue.
   B.   Main stem with a single terminal racemelike inflorescence; corolla 5–8
       mm. wide, mostly bright blue; leaves ovate to oblong
                                          3. *V. serpyllifolia*
  BB. Main stem with lateral racemes; corolla 7–10 mm. wide, violet-blue to
       lilac; leaves lanceolate to roundish .... 1. *V. americana*

1. **V. americana** Schw. In and about streams, 6000–10,150 ft., throughout the range: Wyman Creek, 7800 ft., *M 2037*; Crooked Creek, 9900 ft., *L 3280*; Cottonwood Creek, 9000 ft., *D 1597*; Chiatovich Creek, 7500 ft., *D 2768*; Trail Canyon, 8300 ft., *D 2523*.

2. **V. peregrina** L. ssp. **xalapensis** (Kunth) Penn. Wet places, damp meadows, especially in northern canyon: Chiatovich Creek, 7500 ft., *D 2789*; Trail Canyon, 8300 ft., *D 2522*.

3. **V. serpyllifolia** L. var. **humifusa** (Dickson) Vahl. Meadows, streambanks, northern canyons, 6000–10,300 ft.: Cabin Creek below Chiatovich Flats, 10,300 ft., *D 2551* (JEPS); Indian Creek, 6000 ft., *Lankester 715* (BM).

FAMILY 60. OROBANCHACEAE
1. Orobanche

A.   Flowers on slender pedicels, 3–10 cm. long; plant with several erect
     branches .... 2. *O. fasciculata*
AA. Flowers sessile or on pedicels 3–10 mm. long.
   B.   Inflorescence corymbosely branched; lower flowers on pedicels 3–10
       mm. long; corolla purple, 25–30 mm. long; anthers woolly
                                      1. *O. corymbosa*
  BB. Inflorescence spicate; flowers mostly sessile; corolla yellowish to pinkish,
       15–20 mm. long; anthers glabrous ....3. *O. ludoviciana*

1. **O. corymbosa** (Rydb.) Ferris. Dry flats about sage, pinyon woodland to subalpine forest, throughout the range, 8000–10,400 ft.: 1 mile north of Studebaker Flat on White Mountain Road, 8600 ft., *HM 808*; Silver Canyon, *D 2496*; ridge west of County Line Hill, 10,400 ft., *HM 531*; Cottonwood Creek, 9200 ft., *L 3298*; Station Peak, 10,000 ft., *D 1590*; Chiatovich Creek, 8000 ft., *D 2547-A*; Trail Canyon, 8000 ft., *D 3348*.

2. **O. fasciculata** Nutt. Pinyon woodland to subalpine forest, throughout the range, 8000–10,000 ft.: White Mountain Road, 8000 ft., *Roderick s.n.* (UC); head of Silver Canyon, 9300 ft., *HM 292*; Station Peak, 10,000 ft., *D 1523-A*; Chiatovich Creek, 8000 ft., *D M71*; Trail Canyon, 8000 ft., *D M72*.

3. **O. aff. ludoviciana** Nutt. var. **arenosa** (Suksd.) Cronq. Known only from upper spring of Marble Canyon, at ca. 7000 ft., *D s.n.*

FAMILY 61. CAMPANULACEAE
1. Nemacladus

A.   Corolla lobes united at base into an evident tube, white with pinkish or
     yellowish tips and bases, 2–2.5 mm. long .... 3. *N. sigmoideus*

AA. Corolla lobes ± not united at base, purplish or white with the lobes purplish at tips, 1–2.5 mm. long.
- B. Calyx and ovary enlarged in fruit; plants compact and coarse-stemmed; basal leaves elliptic .... 2. *N. rigidus*
- BB. Calyx and ovary not enlarged in fruit; plants diffuse; basal leaves mostly oblanceolate .... 1. *N. glanduliferous*

1. **N. glanduliferous** Jeps. var. **orientalis** McVaugh. Open hillsides and flats, washes, etc., desert scrub, Inyo Co., below 5700 ft.; below Toll House Springs, *Eastwood & Howell 9594* (CAS); Black Canyon at Marble Canyon, 5700 ft., *D 2730*; Silver Canyon, 4600 ft., *D 3449*.

2. **N. rigidus** Curran. Known only from Black Canyon at Marble Canyon, 5700 ft., *D 2730-A*.

3. **N. sigmoideus** Robbins. Washes and flats, desert scrub to pinyon woodland, 5000–7000 ft., Inyo Co.: Cedar Flat, 7000 ft., *D 3290*; first canyon south of Silver Canyon, 5000 ft., *HM 726*.

FAMILY 62. RUBIACEAE
1. Galium

- A. Plants annual .... 1. *G. aparine*
- AA. Plants perennial.
  - B. Plants low, 2–11 cm. tall, erect or matted, with little or no wood above ground; pubescence of exceedingly fine abundant minute hairs; lower leaves ovate to orbicular, 0.3–8 mm. long .... 3. *G. hypotrichium*
  - BB. Plants ± suffrutescent, stems mostly erect, 10–35 cm. tall; glabrous or hispid.
    - C. Corolla campanulate.
      - D. Leaves mostly arcuate, the apex abrupt ...... 5. *G. multiflorum*
      - DD. Leaves mostly plane, graduated to apex .... 2. *G. hilendiae*
    - CC. Corolla rotate.
      - D. Leaves and stems hispid .... 6. *G. munzii*
      - DD. Leaves and stems glabrous .... 4. *G. matthewsii*

1. **G. aparine** L. Known only from talus slope, Lone Tree Creek, 7200 ft., *M 2247*.

2. **G. hilendiae** Dempst. & Ehrend. Dry rocky crevices, desert scrub to pinyon woodland, throughout the range, 5700–9000 ft.: Marble Canyon, 5700 ft., *D M69*; Silver Canyon, 5800 ft., *L 2864*; Wyman Creek, 8.7 miles east of White Mountain Road, 7900 ft., *L 3035*; Chiatovich Creek, 8900 ft., *M 2103* (JEPS).

3. **G. hypotrichium** Gray. rocky areas, pinyon woodland to alpine fell-fields, throughout the range, 6000–12,500 ft.: Cottonwood Creek, 10,900 ft., *Jepson 7880* (JEPS); Mono Co., 12,500 ft., *Shockley 456* (JEPS); Milner Creek, 12,000 ft., *HM 897*; Indian Creek, 6000 ft., *Lankester 788* (BM); Trail Canyon, 10,000 ft., *D 3359*.

4. **G. matthewsii** Gray. Known only from Black Canyon, 6100 ft., *M 2113*.

148

3. **G. multiflorum** Kell. f. **hirsutum** (Gray) Ehrend. Rocky places, pinyon woodland, 7000–9000 ft.: upper end of Marble Canyon, 7000 ft., *D 2854*; 1 mile below Roberts Ranch, Wyman Creek, ca. 7500 ft., *D s.n.*; canyon from Dead Horse Meadows Road to Cottonwood Creek, 7700 ft., *M 2060*.

FAMILY 63. CAPRIFOLIACEAE

A. Leaves pinnate, 6–15 cm. long; corolla rotate, white . . . . . . 1. *Sambucus*
AA. Leaves entire, 0.5–2.0 cm. long; corolla campanulate or salverform, pink
2. *Symphoricarpos*

1. **Sambucus**

1. **S. caerulea** Raf. Occasional, dry flats, washes to wet places, pinyon woodland to subalpine forest, throughout the range, 7000–10,000 ft.: Silver Canyon, 8800 ft., *L 3884*; Wyman Creek, 7350 ft., *L 2811*; Cottonwood Creek, 9800 ft., *HM 894*.

2. **Symphoricarpos**

A. Leaves lanceolate to elliptical, acute to obtuse, 0.5–1.5 cm. long; corolla 11–13 mm. long; style usually pilose . . . . 1. *S. longiflorus*
AA. Leaves oval, acutish at ends, 1–2 cm. long; corolla 7–9 mm. long; style glabrous . . . . 2. *S. vaccinoides*

1. **S. longiflorus** Gray. Dry rocky slopes, desert scrub to upper pinyon woodland, throughout the range, 5000–9700 ft.: below Toll House Springs, *Eastwood & Howell 9584* (CAS); Wyman Creek: 8100 ft., *HM 871*; Crooked Creek, 3 miles east of lab, 9700 ft., *HM 877*; Cottonwood Creek, 9500 ft., *D 1651*.
2. **S. vaccinoides** Rydb. Known only from ridge south of Queen Mine on decomposed granite, 10,500 ft., *Ferris 6746* (DS).

FAMILY 64. VALERIANACEAE
1. **Valeriana**

1. **V. capitata** Pall. ex Link. ssp. **pubicarpa** (Rydb.) Mey. Dry rocky slopes and canyons, northern canyons, 7000–9500 ft.: Indian Creek, 7500 ft., *Lankester 852* (BM); Davis Ranch, 7000 ft., *Shockley 518* (JEPS); Davis Creek, 9500 ft., *D 3102*.

FAMILY 65. COMPOSITAE
KEY TO GENERA
(*Adapted from Abrams*)

A. Anthers tailed at base; plants thistlelike . . . . 39. *Cirsium*
AA. Anthers not tailed at base, or, if so, plants not thistlelike.
  B. Flowers all perfect, with strap-shaped corollas. (Tribe: Cichorieae)
    C. Bristles of pappus plumose or of stout awns with several rigid bristles near the base.

149

D. Involucres strongly imbricated, phyllaries with broad scarious margins .... 41. *Anisocoma*
DD. Involucres ± not imbricated, phyllaries without or with only narrowly scarious margins.
  E. Pappus of stout awns with rigid bristles at base
                                              43. *Chaetadelpha*
  EE. Pappus of plumose bristles .... 50. *Stephanomeria*
CC. Bristles of pappus capillary, rarely barbellate.
  D. Achenes flattened, sometimes obscurely.
    E. Achenes not beaked .... 49. *Sonchus*
    EE. Achenes beaked .... 46. *Lactuca*
  DD. Achenes angulate or terete.
    E. Ligules pink or purplish, involucre 3–5-flowered
                                              47. *Lygodesmia*
    EE. Ligules white, cream or yellow.
      F. Stems leafless; heads on scapose peduncles.
        G. Leaves pinnatifid, sinuate-dentate or rarely entire, achenes 4–5-ribbed .... 51. *Taraxacum*
        GG. Leaves entire to laciniate or rarely denticulate; achenes 10–15-ribbed .... 40. *Agoseris*
      FF. Stems leafy; heads not on scapose peduncles.
        G. Achenes beakless .... 48. *Malacothrix*
        GG. Achenes beaked.
          H. Achenes striate .... 44. *Crepis*
          HH. Achenes rugulose or tuberculate.
            I. Inflorescence glandular; erect annuals; achenes tapering to the beak .... 42. *Calycoseris*
            II. Inflorescence not glandular; depressed annuals; achenes abruptly beaked .... 45. *Glyptopleura*
BB. Flowers ± regular and tubular when perfect; marginal flowers often female or neutral or strap-shaped.
  C. Pappus ± absent or vestigial.
    D. Rays absent or vestigial.
      E. Heads unisexual; female involucre ± burlike.
        F. Fruiting involucres with conspicuous scarious wings; leaves linear-filiform .... 4. *Hymenoclea*
        FF. Fruiting involucres without conspicuous wings; leaves not linear-filiform .... 1. *Ambrosia*
      EE. Heads not unisexual; female involucre not burlike.
        F. Phyllaries usually of one series.
          G. Leaves oval to ovate, subentire, 4–6 mm. long
                                              13. *Laphamia*
          GG. Leaves oblanceolate, entire, 1–4 cm. long, or pinnately parted and 8–18 mm. long .... 5. *Iva*
        FF. Phyllaries in 2 or more imbricated series .... 27. *Artemisia*

DD. Rays present.
   E.   Ligules white .... 26. *Achillea*
   EE. Ligules yellow.
      F.   Leaves broadly ovate, ca. 3 cm. wide .... 2. *Encelia*
      FF. Leaves linear to linear-lanceolate, 2–5 mm. wide
                              7. *Viguiera*
CC. Pappus present on at least some of the achenes.
   D.   Rays lacking, sometimes vestigial.
      E.   Pappus of paleae or flattened scales or stiff bristles or awns.
         F.   Lower leaves opposite .... 14. *Pericome*
         FF. Lower leaves mostly alternate.
            G.   Phyllaries in one series .... 8. *Chaenactis*
            GG. Phyllaries in two or more series ...... 28. *Hymenopappus*
      EE. Pappus of capillary bristles or rarely with outer scales.
         F.   Phyllaries hyaline or scarious; plants ± white-wooly.
            G.   Cespitose, mat-forming fibrous-rooted perennials
                         35. *Antennaria*
            GG. Erect, tap-rooted annuals or biennials .. 36. *Gnaphalium*
         FF. Phyllaries partly scarious or hyaline or completely herbaceous.
            G.   Plants shrubby .
               H.   Phyllaries 4–6 in one series ....34. *Tetradymia*
               HH. Phyllaries more than 6.
                  I. Leaves needlelike, 2–3 cm. long .. 30. *Lepidospartum*
                  II. Leaves not needlelike.
                     J. Phyllaries in distinct vertical ranks
                         17. *Chrysothamnus*
                     JJ. Phyllaries not in distinct vertical ranks.
                        K.   Flowers yellow .... 21. *Haplopappus*
                        KK. Flowers white to creamy or pink-purple
                         37. *Brickellia*
         GG. Plants herbaceous.
            H.   Plants annual; white-woolly, aromatic
                         31. *Psathyrotes*
            HH. Plants biennial or perennial.
               I. Phyllaries uniseriate; plant scapose, 1–10 cm. high
                         32. *Raillardella*
               II. Phyllaries in 2 or more series, imbricate.
                  J. Flowers white to pink to red-purple
                         38. *Eupatorium*
                  JJ. Flowers yellow.
                     K.   Phyllaries in one or 2 series, little imbricated; style appendages to 0.5 mm. long; plant 1–3 dm. high, cespitose .... 19. *Erigeron*
                     KK. Phyllaries imbricated in 2 or more series; style appendages usually at least 0.7 mm. long
                       21. *Haplopappus*

DD. Rays present.
  E.   Pappus of awns or chaffy scales or scales and bristles.
    F.   Rays yellow to orange or brownish.
      G. Receptacle chaffy or bristly .... 3. *Helianthus*
      GG. Receptacle naked or foveate or alveolate-fimbrillate or hairy.
        H.   Involucre of 2 or more series of graduated phyllaries.
          I.   Heads 1.5–3 cm. wide .... 15. *Acamptopappus*
          II. Heads ca. 1 mm. wide .... 20. *Gutierrezia*
        HH. Involucre of 1–3 series of non-graduated phyllaries.
          I.   Phyllaries in one series.
            J.   Plants 2–5 cm. high .... 9. *Eatonella*
            JJ. Plants 15–30 cm. high .... 10. *Eriophyllum*
          II. Phyllaries in more than one series.
            J.   Rays 12–14; plants ± glandular .. 14. *Hymenoxys*
            JJ. Rays 25–50; plants strongly glandular and ± succulent .... 12. *Hulsea*
    FF. Rays white to red to purple.
      G. Outermost achenes completely enfolded by the subtending phyllary; ligules white, fading rose-purple, 6–15 mm. long 6. *Layia*
      GG. Outermost achenes not enfolded by the subtending phyllary.
        H.   Annual; densely woolly; rays purplish, mostly up to 0.7 cm. long .... 9. *Eatonella*
        HH. Perennial; woolly to strigose hirsute; rays white to lavender to bluish-violet, 0.5–2 cm. long 25. *Townsendia*
EE. Pappus of capillary bristles or weakly plumose or rarely also with outer scales.
  F.   Rays yellow.
    G. Phyllaries numerous, ± imbricated.
      H.   Involucre 4–6.5 mm. high; perennial herbs from a woody caudex .... 24. *Solidago*
      HH. Involucre 6–18 mm. high, or if shorter, then plants shrubby .... 21. *Haplopappus*
    GG. Phyllaries few, in one or two series.
      H.   Leaves opposite, at least near base ...... 29. *Arnica*
      HH. Leaves alternate or basal .... 33. *Senecio*
  FF. Rays white to pink to purplish or blue.
    G. Rays white, very inconspicuous, scarcely exceeding the pappus and disk flowers; annual to 2 m. high 18. *Conyza*
    GG. Rays conspicuous, much exceeding the disk flowers.
      H.   Phyllaries slightly or not graduated, in 1 or 2 series; style-appendages usually less than 0.6 mm. long 19. *Erigeron*
      HH. Phyllaries graduated and ± imbricated in 3 or more

series; style-appendages usually more than 0.5 mm. long.
I. Biennial or short-lived perennial from a taproot; leaves
    subentire to deeply incised-dentate, toothed
                                          23. *Machaeranthera*
II. Perennials from a rhizome or fibrous root system.
    J. Leaves to ca. 1 cm. long; plants tufted, heathlike
                                          22. *Leucelene*
    JJ. Leaves usually 3–20 cm. long; plants mostly erect
                                          16. *Aster*

Tribe 1—HELIANTHEAE*
1. Ambrosia

A. Plants annual, with opposite leaves below; petioles to 6 cm. long; leaf-
    surfaces green, sparsely tomentulose to strigose or hispid
                                          1. *A. acanthicarpa*
AA. Plants perennial; leaves alternate; petioles 0.3–2 cm. long; leaf-surfaces
    gray-green, puberulous to white-woolly tomentose below.
    B. Leaves entire to pinnately-lobed; inflorescence spicate to ± racemose
                                          3. *A. eriocentra*
    BB. Leaves pinnately to tripinnately lobed; inflorescence racemose-pani-
        culate .... 2. *A. dumosa*

1. **A. acanthicarpa** Hook. Weed along lower margins of the range, below
6000 ft.: mouth of Birch Creek, 5100 ft., *L 2978*.
2. **A. dumosa** (Gray) Payne. Alluvium and slopes, southern end of range,
below 5000 ft.: west base of Westgard Pass, 4500–5000 ft., *HM 780*.
3. **A. eriocentra** (Gray) Payne. Slopes and washes, desert scrub, southern
end of the range, 4500–5000 ft.: west base of Westgard Pass, 4500–5000 ft.,
HM 798.

2. Encelia

1. **E. virginensis** A. Nels. ssp. **actoni** (Elmer) Keck. Slopes and washes,
desert scrub, southern end of range, below 6000 ft.: Westgard Pass: 7.4 miles
west of White Mountain Road, 5000 ft., *L 2640*; Black Canyon, 4000 ft., *D
2652*; Birch Creek, 2.9 miles north of Deep Springs Valley Road, 5500 ft.,
L 2981.

3. Helianthus

1. **H. annuus** L. ssp. **lenticularis** (Dougl.) Ckll. Weed, apparently introduced at Toll House Springs and other disturbed places, throughout the range
at lower elevations: Toll House Springs, 5971 ft., *L 3328*.

* Genera are listed alphabetically by tribe. They are numbered consecutively,
as given in the key to genera.

4. Hymenoclea

1. **H. salsola** Torr. & Gray. Open sandy areas, roadsides, etc., desert scrub, below 5600 ft.: Westgard Pass, 7.4 miles west of White Mountain Road, 5000 ft., *L 2667*; first canyon south of Silver Canyon, 5000 ft., *HM 698*; Silver Canyon, 4600 ft., *D 3458*; mouth of Wyman Creek, *D M83*.

5. Iva

A. Perennial herb; stems several, 18–60 cm. high; leaves entire
1. I. axillaris

AA. Annual; stems single, 7–15 cm. high; leaves ternately bipinnatifid
2. I. nevadensis

1. **I. axillaris** Pursh. Alkaline places and dry flats, desert scrub to pinyon woodland, throughout the range, below 6000 (8000) ft.: Toll House Springs, 5971 ft., *L 3333*; Antelope Springs, 5600 ft., *L & M 2998, D 3292*; Chiatovich Creek, 8000 ft., *D 2573*.

2. **I. nevadensis** Jones. Sandy alkaline washes and flats, desert scrub, scattered throughout the range, below 6500 ft.: Wyman Creek, 6400 ft., *HM 873*; north of Pinyon Hill, 6500 ft., *D 2868*; Benton Station, *Jones s.n.* (POM); frequent west of Benton and between Benton and Bishop in foothills.

6. Layia

1. **L. glandulosa** (Hook.) Hook. & Arn. Sandy open places, slopes and flats, desert scrub to pinyon woodland, throughout the range, 5000–8000 ft.: Westgard Pass, 3.8 miles west of White Mountain Road, 6450 ft., *L 2733*; Deep Springs Valley, 6300 ft., *HM 687*; Black Ace Mine, south end of Cedar Flat, 7250 ft., *HM 36*; 3 miles below Roberts Ranch, Wyman Creek, 7000 ft., *D 3052*; 1 mile north of B & B Mine, Trail Canyon, ca. 8000 ft., *D 3258*.

7. Viguiera

1. **V. multiflora** (Nutt.) Blake var. **nevadensis** (A. Nels.) Blake. Frequent, dry open hillsides and washes, desert scrub to pinyon woodland, southern canyons, 5900–8000 ft.: Westgard Pass: Toll House Springs, 5900 ft., *HM 76*; 3.7 miles north of Westgard Pass on White Mountain Road, 7800 ft., *Everett & Balls* 21933 (UC).

Tribe 2. HELENIEAE
8. Chaenactis

A. Biennials or perennials, 1.5–4 dm. high; stems reddish . .2. *C. douglasii*
AA. Annuals.
  B. Phyllaries attenuate at apex with slender, terete, colored tips
1. C. carphoclinia
  BB. Phyllaries acute or obtuse at apex.
    C. Pappus of 2 series of paleae.
      D. Corolla 10–12 mm. long; stamens included . . . . 3. *C. macrantha*

DD. Corolla 6–8 mm. long; stamens exserted .... 5. *C. xantiana*
CC. Pappus of one series of paleae .... 4. *C. stevioides*

1. **C. carphoclinia** Gray var. **attenuata** (Gray) Jones. Washes and flats, desert scrub of Inyo Co., below 5500 ft.: Westgard Pass: west side, 4500 to 5000 ft., *HM 293*; first canyon south of Silver Canyon, 5000 ft., *HM 712*; Silver Canyon, 4600 ft., *D 3452*.

2. **C. douglasii** (Hook.) Hook. & Arn. ssp. **rubricaulis** (Rydb.) Ferris. Frequent, dry washes, slopes and flats, desert scrub to subalpine forest, throughout the range, 6500–10,500 ft.: 1.7 miles east of Toll House Springs, 6500 ft., *HM 155*; Silver Canyon: 8000 ft., *D 1515*; hill west of head of Wyman Creek, 10,500 ft., *HM 256*; near Pinyon Hill, 6500 ft., *D s.n.*; near Trail Canyon, 7500 ft., *D 3084* (RSA).

3. **C. macrantha** D. C. Eat. Dry slopes or washes, desert scrub, Mono Co. south, below 5500 ft.: west base of Westgard Pass, 4500–5000 ft., *HM 795*; near Antelope Springs at mouth of Payson Canyon, 5500 ft., *D 3297*; second ridge south of Silver Canyon, 5500 ft., *HM 148*; Silver Canyon, 4600 ft., *D 3450*; directly below Devernois Ranch, 4800 ft., *Peirson 12465* (UC).

4. **C. stevioides** Hook. & Arn.

A.   Pappus acute; about ⅔ as long as the corolla ...... 4a. var. *stevioides*
AA. Pappus obtuse, ⅓ or less as long as the corolla .... 4b. var. *brachypappa*

4a. Var. **stevioides**. Sandy flats and washes, desert scrub, Inyo Co., below 6500 ft.: Westgard Pass, 3.8 miles west of White Mountain Road, 6450 ft., *L 2732*; near school, Deep Springs Valley, *Raven 7027* (CAS); base of mountains, east of Laws, *Heller 8237* (CAS); Silver Canyon, 5000 ft., *D 2642*.

4b. Var. **brachypappa** (Gray) Hall. Dry washes and slopes, desert scrub, Inyo Co., below 5500 ft.: near west mouth of Westgard Pass, *Wiggins 8816* (JEPS); first canyon south of Silver Canyon, 5000 ft., *HM 713*; Silver Canyon, 5500 ft., *Benson 5941* (POM).

5. **C. xantiana** Gray. Dry, sandy open places, desert scrub to lower pinyon woodland, 4200–7000 ft.: Wyman Creek, 3 miles below Roberts Ranch, 7000 ft., *D 3053*; observed on Westgard Pass, 4200 ft.

9. Eatonella
1. **E. nivea** (D.C. Eat.) Gray. Dry slopes, desert scrub to pinyon woodland, below 8500 ft.: Chiatovich Creek, 8500 ft., *D 3076*; known from Benton and Bishop areas.

10. Eriophyllum
A.   Perennial; stems from a caudex 1.5–2 dm. high; not densely woolly; ray
     flowers 7–16 mm. long .... 1. *E. lanatum*
AA. Annual, 1–5 cm. high; densely woolly; heads discoid ......2. *E. pringlei*

1. **E. lanatum** (Pursh) Forbes var. **integrifolium** (Hook.) Smiley. Rare, northern canyons on rocky slopes, 10,000–10,500 ft.: Davis Creek, 10,000 ft., *D 3109*.

2. **E. pringlei** Gray. Sandy soil, desert scrub, below 6500 ft.: road to Queen Canyon, Queen Valley, 6400 ft., *M 2744*.

11. Hulsea

1. **H. algida** Gray. Rocky areas, subalpine forest to alpine fell-fields, throughout the range, 10,000–14,230 ft.: near cave, Crooked Creek, 10,000 ft., *L 3088*; White Mountain Road, 13,500 ft., *L 3252*; White Mountain Peak: 14,200 ft., *D 1670*; Pellisier Flats, 1 mile south of Jump-Off, 13,500 ft., *M 2194.*

12. Hymenoxys

1. **H. cooperi** (Gray) Ckll. var. **canescens** (D.C. Eat.) Parker. Frequent, dry open flats and rocky places, pinyon woodland to alpine fell-fields, throughout the range, 7500–11,800 ft.: north of Schulman Grove on White Mountain Road, 10,000 ft., *HM 381*; Wyman Creek, 0.1 mile east of White Mountain Road, 10,000 ft., *L 3055*; Crooked Creek Ranger Station, 9500 ft., *D 1560*; south of Sheep Meadow, 11,800 ft., *HM 574*; south ridge, Cottonwood Creek, 10,250 ft., *HM 264*; Chiatovich Flats, 10,300 ft., *D 2555*; Trail Canyon, 7500 ft., *D 2745*.

13. Laphamia

1. **L. megacephala** Wats. Rocky places, crevices, etc., desert scrub to pinyon woodland, Inyo Co., 6000–8000 ft.: Black Canyon, 6500 ft., *D 1750*; Silver Canyon: *Grinnell s.n.* (JEPS); 6000 ft., *HM 304*; 8000 ft., *Jepson 7409* (JEPS).

14. Pericome

1. **P. caudata** Gray. Dry washes and streambanks, sometimes in moist areas, desert scrub to lower pinyon woodland, below 6000 ft.: 4 miles east of Laws in Silver Canyon, 5300 ft., *Anderson 2008* (RSA); mouth of Wyman Creek, 5350 ft., *Ferris 6631* (POM); 8 miles south of Benton Station, *Canfield s.n.* (RSA).

Tribe 3. ASTEREAE
15. Acamptopappus

1. **A. shockleyi** Gray. Dry flats and washes, desert scrub, especially in Inyo Co., below 6000 ft.: Payson Canyon, 6000 ft., *D 3295*; Black Canyon, 5700 ft., *D 2674* (JEPS); Fish Lake Valley, 4900 ft., *Lankester 766*.

16. Aster

A.   Heads solitary at tips of tufted stems and branches; pappus in two series
5. *A. scopulorum*

AA. Heads several; pappus usually in one series.
B.   Branches of inflorescence and phyllaries densely glandular
1. *A. campestris*

BB. Branches of inflorescence and phyllaries not glandular.
    C.   Inflorescence a naked cyme or cymose panicle .... 4. *A. occidentalis*
    CC. Inflorescence a leafy panicle.
        D.   Plant 1–1.5 m. high; stem pubescence in decurrent lines from
            leaf-bases .... 3. *A. hesperius*
        DD. Plants up to 1 m. high; stem pubescence beneath heads uniform
            or glabrate .... 2. *A. eatoni*

1. **A. campestris** Nutt. var. **bloomeri** (Gray) Gray. Rare, drier spots of meadows, pinyon woodland: known only from Roberts Ranch, Wyman Creek, 8000 ft., *D 3149*.

2. **A. eatonii** (Gray) Howell. Wet places along streams, desert scrub to pinyon woodland, throughout the range, 5000–8000 ft.: Silver Canyon, 5000 ft., *Wolf 3855* (RSA); Roberts Ranch, Wyman Creek, 8000 ft., *D 3141*; Cottonwood Creek, just below narrows, 6100 ft., *M 2160*; north base of Mustang Mountain, *Roos 2432* (POM).

3. **A. hesperius** Gray. Streambanks and meadows, desert scrub to upper pinyon woodland, Mono Co. south, 5400–9200 ft.: Silver Canyon, 5400 ft., *L 3883*; Cottonwood Creek, 9200 ft., *L 3297*.

4. **A. occidentalis** (Nutt.) Torr. & Gray. Wet places, meadows, pinyon woodland to subalpine forest: Crooked Creek, 9300 ft., *J. & L. Roos 5863* (RSA).

5. **A. scopulorum** Gray. Dry, rocky hillsides; probably widely scattered throughout the range in desert scrub and pinyon woodland, but our collections only from northern slopes: Trail Canyon, 8000 ft., *D 2699*; Montgomery Pass, 7000 ft., *DeDecker 232* (RSA).

17. Chrysothamnus

A.   Leaves resinous-punctate, terete.
    B.   Phyllaries with a thick, green, glandular spot at the tip
                                  4. *C. teretifolius*
    BB. Phyllaries scarcely or not at all glandular-thickened above
                                  3. *C. paniculatus*
AA. Leaves not resinous-punctate, variously shaped.
    B.   Twigs not tomentose; involucre 5–7 mm. high.
        C.   Phyllaries in obscure vertical ranks ....5. *C. viscidiflorus*
        CC. Phyllaries in 5 sharply defined vertical ranks ...... 1. *C. axillaris*
    BB. Twigs tomentose; leaves tomentose to subglabrous; involucre 6–13 mm.
        high .... 2. *C. nauseosus*

1. **C. axillaris** Keck. Desert slopes and canyons, 5000–6000 ft., described by Keck as an endemic to the White–Inyo Mts. region, Deep Springs Valley and Esmeralda Co., Nevada.

2. **C. nauseosus** (Pall.) Britt.
A.   Achenes densely pubescent.
    B.   Outer phyllaries ± pubescent or tomentose.
        C.   Plants yellow-green with glandular-pubescent inflorescences
                                    2d. ssp. *viscosus*

CC. Plants grayish or whitish, and ± non-glandular .. 2b. ssp. *hololeucus*
BB. Outer phyllaries sometimes glandular but not hairy .. 2a. ssp. *consimilis*
AA. Achenes ± glabrous .... 2c. ssp. *leiospermus*

2a. Ssp. **consimilis** (Greene) Hall & Clem. Alkaline places, desert scrub to pinyon woodland, around the base of the range, below 8000 ft.: Toll House Springs, *L 3336*; Silver Canyon, 7.7 miles east of Laws, 8000 ft., *Munz 12689* (RSA); 8 miles south of Benton Station at Taylor's Ranch, *Canfield s.n.* (RSA).

2b. Ssp. **hololeucus** (Gray) Hall & Clem. Sandy soils, slopes and canyons, desert scrub to pinyon woodland, below 8000 ft.: Silver Canyon, 7.7 miles east of Laws, 8000 ft., *Munz 12695* (RSA); Wyman Creek, 7500 ft., *D 3044*; Benton, 5700 ft., *Hall 10654* (UC).

2c. Ssp. **leiospermus** (Gray) Hall & Clem. Dry slopes, pinyon woodland, ca. 7000 ft.: Silver Canyon: 7000 ft., *Wolf 2585* (UC); 7200 ft., *HM 485*.

2d. Ssp. **viscosus** Keck. Sandy places in washes and flats, desert scrub, Inyo Co., 4500 to 6000 ft.: Toll House Springs, 5971 ft., *L 3335*; Silver Canyon, 4500 ft., *L 2854*.

3. **C. paniculatus** (Gray) Hall. Known only from dry slopes and washes, about 1.5 miles below Marble Canyon in Black Canyon, 5000 ft., *D 3023*.

4. **C. teretifolius** (Dur. & Hilg.) Hall. Dry rocky slopes and washes, desert scrub to lower pinyon woodland, Milner Creek south, below 8000 ft.: 1.3 miles east of Toll House Springs, 6500 ft., *HM 162*; second ridge south of Silver Canyon, 7000 ft., *HM 139*; Silver Canyon: 7000 ft., *M 2292-A*; 7200 ft., *Wolf 2581* (UC).

5. **C. viscidiflorus** (Hook.) Nutt.

A. Leaves glabrous, sometimes viscid.
B. Shrubs 4–12 dm. high; leaves 2–10 mm. wide or sometimes narrower
5a. ssp. *viscidiflorus*
BB. Shrubs 1–3.5 dm. high; leaves 0.5–2 mm wide ...... 5d. ssp. *pumilus*
AA. Leaves slightly to densely pubescent.
B. Leaves slightly pubescent, up to 1 mm. wide, linear-filiform
5b. ssp. *elegans*
BB. Leaves ± densely pubescent, 1–2 mm. wide ...... 5c. ssp. *puberulus*

5a. Ssp. **viscidiflorus.** Frequent, dry slopes and washes, desert scrub to pinyon woodland, 5700–9300 ft.: Westgard Pass, 3.8 miles west of White Mountain Road, 6450 ft., *L 2745*; Black Canyon near Marble Fork, 5700 ft., *D 1754-A*; head of Silver Canyon, 9300 ft., *HM 283*; Wyman Creek, 5.7 miles east of White Mountain Road, 8200 ft., *L 3045*.

5b. Ssp. **elegans** (Greene) Hall & Clem. Known only from the mouth of Mollie Gibson Canyon, in wash at 6960 ft., *L 2962*.

This plant is intermediate between ssp. *puberulus* and ssp. *elegans* but closer in morphology to the latter.

5c. Ssp. **puberulus** (D.C. Eat.) Hall & Clem. Dry slopes and flats, desert scrub to subalpine forest, 5000–10,000 ft.: Payson Canyon, 6500 ft., *HM 361*; Black Ace Mine, Cedar Flat, 7200 ft., *HM 804*; 3 miles northwest of Cedar

Flat, 8500 ft., *J. & L. Roos 5091* (UC); head of Black Canyon, 9500 ft., *HM 326*; Silver Canyon, 5800 ft., *L 2867*; Benton, 5600 ft., *Hall 10677* (UC).

5d. Ssp. **pumilus** (Nutt.) Hall & Clem. Dry rocky slopes, pinyon woodland to subalpine forest, 8000–10,200 (12,650) ft.: southeast rim of Reed Flat, 10,100 ft., *J. & L. Roos 5113* (RSA); Wyman Creek, 5.7 miles east of White Mountain Road, 8200 ft., *L 3044*; Crooked Creek, ca. 4 miles east of lab, *Tucker 2249* (DAV).

18. Conyza

1. **C. canadensis** (L.) Cronq. Weed, alluvium and disturbed places, 4500–6500 ft.: Wyman Creek: 5900 ft., *M 2155*; 6500 ft., *D 3169*; Marble Creek (Nevada), 5500 ft., *Lankester 828* (BM).

19. Erigeron

A. Pistillate corollas numerous, filiform, with erect narrow rays 2–3 mm. long and 0.25–0.5 mm. wide .... 8. *E. lonchophyllum*

AA. Pistillate corollas absent to numerous with absent to well-developed rays not short, narrow, and erect.

  B. Leaves ± uniform in size; phyllaries strongly imbricate; rays ± blue; internodes numerous and short ....3. *E. breweri*

  BB. Basal leaves larger than cauline leaves; phyllaries equal or imbricate; internodes not numerous or short.

   C. Achenes 6–10-nerved; basal leaves tufted; phyllaries strongly imbricate, silvery-strigose .... 2. *E. argentatus*

   CC. Achenes usually 2-nerved, or if more, then phyllaries equal and not silvery-strigose.

    D. Leaves mostly 3-lobed or 2–4-ternate.

     E. Leaves mostly with 3 short, broad, obtuse lobes .. 11. *E. vagus*

     EE. Leaves trifid or 2–4 times ternate with slender lobes

6. *E. compositus*

    DD. Leaves not 3-lobed, usually entire.

     E. Stem pubescence absent or closely appressed; pulvinate-cespitose with basal leaves .... 5. *E. compactus*

     EE. Stem pubescence widely spreading.

      F. Heads solitary or rarely 2, radiate; plants usually found in alpine or subalpine.

       G. Plants with cauline leaves; style-appendages short and blunt, 0.1–0.15 mm. long; mostly above 11,000 ft.

10. *E. pygmaeus*

       GG. Plants ± scapose; style-appendages lanceolate, acute, 0.3–0.5 mm. long; mostly below 12,000 ft. .... 4. *E. clokeyi*

      FF. Heads 1–many, radiate or disciform; plants usually found below 10,000 ft.

       G. Heads disciform, yellow .... 1. *E. aphanactis*

GG. Heads obviously radiate (rarely disciform in *E. divergens*).
  H.   Leaves oblanceolate, to 8 cm. long and 8 mm. wide; disk-
       corollas 3.5–5 mm. long . . . . 9. *E. pumilus*
  HH. Leaves oblanceolate or spatulate, to 2.5 cm. long; disk-
       corollas 2–3 mm. long . . . . 7. *E. divergens*

1. **E. aphanactis** (Gray) Greene. Common, dry rocky slopes and washes, desert scrub to upper pinyon woodland, throughout the range, 5900–9500 ft.: Westgard Pass: 5.4 miles west of White Mountain Road, 5900 ft., *L 2671, 2675*; mouth of Mollie Gibson Canyon, 6960 ft., *L 2961*; Silver Canyon: 6500 ft., *L 2834*; 9300 ft., *HM 288*; Indian Creek, 6500 ft., *Linsdale s.n.* (UC); near B & B Mine, Trail Canyon, 7500 ft., *D M122*.

2. **E. argentatus** Gray. Rocky slopes and flats, pinyon woodland, Inyo Co., 7000–8500 ft.: east side of Westgard Pass, 7000 ft., *Hovanitz s.n.* (UC); White Mountain Road, 7300 ft., *L 2907*; near Studebaker Flats, White Mountain Road, 8500 ft., *HM 759*.

3. **E. breweri** Gray var. **porphyreticus** (Jones) Cronq. Dry rocky places, slopes, washes, etc., desert scrub to pinyon woodland, throughout the range, 5000–8500 ft.: Westgard Pass, 4 miles west of White Mountain Road, 6400 ft., *L 2706*; Black Canyon at Marble Canyon, 5700 ft., *D M123*; Silver Canyon, 6000 ft., *HM 131*; Wyman Creek: 7100 ft., *L 2779*; 8300 ft., *L 2799*; also known from Indian Creek.

4. **E. clokeyi** Cronq. Common, rocky slopes and meadows, pinyon woodland to alpine fell-fields, throughout the range, 8000–12,100 ft.: north of Schulman Grove on White Mountain Road, 10,000 ft., *HM 383*; head of Silver Canyon, 9300 ft., *HM 286*; Wyman Creek, 5.7 miles east of White Mountain Road, 8200 ft., *L 3046*; meadow ½ mile westsouthwest of Crooked Creek Lab, 10,200 ft., *L 3144*; Big Prospector Meadow, 10,500 ft., *J. & L. Roos 5100* (UC); southeast slope of Sheep Mountain, 11,450 ft., *L 3180*; McAfee Meadow, 11,700 ft., *D 2835*; Chiatovich Creek, 8500 ft., *D 3112*; Chiatovich Flats, 10,300 ft., *D 2556*.

5. **E. compactus** Blake. Dry slopes in pinyon woodland, Westgard Pass, 6000–7500 ft.: Cedar Flat, 7000 ft., *D 3284*.

6. **E. compositus** Pursh.
A.   Leaves mostly 1-ternate; plants small and compact . . . . 6a. var. *discoideus*
AA. Leaves 2–3-ternate; plants 1–2.5 dm. tall . . . . 6b. var. *glabratus*

6a. Var. **discoideus** Gray. Rocky places, subalpine forest to alpine fell-fields, 9000–14,000 ft.: Crooked Creek Ranger Station, 9500 ft., *D 1533*; Crooked Creek, 9900 ft., *L 3275*; White Mountain Peak, 14,000 ft., *D 2613*.

6b. Var. **glabratus** Macoun. Rocky places and grassy meadows, subalpine forest to alpine fell-fields, throughout the range, 9500–14,000 ft.: Wyman Creek, 9500 ft., *D 1742*; Crooked Creek, 9900 ft., *HM 817*; northwest corner of Sagehen Flat, 10,250 ft., *L 3169*; McAfee Meadow, 11,700 ft., *D M94*; Pellisier Flats, 12,400 ft., *M 2199*.

7. **E. divergens** Torr. & Gray. Rare in moist areas, desert scrub, 5500–6500 ft.: Deep Springs, 5500 ft., *Buechner C55* (RSA); Antelope Springs, 5600 ft., *L 3003*; Black Canyon, 6200 ft., *M 2116*.

8. **E. lonchophyllus** Hook. Meadows and grassy streamsides, 8000–10,000 ft.: Roberts Ranch, Wyman Creek, 8000 ft., *D 3163*; Crooked Creek, 9400 ft., *M 2258*; Cottonwood Creek: 8900 ft., *L 2926, 2927*; south fork, 9800 ft., *HM 463*.

9. **E. pumilus** Nutt. ssp. **concinnoides** Cronq. Dry rocky slopes, 9500–10,500 ft.: 8.5 miles north of Westgard Pass on White Mountain Road, 9800 ft., *Everett & Balls* 21930 (RSA); also known from east of Campito Meadow, *Billings 1693* (prob. RENO).

10. **E. pygmaeus** (Gray) Greene. Rocky slopes, alpine fell-fields, throughout the range, 11,000–13,500 ft.: southeast slope of Sheep Mountain, 11,450 ft., *L 3181*; White Mountain summit, 13,400 ft., *HM 507*; Pellisier Flats, 12,800 ft., *M 2214*.

11. **E. vagus** Pays. Rocky slopes, alpine fell-fields throughout the range, 13,000–14,240 ft.: White Mountain Peak: 13,500 ft., *L 3254*; 14,100 ft., *L 3240, M 2227*; Pellisier Flats, east slope of Mt. Dubois, 13,450 ft., *M 2269*.

20. Gutierrezia

1. **G. microcephala** (DC.) Gray. Desert slopes and alluvium, Inyo Co., 6000–7000 ft.: Silver Canyon, 7000 ft., *Wolf 2589* (UC); near mouth of Wyman Creek, 6000 ft., *Ferris 6910* (UC); Wyman Creek, 7000 ft., *D 3151*.

21. Haplopappus

A. Herbaceous perennial with a basal rosette of linear-lanceolate to oblanceolate, entire to laciniate leaves, 3–10 cm. long . . . . 2. *H. apargioides*
AA. Woody perennials without a basal rosette of leaves.
   B. Plants cespitose, matted, with leaves 1–6 cm. long with scabrid margins
                                       1. *H acaulis*
   BB. Plants not cespitose or matted.
      C. Leaves oblong to spatulate to linear-oblanceolate, 1–3 cm. long, 1.5–6 mm. wide; plants 1–4 dm. high; style-branch appendages more than twice as long as stigmatic region.
         D. Heads discoid; twigs closely white-tomentose . . 5. *H. macronema*
         DD. Heads radiate; twigs not closely white-tomentose
                                     6. *H. suffruticosus*
      CC. Leaves linear-spatulate, 6–15 mm. long and up to 1.5 mm. wide, or cuneate to suborbicular-obovate, 5–20 mm. long and 3–10 mm. wide; plants 1–15 dm. high; style-appendages equally or shorter than the stigmatic region.
         D. Leaves linear-spatulate, 6–15 mm. long and up to 1.5 mm. wide; phyllaries 2–3-seriate . . . . 3. *H. cooperi*
         DD. Leaves cuneate to suborbicular-obovate, 5–20 mm. long, 3–10 mm. wide; phyllaries 4–6-seriate . . . . 4. *H. cuneatus*

1. **H. acaulis** (Nutt.) Gray. Frequent, dry hillsides and flats, desert scrub to upper subalpine forest and alpine fell-fields, throughout the range, 7000–12,000 ft.: north of Schulman Grove on White Mountain Road, 10,000 ft., *HM 382;* Wyman Creek, 9500 ft., *D 1743;* southeast slope of Sheep Mountain, 11,450 ft., *L 3183;* head of Cottonwood Creek, 11,500 ft., *D 2595;* Trail Canyon, 8000 ft., *D 2700;* east slope of Montgomery Pass, *Eastwood & Howell 9529* (CAS).

2. **H. apargioides** Gray. Common, meadows and flats, subalpine forest to alpine fell-fields, throughout the range, 8700–13,400 ft.: northwest corner of Sagehen Flat, 10,250 ft., *L 3159;* upper Cottonwood Creek, 11,700 ft., *D 2608;* McAfee Meadow, 11,700 ft., *D 2823;* White Mountain Peak, 13,400 ft., *HM 506;* south end of Pellisier Flats, 12,500 ft., *M 2203;* Queen Canyon, 8700 ft., *M 2763.*

3. **H. cooperi** (Gray) Hall. Common, slopes and flats, desert scrub to pinyon woodland, 4000–6500 ft.: Westgard Pass, 7.4 miles west of White Mountain Road, 5000 ft., *L 2657;* Black Canyon, 5700 ft., *D s.n.;* first canyon south of Silver Canyon, 5000 ft., *HM 695.*

4. **H. cuneatus** Gray. Rocky crevices, desert scrub to pinyon woodland, southern canyons, 5000–8000 ft.: Marble Canyon at Black Canyon, 5700 ft., *D 3021;* Silver Canyon, 7200 ft., *Wolf 2580* (UC); 1 mile below Roberts Ranch, Wyman Creek, 8000 ft., *D 1694.*

5. **H. macronema** Gray. Common, rocky slopes and flats, meadows, subalpine forest and alpine fell-fields, 9900–12,500 ft.: Crooked Creek, 9900 ft., *L 3272;* south of Sheep Meadow, 11,800 ft., *HM 572;* head of Cottonwood Creek, 11,500 ft., *D 2606;* cliff above Indian Creek on Pellisier Flats, 12,400 ft., *M & L 2203-A.*

6. **H. suffruticosus** (Nutt.) Gray. Slopes and flats, subalpine forest to alpine fell-fields, throughout the range, 10,500–12,500 ft.: Sagehen Flat, 10,500 ft., *HM 444;* upper Cottonwood Creek, 11,500 ft., *D 2607;* McAfee Meadow, 11,700 ft., *D 2824;* Barcroft Lab, 12,500 ft., *Tucker 2268* (DAV).

22. Leucelene

1. **L. ericoides** (Torr.) Greene. Dry open slopes and flats, 7000–9000 ft.: Wyman Creek, 7000 ft. *M 2050;* 1 mile below Roberts Ranch, 8000 ft., *D 1699.*

23. Machaeranthera

A. Plants suffruticose, about 6 dm. tall; heads solitary . . . . 3. *M. tortifolia*
AA. Plants herbaceous biennials or perennials, 0.5–6 dm. tall; heads few in in an inflorescence.
B. Phyllaries 2–5 seriate; heads 6–8 mm. high . . . . 2. *M. shastensis*
BB. Phyllaries 6–8-seriate; heads 8–15 mm. high . . . . 1. *M. canescens*

1. **M. canescens** (Pursh) Gray. Open hillsides, flats, around springs and meadows, pinyon woodland to subalpine forest, throughout the range, 7000–10,300 ft.: spring of Marble Canyon, 7000 ft., *D M34;* 1 mile below Roberts

Ranch, Wyman Creek, 8000 ft., *D 1702;* meadow ½ mile westsouthwest of Crooked Creek Lab, 10,200 ft., *L 3143;* Cottonwood Creek, 9200 ft., *L 3295;* Chiatovich Flats, 10,300 ft., *D 2561.*

2. **M. shastensis** Gray var. **montana** (Greene) Cronq. & Keck. Dry slopes and ridges, subalpine forest, 9500–10,250 ft.: White Mountain Road, 9800 ft., *HM 341;* head of Wyman Creek, 10,000 ft., *L 3886;* ridge between Crooked Creek and Cottonwood Creek, 10,250 ft., *HM 427.*

3. **M. tortifolia** (Gray) Cronq. & Keck. Dry places, slopes and washes, desert scrub, Inyo Co., below 6000 ft.: Westgard Pass, 8.5 miles west of White Mountain Road, 4600 ft., *L 2638;* Black Canyon, 4500 ft., *D 2624;* first canyon south of Silver Canyon, 5000 ft., *HM 696;* ridge north of Silver Canyon, 5800 ft., *HM 199.*

24. Solidago

A.   Stems 0.5–4 dm. high; petioles not clasping; mostly above 9000 ft.

1. S. *multiradiata*

AA.   Stems 4–13 dm. high; petioles ± clasping; mostly below 7000 ft.

2. S. *spectabilis*

1. **S. multiradiata** Ait. Common, dry rocky open areas or meadows, pinyon woodland to alpine fell-fields, throughout the range, 9000–13,000 ft.: Sheep Mountain, 11,600 ft., *Jepson 7402* (JEPS); south fork of Cottonwood Creek, 9800 ft., *HM 462;* McAfee Meadow, 11,800 ft., *HM 607;* Barcroft Lab, 12,650 ft. *Bacigalupi et al. 8125* (JEPS); east slope, Pellisier Flats, 12,800 ft., *M & L 2215.*

2. **S. spectabilis** (D.C. Eat) Gray. Wet areas, springs, meadows, desert scrub to lower pinyon woodland, throughout the range, 5000–7000 ft.: Antelope Springs, *Hurd 60-84* (UC); upper spring, Marble Canyon, 7000 ft., *D 2890;* Cottonwood Creek, 6100 ft., *M 2163;* Chiatovich Creek, 2 miles west of Kellogg Ranch, 5100 ft., *Archer 7183* (UC).

25. Townsendia

A.   Plants densely woolly-villous throughout ....1. *T. condensata*

AA.   Plants not densely woolly-villous.

B.   Involucre 4–7-seriate, the phyllaries lanceolate to linear, acute

2. *T. leptotes*

BB.   Involucre ± 3-seriate, the phyllaries oblong, acute to subacuminate

3. *T. scapigera*

1. **T. condensata** D.C. Eat. Rare, gravelly ridges and flats, alpine fell-fields, higher elevations: White Mountain Road, 11,400 ft., *L 3129.*

2. **T. leptotes** (Gray) Osterh. Stony slopes and meadows, alpine fell-fields, 11,000–12,500 ft.: entrance to Patriarch Grove, 11,200 ft., *HM 624;* White Mountain, 11,500 ft., *D 1661;* south of Sheep mountain, 11,800 ft., *HM 578;* Barcroft Meadows, 12,450 ft., *Bacigalupi et al. 8138* (JEPS).

3. **T. scapigera** D. C. Eat. Uncommon, rocky slopes and flats, sometimes sandy places, desert scrub to subalpine forest, throughout the range, 5000–10,000 ft.: Westgard Pass, 6900 ft., *L 2904;* 1 mile south of Reed Flat, 10,000 ft., *J. & L. Roos 5120* (RSA); between Pinchot Creek and Pinyon Hill on road to B & B Mine, 6700 ft., *D 2758;* road to B & B Mine, ½ mile south of Fish Lake Valley Road, *D 3260.*

Tribe 4. ANTHEMIDEAE
26. Achillea

1. **A. lanulosa** Nutt. ssp. **alpicola** (Rydb.) Keck. Sporadically common in meadows, pinyon woodland to subalpine forest, Mono Co. north, 8700–9500 ft.: Cottonwood Creek, 8900 ft., *L 2933;* meadow of Poison and Cottonwood creeks, 9450 ft., *L 3134;* Chiatovich Creek, 8700 ft., *D 3117.*

27. Artemisia

A. Plants herbaceous, at most only woody at base.
  B. Leaves entire to lobed to bipinnatifid; pistil of disk florets fertile.
    C. Lower leaves bipinnatifid with some segments toothed, tomentose beneath at least when young, glabrate and green above; ray florets 9–12 . . . . .4. *A. michauxiana*
    CC. Lower leaves entire to bipinnatifid, the lobes entire or toothed, white-tomentose on both sides or floccose to glabrate above or rarely glabrous throughout; ray florets 5–12 . . . . .3. *A. ludoviciana*
  BB. Leaves entire, occasionally 3-parted; pistil of disk florets infertile; plants ± strongly odoriferous . . . . .2. *A. dracunculus*
AA. Plants shrubby.
  B. Plants spinescent . . . . .6. *A. spinescens*
  BB. Plants not spinescent.
    C. Outer phyllaries acute to acuminate; inner phyllaries usually glabrous; florets 8–20 per head; plants often root sprouting
                                                  5. *A. rothrockii*
    CC. Outer phyllaries obtuse to acute; inner phyllaries usually canescent (glabrous in *A. arbuscula* ssp. *nova*); florets 3–12 per head; plant seldom root-sprouting.
      D. Leaves mostly 3 or more times as long as wide, linear to cuneate or with divergent apical lobes . . . . .7. *A. tridentata*
      DD. Leaves mostly as long as to 3 times as long as wide, broadly cuneate or flabelliform . . . . .1. *A. arbuscula*

1. **A. arbuscula** Nutt.
A. Plants with larger heads with 6–11 florets; inner phyllaries canescent or ± glabrous; plant grayer . . . . .1a. ssp. *arbuscula*
AA. Plants with small heads with 3–5 florets; inner phyllaries ± glabrous; plant greener . . . . .1b. ssp. *nova*

1a. Ssp. **arbuscula**. Dry slopes and flats, subalpine forest and lower alpine fell-fields, throughout the range, 10,800–12,200 ft.: entrance to Patriarch Grove, 11,000 ft., *HM 665*; north of Crooked Creek Lab, 10,800 ft., *HM 891*; head of Poison Creek, 10,800 ft., *HM 832*; east slope of Sheep Mountain, 12,100 ft., *HM 585*; between gate and Barcroft Lab, 12,000 ft., *HM 667*.

1b. Ssp. **nova** (A. Nels.) Ward. Dy slopes and flats, pinyon woodland to alpine fell-fields, throughout the range, 7200–12,500 ft.: summit of Westgard Pass, 7271 ft., *Beetle 12896* (UC); Cedar Flat, 7600 ft., *Smith 1261* (JEPS); White Mountain Road, 8000 ft., *HM 668*; Pellisier Flats, south end, 12,500 ft., *Mitchell and LaMarche 2208* (UC).

2. **A. dracunculus** L. Dry slopes and washes, desert scrub to subalpine forest, throughout the range, 6500–12,200 ft.: 1.7 miles northeast of Toll House Springs, 6500 ft., *HM 152*; Marble Canyon, 7000 ft., *D 2887*; Wyman Creek, 5.7 miles east of White Mountain Road, 8200 ft., *L 3047*; northwest corner of Sagehen Flat, 10,300 ft., *L 3160*; Sheep Mountain, 12,200 ft., *D 2596*; Chiatovich Creek, 10,300 ft., *D 2575*.

3. **A. ludoviciana** Nutt.

A. Leaves entire to lobed, white-tomentose on both sides or floccose to green and glabrate above ....3a. ssp. *ludoviciana*
AA. Leaves parted into toothed lobes, commonly glabrate above and white-tomentose below but sometimes tomentose or glabrous throughout
3b. ssp. *incompta*

3a. Ssp. **ludoviciana**. Dry open places, desert scrub, 5500–6500 ft.: Toll House Springs, 5971 ft., *L 3331*; Cottonwood Creek, 6100 ft., *M 2161*.

3b. Ssp. **incompta** (Nutt.) Keck. Dry places, washes, roadsides, etc., desert scrub to alpine fell-fields, 6000–13,500 ft.: Birch Creek (Inyo Co.), 4.8 miles north of Deep Springs Valley Road, 6000 ft., *L 2984*; northeast slope of Sheep Mountain, 11,600 ft., *J & L Roos 5163* (RSA); McAfee Meadow, 12,000 ft., *Maguire & Holmgren 26082* (UC); White Mountain summit: 13,500 ft., *L 3249*.

4. **A. michauxiana** Besser. Dry streambeds, sandy washes, subalpine forest to alpine fell-fields, throughout the range, 9000–13,600 ft.: Sheep Mountain, 12,200 ft., *Jepson 7315* (JEPS); Cottonwood Creek: 9000 ft., *D 1598*; McAfee Meadow, 11,500 ft., *D 2834* (RSA); 3 miles south of Barcroft Lab, 11,500 ft., *Cook s.n.* (UC); White Mountain Peak, 13,600 ft., *J & L Roos 5143* (RSA).

5. **A. rothrockii** Gray. Uncommon, washes and slopes, subalpine forest to alpine fell-fields, 10,000–12,400 ft.: Crooked Creek Lab, 10,200 ft., *Tucker 2224* (DAV); Big Prospector Meadow, 10,500 ft., *J & L Roos 5099* (RSA); Pellisier Flats, above head of Indian Creek, 12,400 ft., *M 2205*; Davis Creek, 10,500 ft., *D 3110*.

6. **A. spinescens** D. C. Eat. Common locally, flats and slopes, desert scrub, 4200–6700 ft.: Westgard Pass, 4200 ft., *HM 21*; first canyon south of Silver Canyon, 5000 ft., *HM 697*; Silver Canyon, 6700 ft., *D s.n.* (CAS).

7. **A. tridentata** Nutt. Very common, slopes and flats, pinyon woodland to subalpine forest, throughout the range, 6000–10,800 ft.: Silver Canyon, 7000 ft., *M 2322;* White Mountain Road, 10,100 ft., *HM 670;* north of Crooked Creek Lab, 10,800 ft., *HM 890;* Cottonwood Creek, 9500 ft., *D 1654.*

28. Hymenopappus
1. **H. filifolius** Hook. var. **nanus** (Rydb.) Turner. Dry places, slopes and washes, 6000–10,000 ft.: Mollie Gibson Canyon, 7950 ft., *L 2940;* canyon off Black Canyon, 8000 ft., *M 2141.*

Tribe 5. SENECIONEAE
29. Arnica
A. Cauline leaves mostly 2–5-pairs, exclusive of those of the basal cluster.
B. Heads discoid . . . . 4. *A. parryi*
BB. Heads radiate . . . . 3. *A. mollis*
AA. Cauline leaves mostly 5–12 pairs.
B. Involucral bracts bearing tufts of long hairs near the tip; stems solitary; herbage ± villous-puberulent to villous-hirsute to minutely puberulent
1. *A. chamissonis*
BB. Involucral bracts not more hairy at tip than below; stems numerous; plants tufted . . . . 2. *A. longifolia*
1. **A. chamissonis** Less. ssp. **foliosa** (Nutt.) Maguire.

A. Herbage ± villous-puberulent to villous-hirsute; phyllaries narrow-obtuse; leaves not thin, minutely denticulate . . . . 1a. var. *foliosa*
AA. Herbage ± minutely puberulent; leaves thin, sharply denticulate
1b. var. *jepsoniana*

1a. Var. **foliosa.** Moist places, meadows, 9000–11,000 ft., subalpine forest: Crooked Creek Lab, 10,150 ft., *Blakley & Muller 3551* (JEPS); north fork, 10,500 ft., *Maguire & Holmgren 26149* (UC); meadow at head of Crooked Creek, 10,500 ft., *Maguire & Holmgren 26057.*
These plants are extremely variable in the White Mountains. The Maguire and Holmgren collections above show many characters which intergrade with var. **bernardina** (Greene) Jepson.
1b. Var. **jepsoniana** Maguire. Known from scattered dense patches in meadows and near streams, Chiatovich Creek, 8000 ft., *D 3100* (NY).
2. **A. longifolia** D.C. Eat. ssp. **myriadenia** (Piper) Maguire. Streamsides, wet places, subalpine forest in northern canyons: steep canyon in Lone Tree Creek, 9100 ft., *M 2254.*
3. **A. mollis** Hook. Reported by Munz in the supplement to *A California Flora* as occuring in the White Mountains.
4. **A. parryi** Gray ssp. **sonnei** (Greene) Maguire. Open meadows and along streams, Mono Co. north, 8000–10,000 ft.: Crooked Creek, 9900 ft., *L 3271;* Trail Canyon, ca. 8300 ft., *D 2499.*

30. Lepidospartum

1. **L. latisquamum** Wats. Frequent, open washes, dry slopes, desert scrub to pinyon woodland, Mono Co. south, 5500–7500 ft.: west side of Westgard Pass, 6000 ft., *J & L Roos 5082* (UC); east side of Westgard Pass, 6400 ft., *Wolf 3225* (UC); upper end of Marble Canyon, 7000 ft., *D 2853;* Silver Canyon, north fork at 7000 ft., *Wolf 2584* (UC).

31. Psathyrotes

A. Plants short-woolly and scurfy; outer involucral bracts ± oblong-obovate, the green tip 1.5–3 mm. wide . . . . .2. *P. ramosissima*
AA. Plants scurfy-pubescent, not woolly; outer involucral bracts nearly linear, the green tip 0.4–1.3 mm. wide . . . . .1. *P. annua*

1. **P. annua** (Nutt.) Gray. Uncommon, dry, often alkaline places, desert scrub throughout the range, below 6500 ft.: Silver Canyon, 5850 ft., *Alexander & Kellogg 4267* (UC); mouth of Pinchot Creek, 6500 ft., *D 3274.*
2. **P. ramosissima** (Torr.) Gray. Dry places, desert scrub, throughout the range, below 6300 ft.: Payson Canyon, 5913 ft., *L 2968;* Queen Valley at mouth of Queen Canyon, 6300 ft., *M 2743.*

32. Raillardella

1. **R. argentea** (Gray) Gray. Dry ridges, flats and meadows, alpine fell-fields, 11,500–12,600 ft.: meadow north of Sheep Mountain, 11,650 ft., *Jepson 7404* (JEPS); White Mountain Peak, 12,000 ft., *Shockley 449* (UC); ridge northwest of Mt. Barcroft, 12,600 ft., *HM 896.*

33. Senecio

A. Plants with leaves well distributed along the stem, basal leaves lacking.
  B. Leaves oblanceolate to lanceolate, 1–4 cm. wide . . . . .6. *S. serra*
  BB. Leaves narrowly linear, 0.5–5 mm. wide, dissected into lateral segments or leaves entire, linear and 1.5–5 mm. wide.
    C. Involucral bracts about 21, rarely 13; leaves ± divided into lateral segments . . . . .2. *S. douglasii*
    CC. Involucral bracts 13, sometimes 8; leaves rarely divided into lateral segments . . . . .7. *S. spartioides*
AA. Plants with mostly basal leaves.
  B. Fibrous-rooted perennial from a short erect crown; herbage hirsute to arachnoid-villous . . . . .3. *S. integerrimus*
  BB. Plants taprooted or fibrous-rooted from a single or branched caudex or rhizome.
    C. Leaves saliently dentate or rarely subentire; herbage tomentulose when young, ± glabrate with age . . . . .5. *S. scorzonella*
    CC. Leaves not saliently dentate.
      D. Basal leaves pinnatifid or lyrate-pinnatifid, commonly with toothed segments.

E. Plants glabrous except for small tufts of wool in leaf-axils; involucre 5–6 mm. high; rays ca. 13 . . . . .8. *S. stygius*
EE. Plants tomentulose, ± glabrous in age; involucre 6–8 mm. high; rays ca. 8 . . . . .4. *S. multilobatus*
DD. Basal leaves entire to subpinnately lobed.
E. Heads several; stems strongly white-tomentose . . . .1. *S. canus*
EE. Heads 1–6; stems thinly tomentulose or glabrate in age
9. *S. werneriaefolius*

1. **S. canus** Hook. Open rocky areas, pinyon woodland to subalpine forest, 7500–11,000 ft.: Wyman Creek, 7800 ft., *L 2768;* Crooked Creek, 3 miles east of the lab, 9700 ft., *HM 875;* ½ mile north of Crooked Creek Lab, 10,300 ft., *HM 548;* ¾ mile west of Barcroft gate, 11,000 ft., *HM 651.*
2. **S. douglasii** DC var. **monoensis** (Greene) Jeps. Dry washes, talus slopes, desert scrub to lower pinyon woodland, throughout the range, 5000–7000 ft.: Black Canyon, 5700 ft., *D s.n.;* Coldwater Canyon, *Brandegee s.n.* (UC); Silver Canyon, 5150 ft., *Alexander & Kellogg 4261* (UC); Silver Canyon, 6600 ft., *M 2004;* Cottonwood Creek, *Austin 126* (UC).
3. **S. integerrimus** Nutt.

A. Leaves subentire to toothed or slightly lobed; heads mostly few; involucre 7–12 mm. high, its bracts with pale or purplish tips; rays to 2 cm. long
3b. var. *major*
AA. Leaves entire to irregularly dentate; heads several or numerous; involucre 5–10 mm. high, its bracts black-tipped; rays 6–15 mm. long
3a. var. *exaltatus*

3a. Var. **exaltatus** (Nutt.) Cronq. Wet to dry meadows, pinyon woodland to subalpine forest, throughout the range, 7500–10,600 ft.: ½ mile southwest of Patriarch Road on White Mountain Road, 10,600 ft., *McHargue s.n.* (RSA); Crooked Creek Ranger Station, 9800 ft., *D 1580;* Indian Creek, 7500 ft., *Lankester 853* (BM); Chiatovich Creek, 8000 ft., *D 3063.*
3b. Var. **major** (Gray) Cronq. Hillsides, locally common, subalpine forest and alpine fell-fields, 10,000–12,000 ft.: Crooked Creek, 10,000 ft., *J & L Roos 5870* (RSA); Campito Meadow, 10,200 ft., *Jepson 7293* (JEPS); Sheep Mountain, 11,800 ft., *Jepson 7392* (JEPS); McAfee Meadow, 11,700 ft., *Jepson 7401* (JEPS).
4. **S. multilobatus** Torr. & Gray. Frequent, dry places, desert scrub to subalpine forest, throughout the range, 6500–10,500 ft.: Westgard Pass, 6500 ft., *L 2905;* hill west of head of Wyman Creek, 10,500 ft., *HM 527;* Crooked Creek, 9300 ft., *HM 93;* northwest corner of Sagehen Flat, 10,250 ft., *L 3154;* Cottonwood Creek, 9700 ft., *L 2911;* Chiatovich Flats, 10,300 ft., *D 2558.*
5. **S. scorzonella** Greene. Dry places to moist meadows, subalpine forest to alpine fell-fields, 9800–11,700 ft.: Silver Canyon, 9850 ft., *L 2886;* near cave, Crooked Creek, 10,000 ft., *L 3087;* Cottonwood Creek, 11,700 ft., *D 2591.*

6. **S. serra** Hook. Uncommon, damp places, meadows, etc., pinyon woodland to subalpine forest, throughout the range, 8000–10,300 ft.: Roberts Ranch, Wyman Creek, 8000 ft., *D 3134;* White Mountain Road at road to Crooked Creek. 10,300 ft., *Cook s.n.* (UC); Cottonwood Creek, 8700 ft., *D 2581*

7. **S. spartioides** Torr. & Gray. Sporadically common, dry slopes and meadows, pinyon woodland to subalpine forest, 8000–10,400 ft.: meadow ½ mile westsouthwest of Crooked Creek Lab, 10,200 ft., *L 3148;* Big Prospector Meadow, 10,400 ft., *J & L Roos 5102* (RSA); south of flat above Big Meadows, Chiatovich Creek, ca. 8000 ft., *D 3364;* Trail Canyon at fork to Boundary Peak, ca. 8600 ft., *D 3355.*

8. **S. stygius** Greene. Rare, known only from Chiatovich Creek at 7500 ft., meadows in damp soil, *D 2785.*

9. **S. werneriaefolius** Gray. Wet slopes, alpine fell-fields, known only from Sheep Mountain area, 11,400–12,000 ft.: Sheep Meadow, 11,400 ft., *HM 846;* Sheep Mountain, 12,000 ft., *D 2600.*

34. Tetradymia

A. Achenes with long, soft white hairs, nearly equaling or concealing the pappus; primary leaves modified into slender rigid spines, 2–3 cm. long; heads peduncled . . . . .1. *T. axillaris*
AA. Achenes glabrous or villous, the hairs much shorter than the pappus.
    B. Primary leaves mostly 5–10 mm. long, subulate; secondary leaves fasciculate; leaves early glabrate and greenish . . . . .3. *T. glabrata*
    BB. Primary leaves 10–20 mm. long, linear to lance-linear rarely fasciculate, white-tomentose . . . . .2. *T. canescens*

1. **T. axillaris** A. Nels. Dry slopes and flats, desert scrub, below 6000 ft.: 2.9 miles east of Big Pine on Westgard Pass Road, 4200 ft., *HM 1;* 5.4 miles west of White Mountain Road, Westgard Pass, 5900 ft., *L 2677;* Black Canyon, 5700 ft., *D. s.n.;* Silver Canyon, 5000 ft., *M 2003.*

2. **T. canescens** DC. Frequent, dry slopes and flats, pinyon woodland to subalpine forest, throughout the range, 7000–10,000 ft.: 2 miles below Roberts Ranch, Wyman Creek, 8000 ft., *D 1713;* 4.8 miles east of Crooked Creek Lab, 9500 ft., *Bacigalupi et al 8078* (JEPS); near Trail Canyon, 7200 ft., *D 2528.*

3. **T. glabrata** Gray. Dry, gravelly hillsides and alluvium, especially Inyo Co., desert scrub, below 6000 ft.: Westgard Pass, 5900 ft., 5.4 miles west of White Mountain Road, *L 2682.* Black Canyon, 5700 ft., *D s.n.;* first canyon north of Silver Canyon, 5200 ft., *HM 202.*

Tribe 6. INULEAE
35. Antennaria

A. Terminal portion of outer phyllaries blackish-green or brown.
    B. Tips of phyllaries blackish-green, acute . . . . .1. *A. alpina*
    BB. Tips of phyllaries brownish, obtuse . . . . .3. *A. umbrinella*
AA. Terminal portion of outer phyllaries white or rose . . . . .2. *A. rosea*

1. **A. alpina** (L.) Gaertn. var. **media** (Greene) Jeps. Sporadically common

on meadows and flats, upper subalpine forest to alpine fell-fields, throughout the range, 11,500–13,000 ft.: northeast slope of Sheep Mountain, 12,100 ft., *M 2224;* head of Cottonwood Creek, 11,700 ft., *D 2594;* McAfee Meadow 12,000 ft., *D 1667;* southeast of White Mountain Peak, 13,000 ft., *HM 523;* south slope of Mt. DuBois, Pellisier Flats, *M 2189.*

2. **A. rosea** Greene. Common, dry places to around springs and damp places, pinyon woodland to subalpine forest and occasionally higher, throughout the range, 6000–10,000 (11,000) ft.: Cottonwood Creek, 8900 ft., *L 2930;* Indian Creek, ca. 6000 ft., *Lankester 751* (BM); Chiatovich Creek, 8900 ft., *M 2091;* Trail Canyon, 8300 ft., *D 2517*

3. **A. umbrinella** Rydb. Meadows, subalpine forest to alpine fell-fields, 9500–12,500 ft.: Crooked Creek Ranger Station, 9500 ft., *D 1570;* south of Sheep Meadow, 11,800 ft., *HM 573;* hill above McAfee Meadow, 12,500 ft., *Tucker 2258* (DAV); Barcroft Lab, 12,500 ft., *Cook s.n.* (UC).

36. Gnaphalium

A.   Heads or glomerules not leafy-bracted; corollas yellow; basal leaves 2–9.5 cm. long; heads 180–230-flowered with involucres 4–6 mm. high

1. *G. chilense*

AA. Heads or glomerules leafy-bracted; corollas whitish; leaves 0.5–4.5 cm. long; heads 120–130-flowered; ca. 3 mm. high. . . . . 2. *G. palustre*

1. **G. chilense** Spreng. Uncommon, wet places at lower elevations throughout the range: upper spring, Marble Canyon, 7000 ft., *D 2889.*

2. **G. palustre** Nutt. Rare, damp streambanks: Chiatovich Creek, ca. 8000 ft., *D s.n.*

Tribe 7. EUPATORIEAE
37. Brickellia

A.   Plants 5–9 dm. high; leaves ovate-lanceolate, 3.0–9.0 cm. long; heads 3–5-flowered . . . . .1. *B. multiflora*

AA. Plants 1–5 dm. high; leaves elliptic to oval, 1–4 cm. long; heads 40–50-flowered . . . . .2. *B. oblongifolia*

1. **B. multiflora** Kell. Common, dry washes and streamsides, desert scrub to pinyon woodland, Inyo Co., 4300–7000 ft.: Black Canyon at Marble Canyon, 5600 ft., *D 3019;* Silver Canyon, 4800 ft., *Wolf 2604* (UC); Silver Canyon, 4.6 miles east of Laws, 7000 ft., *Munz 12681* (RSA).

2. **B. oblongifolia** Nutt. var. **linifolia** (D.C. Eat.) Rob. Rocky canyon washes, desert scrub to pinyon woodland, 6000–7000 ft.: Westgard Pass, 6500 ft., *McHargue s.n.* (RSA); Birch Creek, 4.8 miles north of Deep Springs Valley Road, 6000 ft., *L 2985.*

38. Eupatorium

1. **E. occidentale** Hook. Rocky areas in northern canyons: Lone Tree Creek, 8400 ft., *M 2243;* also observed in Milner Creek.

Tribe 8. CYNAREAE
39. Cirsium

A. Plants acaulescent ....1. *C. drummondii*
AA. Plants caulescent.
   B. Flowers pinkish or light red; phyllaries with a definite dorsal glutinous
      ridge; leaves with white-arachnoid tomentum........2. *C. mohavense*
   BB. Flowers light red-purple; phyllaries with a faint dorsal glutinous ridge;
      leaves with thin arachnoid tomentum, sometimes deciduous above
                              3. *C. nidulum*

1. **C. drummondii** Torr. & Gray. Frequent, meadows, desert scrub to subalpine forest, throughout the range, 5700-10,150 ft.: Black Canyon, 5700
ft., *D s.n.;* Wyman Creek, 8300 ft., *L 2800;* east end of Crooked Creek Road,
9000 ft., *HM 102;* Crooked Creek Lab, 10,150 ft., *Blakley & Muller 3558*
(UC); Trail Canyon, 8300 ft., *D 2504.*

2. **C. mohavense** (Greene) Petr. Moist places, canyons of Inyo Co., below
7000 ft., upper end of Marble Canyon, 7000 ft., *D 2852;* Silver Canyon, 5100
ft., *L 2829;* Silver Canyon, 7000 ft., *D 1510* (JEPS).

3. **C. nidulum** (Jones) Petr. Rocky washes and hillsides, pinyon woodland
to subalpine forest, Mono Co. south, 7000–10,400 ft.: Payson Canyon, 7000
ft., *Lankester 868* (BM); Wyman Creek: 7100 ft., *L 2776;* 10,000 ft., *D 2619;*
½ mile south of Crooked Creek Lab on White Mountain Road, 10,400 ft.,
HM 550-A.

Tribe 9. CICHORIEAE
40. Agoseris

A. Flowers orangish or pinkish, drying purple; ligules 6–9 mm. long
                              1 *A. aurantiaca*
AA. Flowers yellow, drying pinkish or purple; ligules 7–14 mm. long
                              2. *A. glauca*

1. **A. aurantiaca** (Hook.) Greene. Known only from Roberts Ranch, Wyman
Creek, 8000 ft., *D 3150* (JEPS).

2. **A. glauca** (Pursh) Greene.

A. Ligules mostly 11–14 mm. long; achene-beak 4.5–9.0 mm. long; pappus
    14–17 mm. long ....2a. var. *laciniata*
AA. Ligules mostly 7–9 mm. long; achene-beak 0–4.5 mm. long; pappus 10–
    15 mm. long ....2b. var. *monticola*

2a. Var. **laciniata** (D.C. Eat.) Smiley. White Mountain Road at Wyman
Creek, 10,000 ft., *Cook s.n.* (UC). The characters of this variety intergrade with
those of the following:

2b. Var. **monticola** (Greene) Q. Jones. Frequent, in and around meadows,
throughout the range, 7500–12,800 ft.: head of Wyman Creek, 10,500 ft., *J.
& L. Roos 5896* (RSA); edge of Reed Flat, 10,300 ft., *Munz 21016* (UC);
Crooked Creek Lab, 10,200 ft., *Cook s.n.* (UC); intersection of Poison and

Cottonwood creeks, 9450 ft., *L 2917;* Pellisier Flats, 12,800 ft., *M 2213;* Chiatovich Creek, 7500 ft., *D 2770;* Chiatovich Creek, 10,800 ft., *M 2100;* Trail Canyon, 8300 ft., *D 2502.*

41. Anisocoma
1. **A. acaulis** Torr. & Gray. Washes and sandy places, scattered throughout, below 7000 ft.: near Trail Canyon, 7000 ft., *D s.n.;* also collected west of Laws.

42. Calycoseris
1. **C. parryi** Gray. Washes and slopes, desert scrub, below 6500 ft.: west base of Westgard Pass, 4500–5000 ft., *HM 787;* Black Canyon, 5700 ft., *D s.n.;* road between Deep Springs Valley and Oasis, 6374 ft., *J. & H. Grinnell 1051a* (UC); first canyon south of Silver Canyon, 5000 ft., *HM 719.*

43. Chaetadelpha
1. **C. wheeleri** Gray. On alluvium, lower elevations at base of the range: directly below old Devernois Ranch, 4800 ft., *Peirson 12457* (RSA).

44. Crepis
A. Stems and leaves glabrous or glandular-hispid; cauline leaves reduced to bracts . . . . .3. *C. runcinata*
AA. Stems and leaves tomentose; cauline leaves few and reduced above.
B. Stems 1–4 dm .high; achenes 10 18-ribbed; heads 12–30-flowered
                                   2. *C. occidentalis*
BB. Stems 3–7 dm. high; achenes 10–12-ribbed; heads mostly 7–12-flowered . . . . .1. *C. intermedia*

1. **C. intermedia** Gray. Frequent, dry slopes and moist areas, desert scrub to subalpine forest, throughout the range, 6000–10,000 ft.: White Mountain Road, 8800 ft., *HM 347;* north of Schulman Grove, 10,000 ft., *HM 377;* Silver Canyon, 7100 ft., *L 2858;* head of Wyman Creek, 9750 ft., *HM 318;* Crooked Creek Ranger Station, 9500 ft., *D M125;* Poison Creek at Cottonwood Creek, 9450 ft., *L 3135;* Chiatovich Creek, 8000 ft., *D 2894.*

2. **C. occidentalis** Nutt.

A. Herbage with some glandular-pubescence; inner phyllaries 8–13
                              2a. ssp. *occidentalis*
AA. Herbage without glandular-pubescence; inner phyllaries 8 .2a. ssp. *pumila*

2a. **Ssp. occidentalis.** Dry rocky places, 6500–8000 ft.: Trail Canyon: 6500 ft., *Jaeger s.n.* (RSA); at first saddle on way to B & B Mine, 7600–8000 ft., *D 3257.*

2b. **Ssp. pumila** (Rydb.) Babc. & Stebb. Westgard Pass region in pinyon woodland: above "The Narrows," Westgard Pass, 6800 ft., *L 2754;* 1 mile east of Westgard Pass, *Kerr s.n.* (RSA).

172

3. **C. runcinata** Torr. & Gray. ssp. **hallii** Babc. & Stebb. Alkaline spots, open spots in sage or meadows, desert scrub to pinyon woodland, 4500–8300 ft.: Benton, *Hall 12281* (UC) (TYPE); Trail Canyon, 8300 ft., *D 2501.*

45. Glyptopleura

1. **G. marginata** D.C. Eat. Open areas, northeastern canyons and flats, ca. 6500 ft.: north of Pinyon Hill, 6500 ft., *D 2760;* mouth of Pinchot Creek, 6500 ft., *D 3264.*

46. Lactuca

1. **L. serriola** L. var. **integrata** Gren. & Godr. Occasional weed: Toll House Springs, 5971 ft., *L 3334.*

47. Lygodesmia

A. Perennial with rigid spine-tipped branches; pappus bristles 6–10 mm. long . . . .**2. *L. spinosa***
AA. Annual, without spine-tipped branches; pappus-bristles 2–2.5 mm. long
1. *L. exigua*

1. **L. exigua** Gray. Dry places, desert scrub, especially of Inyo Co., below 5000 ft.: west base of Westgard Pass, 4500–5000 ft., *HM 796;* first canyon south of Silver Canyon, 5000 ft., *HM 728;* Silver Canyon, 4600 ft., *D 3451.*
2. **L. spinosa** Nutt. Dry places, washes, roadsides, etc., desert scrub to pinyon woodland, 5000–8800 ft.: Westgard Pass, 7000 ft., *HM 396;* Marble Canyon at upper spring, 7000 ft., *D 2884;* White Mountain Road, 8800 ft., *HM 345;* Wyman Creek, 8500 ft., *M 2264.*

48. Malacothrix

1. **M. sonchoides** (Nutt.) Torr. & Gray. Scattered, dry places, desert scrub to lower pinyon woodland, 4900–7000 ft.: near Pinyon Hill, 7000 ft., *D M37;* Pinchot Creek, ca. 6500 ft., *D s.n.;* also known from Fish Lake Valley at 4900 ft.

49. Sonchus

1. **S. asper** L. Weed in riparian areas, 4500–7000 ft.: Toll House Springs, 5971 ft., *L 2700;* Antelope Springs, 5600 ft., *L 3014;* Silver Canyon, 4600 ft., *D s.n..*

50. Stephanomeria

A. Perennial from a woody base . . . .**2. *S. pauciflora***
AA. Annual or rarely biennial . . . .**1. *S. exigua***

1. **S. exigua** Nutt.
A. Pappus-bristles 8–18; stems pale bluish-green. . . . .**1a. var. *exigua***
AA. Pappus-bristles 5-8; stems whitish . . . .**1b. var. *pentachaeta***

1a. Var. **exigua**. Dry places, hillsides, etc., throughout the range, 5000–7500 ft.: west of Westgard Pass, 7300 ft., *D 2874;* Payson Canyon, 5913 ft., *L 2970.*

1b. Var. **pentachaeta** (D.C. Eat.) Hall. Dry places, desert scrub: mouth of Birch Creek, 5050 ft., *L 2971.*

2. **S. pauciflora** (Torr.) Nutt. Desert slopes and washes, 4500–6000 ft.: west base of Westgard Pass, 4500–5000 ft., *HM 779;* Westgard Pass, 5500 ft., *HM 189;* ridge north of Silver Canyon, 5800 ft., *HM 198.*

51. Taraxacum

1. **T. officinale** Wiggers. Weed, throughout the range, below 11,500 ft.: Silver Canyon, 9850 ft., *L 2879;* Wyman Creek, 8300 ft., *L 2791;* Campito Meadow, 11,000 ft., *Tucker 3427* (DAV); Trail Canyon, 8300 ft., *D 2525.*

MONOCOTYLEDONEAE
FAMILY 66. JUNCACEAE

A. Stems filled with papery or spongy pith (sometimes flattened); leaf-sheaths free at margin . . . . .1. *Juncus*

AA. Stems hollow; leaf-sheaths united at the margin . . . . .2. *Luzula*

1. Juncus

A. Inflorescence appearing lateral to the stem, the lowest bract terete, ungrooved and stemlike above it.

B. Flowers 1–3 (5), seeds tailed . . . . .9. *J. parryi*

BB. Flowers many, seeds not tailed.

C. Upper leaf-sheaths with well-developed blades; stems compressed
5. *J. mexicanus*

CC. Upper leaf-sheaths without blades; stems usually terete . . . .
. . . . .1. *J. balticus*

AA. Inflorescence appearing terminal; lowest bract grooved if extending beyond it.

B. Leaf–blades flat, the surface facing the stem . . . . .8. *J. orthophyllus*

BB. Leaf-blades terete or if flat, with edge facing the stem.

C. Blades terete or slightly compressed.

D. Anthers shorter than filaments.

E. Stem 4–10 dm. high; perianth brownish to greenish
11. *J. torreyi*

EE. Stems 1–3 dm. high; perianth brown to black . 4. *J. mertensianus*

DD. Anthers equaling, or longer than filaments.

E. Capsule narrowed into a long beak, well exserted when mature
7. *J. nodosus*

EE. Capsule contracted, not well exserted.

F. Heads single, purplish-black, with spathelike bract
4. *J. mertensianus*

FF. Heads 1–many, brownish with narrow bract . . 6. *J. nevadensis*
CC. Blades flat with edge facing the stem.
 D.   Anthers longer than filaments . . . . 3. *J. macrandrus*
 DD. Anthers shorter than filaments.
  E. Auricles of leaves present, small . . . . 10. *J. saximontanus*
  EE. Auricles absent.
   F.   Stamens usually 6; leaves 3–12 mm. wide . . 12. *J. xiphioides*
   FF. Stamens usually 3; leaves 2–5 mm. wide . . . . . 2. *J. ensifolius*

1. **J. balticus** Willd. Common, streams and meadows, desert scrub to alpine, throughout the range, 5000–12,500 ft.: Toll House Springs, 5971 ft., *L 2720;* Antelope Springs, 5600 ft., *L 2990;* Wyman Creek, 8300 ft., *L 2789;* roadside below Barcroft Lab, 12,450 ft., *Bacigalupi et al. 8165* (JEPS); Chiatovich Creek; 7500 ft., *D s.n.* (RSA); 8000 f., *D 2565.*

2. **J. ensifolius** Wikstr. Known only from Antelope Springs, 5600 ft., *Raven 7038* (CAS).

3. **J. macrandrus** Cov. Sporadic, pinyon woodland in wet places: Black Canyon Spring, 8400 ft., *D 1746;* Trail Canyon, 8300 ft., *D 2515.*

4. **J. mertensianus** Bong. Occasional, moist places, throughout the range, below 11,500 ft.: McAfee Creek, 11,500 ft., *L 3313; L 3322.*

5. **J. mexicanus** Willd. Common, riparian areas, throughout the range, below 12,000 ft.: 3 miles east of Crooked Creek Lab, 9600 ft., *HM 881;* Sagehen Flat, 10,500 ft., *HM 538;* McClouds Camp, Cottonwood Creek, 9500 ft., *D 1609;* south of McAfee Creek, 11,900 ft., *HM 618;* Chiatovich Creek, 8400 ft., *M 2084.*

6. **J. nevadensis** Wats. Occasional, wet places, streambanks, below 10,000 ft.: Cottonwood Creek, 9700 ft., *HM 249.*

7. **J. nodosus** L. Rare. Known only from Antelope Springs, 5600 ft., *L 3024.*

8. **J. orthophyllus** Cov. Streamsides, northern canyons, 6000–8000 ft.: Indian Creek, 6000 ft., *Lankester 780* (BM); Chiatovich Creek, 8000 ft., *D 2570.*

9. **J. parryi** Engelm. Rocky areas, roadsides, meadows, 10,900–12,000 ft.: east base of Sheep Mountain, 10,900 ft., *Bacigalupi et al. 8197* (JEPS); northeast of Piute Trail Pass, 11,800 ft., *L 3287;* McAfee Creek, 11,800 ft., *HM 610.*

10. **J. saximontanus** A. Nels. Infrequent, marshes, streambeds, below 6500 ft.: Antelope Springs, 5600 ft., *L 2989;* Black Canyon, 6200 ft., *M 2121.*

11. **J. torreyi** Cov. Known only from Antelope Springs, 5600 ft., *L 2992.*

12. **J. xiphioides** E. Mey. Known only from Silver Canyon, streambank at 7000 ft., *M 2462.*

2. Luzula

1. **L. spicata** (L.) DC: Alpine meadows and cirques, Mono Co. north, 11,500–12,500 ft.: south of Barcroft Lab, 12,200 ft., *HM 663.*

FAMILY 67. CYPERACEAE

A.   Flowers perfect, or perfect and male; achenes naked.
 B.   Style-base deciduous from the summit of the achene; involucral leaves

present . . . . .3. *Scirpus*
BB. Style-base persistent as a tubercle on the summit of the achene; invo-
lucral leaves absent . . . . .2. *Eleocharis*
AA. Flowers all unisexual; achenes surrounded by a perigynium. . . .1. *Carex*

1. Carex
(Key to species by John Thomas Howell)
A. Spikelet one on each culm, androgynous or unisexual.
  B. Perigynia lightly–densely pubescent . . . . .10. *C. filifolia*
  BB. Perigynia glabrous.
    C. Pistillate scales 1-nerved, covering the 3.5–4.0 mm. long perigynia
23. *C. subnigricans*
    CC. Pistillate scales 3-nerved, much smaller than the 5–6.5 mm. inflat-
ed perigynia . . . . .4. *C. breweri*
AA. Spikelets several to many on each culm (rarely 2).
  B. Styles 2, achenes lenticular.
    C. Spikelets sessile, short, with few perigynia.
      D. Spikelets androgynous, or if unisexual, then the plants dioecious.
        E. Plants open or ± cespitose; rootstocks long, creeping.
          F. Spikelets in dense ± globose heads . . . . . .25. *C. vernacula*
          FF. Spikelets in elongated heads or spikes.
            G. Spikelets generally unisexual, the plant ± dioecious.
              H. Beak of the perigynium from ½ to as long as the body.
                I. Culms less than 2 dm. long, ± smooth; leaves folded,
involute near apex . . . . .6. *C. douglasii*
                11. Culms more than 2 dm. long, ± roughened above,
leaves flat or canaliculate . . . . .20. *C. praegracilis*
              HH. Beak of perigynium ⅓ as long as the body or less
7. *C. eleocharis*
            GG. Spikelets androgynous . . . . .5. *C. dispersum*
        EE. Plants cespitose, rootstock not long and creeping.24. *C. vallicola*
      DD. Spikelets gynaecandrous.
        E. Perigynia visible in the spikelets, the subtending scales shorter.
          F. Perigynia strongly flattened, thin.
            G. Perigynium margin undulate, beak flattened and serrulate,
margined to top . . . . .22. *C. straminiformis*
            GG. Perigynium margin not undulate, beak terete and smooth
at the tip, or rarely ± flattened.
              H. Perigynia lanceolate to lance-ovate, the margin narrow
17. *C. microptera*
              HH. Perigynia ovate (rarely lanceolate), the margin broad
to the base
                I. Culms erect, 3–10 dm. tall . . . . .9. *C. festivella*
                II. Culms decumbent, 1–3 dm. . . . . .12. *C. haydeniana*
          FF. Perigynia plano-convex, thickish . . . . .1. *C. abrupta*
        EE. Perigynia covered, ± concealed by scales.

    F.   Perigynia 1 mm. wide or less, narrowly margined
                       16. *C. leporinella*
    FF. Perigynia 1.5–2.3 mm. wide, conspicuously margined . . . . . .
. . . . .19. *C. phaeocephala*
CC. Spikelets stalked, or if the lateral spikelets are sessile, then elongate
    with many perigynia.
    D.   Lowest bract long-sheathing; perigynia beakless.
      E.   Perigynia granular and whitish, pulverulent at maturity, not
         fleshy . . . . .11. *C. hassei*
      EE. Perigynia not granular or pulverulent, fleshy . . . . . .3. *C. aurea*
    DD. Lowest bract ± sheathless; perigynia short-beaked
                       18. *C. nebrascensis*
BB. Styles 3 or 4; achenes triangular or quadrangular.
    C.   Perigynia pubescent.
      D.   Achenes with sides convex above . . . . .21. *C. rossii*
      DD. Achenes with sides flat or convex . . . . .15. *C. lanuginosa*
    CC. Perigynia glabrous.
      D.   Perigynium or beak granular-roughened . . . . . . .2. *C. albonigra*
      DD. Perigynium smooth or puncticulate.
        E.   Spikelets closely approximate; pistillate scales longer than the
          perigynia . . . . .13. *C. helleri*
        EE. Spikelets discrete or separate, at least the lower; pistillate scales
          equalling the perigynia or shorter.
          F.   Pistillate scales with ± obsolete midvein; perigynia 3–4.5
            mm. long . . . . .8. *C. epapillosa*
          FF. Pistillate scales with conspicuous midvein; perigynia 2.5–3.5
            long . . . . .14. *C. heteroneura*

1. **C. abrupta** Mkze. Occasional, riparian areas, 5000–9500 ft.: McClouds Camp, Cottonwood Creek, 9500 ft., *D 1608;* Birch Creek (Mono Co.), 5800 ft., *D 3481;* Trail Canyon, 8300 ft., *D 2514.*

2. **C. albonigra** Mkze. Sporadic, rocky slopes and meadows, alpine, 11,500–13,000 ft.: meadow west of White Mountain Road, northeast slope of Sheep Mountain, 11,800 ft, *L 3262;* Pellisier Flats, around frost polygons, 12,800 ft., *M 2275.*

3. **C. aurea** Nutt. Wet places, grassy streambeds, east-facing canyons, 6000 to 9500 ft.: Crooked Creek, 9400 ft., *M 2260;* Indian Creek, 6000 ft., *Lankester 781* (BM).

4. **C. breweri** Boott. Known only from McAfee Meadow, 11,800 ft., *HM 613.*

5. **C. disperma** Dewey. Known only from Chiatovich Creek, submerged in water around springs, 7500 ft., *D 2774.*

6. **C. douglasii** Boott. Common meadow plant, pinyon woodland to alpine fell-fields, throughout the range, 6000–12,500 ft.: Wyman Creek, 8300 ft., *L 2798;* Crooked Creek Lab, 10,200 ft., *L 3112;* Indian Creek, 6000 ft., *Lankester 708* (BM).

7. **C. eleocharis** Bailey. High meadows, Mono Co. north, 11,500–13,500 ft.: McAfee Meadow, 11,700 ft., *D s.n.;* south of Piute Trail, *HM 640;* south fork, Perry Aikin Creek, 13,000 ft., *HM 636;* White Mountain Peak, 13,500 ft., *L 3257;* Pellisier Flats, 13,000 ft., *M 2170.*

8. **C. epapillosa** Mkze. Known only from McAfee Meadow, along stream, 11,500 ft., *L 3321.*

9. **C. festivella** Mkze. Meadows and streamsides, throughout the range, 4900–10,100 ft.: Fish Lake Valley, 4900 ft., *Lankester 770* (BM); Crooked Creek Lab, 10,100 ft., *L 3106;* Indian Creek, 6000 ft., *Lankester 741* (BM).

10. **C. filifolia** Nutt. Known only from pine stands near wet meadows, head of Cottonwood Creek, 11,700 ft., *D 2589.*

11. **C. hassei** Bailey. Sporadic, meadows, pinyon woodland to subalpine forest, 7500–10,000 ft.: Crooked Creek Ranger Station, 9500 ft., *D 1574;* Chiatovich Creek, 7500 ft., *D M35.*

12. **C. haydeniana** Olney. Meadows, subalpine forest to alpine, 10,000–13,400 ft.: Crooked Creek, 10,150 ft., *Blakley & Muller 3552* (RSA); Sheep Meadow, 11,400 ft., *HM 841;* White Mountain Peak, 13,400 ft., *HM 502.*

13. **C. helleri** Mkze. Abundant, rocky slopes and flats, throughout the range, 11,400–13,500 ft.: Sheep Meadow, 11,400 ft., *HM 844;* north fork, Cottonwood Creek, 12,000 ft., *Maguire & Holmgren 26101* (UC); McAfee Meadow, 12,000 ft., *D 1677;* Pellisier Flats, southeast of Mt. DuBois, 13,200 ft., *M 2171.*

14. **C. heteroneura** Boott. Occasional, rocky slopes and meadows, alpine, 11,500–13,100 ft.: northeast of Piute Trail Pass, 11,800 ft., *L 3286;* White Mountain Peak, 13,100 ft., *D 2617.*

15. **C. lanuginosa** Michx. Moist places, sporadic throughout the range, 7500–9700 ft.: Roberts Ranch, Wyman Creek, 8000 ft., *M 2054;* Cottonwood Creek, 9700 ft., *HM 250;* Chiatovich Creek, 7500 ft., *D s.n.*

16. **C. leporinella** Mkze. Known only from streamside near cave, Crooked Creek, 10,000 ft., *L 3071; L 3090.*

17. **C. microptera** Mkze. Sporadic, in moist creekbeds, Mono Co. north, 5800–12,600 ft.: plateau north of Barcroft Lab, 12,600 ft., *Bacigalupi et al. 8132* (JEPS); Birch Creek (Mono Co.), 5800 ft., *D 3481.*

18. **C. nebrascensis** Dewey. Moist places, meadows, springs, throughout the range, 5500–8500 ft.: Toll House Springs, *L 2716a;* Antelope Springs, 5600 ft., *L 3025;* Wyman Creek, 8300 ft., *L 2784;* Trail Canyon, 8300 ft., *D 2511.*

19. **C. phaeocephala** Piper. Slopes and meadows, 9000–12,700 ft.: Crooked Creek, 9000 ft., *HM 103;* McAfee Meadow, 12,200 ft., *HM 557;* plateau north of Barcroft Lab, 12,600 ft., *Bacigalupi et al. 8133* (JEPS).

20. **C. praegracilis** Boott. Moist canyons, alkaline places, springs, below 9500 ft.: Toll House Springs, 6000 ft., *Raven 6998* (CAS); Alkali Marsh, Deep Springs Lake, 4800 ft., *D 3299;* McClouds Camp, Cottonwood Creek, 9500 ft., *D 1607.*

21. **C. rossii** Boott. Meadows and flats, 9000–12,000 ft.; Crooked Creek, 9900 ft., *HM 817;* south end, Sagehen Flat, 10,000 ft., *HM 900;* northeast of Piute Trail Pass, 11,800 ft., *L 3288.*

22. **C. straminiformis** Bailey. Known only from Crooked Creek, streambed near cave, 10,000 ft., *L 3225.*

23. **C. subnigricans** Stacey. Locally abundant, forming extensive turf in meadows and flats, throughout the alpine, above 11,000 ft.: north fork, Cottonwood Creek, 11,500 ft., *Maguire & Holmgren 26098* (CAS); north of Barcroft Lab, 13,100 ft., *HM 632;* around polygons, Pellisier Flats, 12,800 ft., *M 2274.*

24. **C. vallicola** Dewey. Known only from moist slopes of north-facing canyon, about ¼ mile above Cottonwood Creek, 9200 ft., *M 2029.*

25. **C. vernacula** Bailey. Meadows, late snow melt areas, alpine fell-fields, 11,500 ft.: McAfee Creek, 11,500 ft., *L 3310;* Barcroft Lab, 13,100 ft., *HM 631;* Pellisier Flats, southeast of Mt. DuBois, 13,200 ft., *M & L 2171* (CAS).

26. **C. subfusca** Boott. Reported by Munz (supplement to *A California Flora*) as from the White Mountains.

2. Eleocharis

A.   Flowers fewer than 8 per spikelet . . . . .2. *E. pauciflorus*
AA. Flowers 10 or more per spikelet.
  B.   Tubercle short-subulate to conic, not continuous with achene apex
                                            1. *E. parishii*
  BB. Tubercle long-subulate, continuous with achene apex . . .3. *E. rostellata*

1. **E. parishii** Britt. Known only from Antelope Springs, 5600 ft., *L 3006.*

2. **E. pauciflorus** (Lightf.) Link. Meadows and springs, pinyon woodland to alpine, throughout the range, 6000–11,800 ft.: Crooked Creek Lab, 10,100 ft., *L 3116;* Sheep Meadow, 11,400 ft., *HM 845;* northeast of Sheep Mountain, 11,800 ft., *L 3261;* Cottonwood Creek, McClouds Camp, 9500 ft., *D 1606;* Trail Canyon: 8000 ft., *D 2703.*

3. **E. rostellata** (Torr.)) Torr. Wet places, springs, streamsides, below 8000 ft.: Antelope Springs, 5600 ft., *L 2994;* Wyman Creek, 7300 ft., *M 2043.*

3. Scirpus

A.   Involucral leaves 2–5 . . . . .2. *S. microcarpus*
AA. Involucral leaf solitary.
  B.   Culms leafy, sharply triangular . . . . .3. *S. olneyi*
  BB. Culm leaves reduced to basal sheaths; culms terete, hollow . .1. *S. acutus*

1. **S. acutus** Muhl. Known only from spring, just north of Black Canyon at 4800 ft. (cattle watering place), *M 2075.*

2. **S. microcarpus** Presl. Sporadic, swampy wet places along streams, below 8000 ft.: Cottonwood Creek, 5600 ft., *M 2164;* Marble Creek (Nevada), 5500 ft., *Lankester 825* (BM); Chiatovich Creek, 8000 ft., *D 2571.*

3. **S. olneyi** Gray. Known only from Antelope Springs, 5600 ft., in marsh, *L 2991; L 3004.*

FAMILY 68. GRAMINEAE

KEY TO TRIBES

A.   Spikelets sessile; inflorescence of one to several spikes.
  B.   Spikes asymmetrical, with spikelets only along one side 6. *Chlorideae*
  BB. Spikes ± symmetrical, with spikelets on two or more sides.
    C.   Glumes falling with the spikelets .... 5. *Zoysieae*
    CC. Glumes persistent, not falling with the spikelets, the entire rachis somewhat articulating .... 2. *Hordeae*
AA. Spikelets stalked, not sessile; the inflorescence a loose-to-compact panicle or raceme.
  B.   Glumes falling with the spikelets .... 4. *Agrostideae*
  BB. Glumes persistent, not falling with spikelets.
    C.   Spikelets 1-flowered .... 4. *Agrostideae*
    CC. Spikelets 2- to many-flowered.
      D.   Lemmas usually shorter than the glumes; awns dorsal. 3. *Aveneae*
      DD. Lemmas exceeding glumes; awns terminal or dorsal.. 1. *Festuceae*

Tribe 1. FESTUCEAE

A.   Plants reedlike, stout and tall .... 8. *Phragmites*
AA. Plants not reedlike, low.
  B.   Plants dioecious.
    C.   Plants densely tufted; dry slopes .... 6. *Hesperochloa*
    CC. Plants not densely tufted; alkaline soils .... 3. *Distichlis*
  BB. Plants monoecious.
    C.   Lemmas 3-nerved.
      D.   Lemmas cleft to near the base .... 1. *Blepharidachne*
      DD. Lemmas cleft to halfway to base .... 11. *Tridens*
    CC. Lemmas at least 5 nerved.
      D.   Lemmas keeled or somewhat rounded on back.
        E.   Spikelets large .... 2. *Bromus*
        EE. Spikelets small .... 9. *Poa*
      DD. Lemmas rounded on back.
        E.   Glumes papery .... 7. *Melica*
        EE. Glumes not papery.
          F.   Nerves of lemma converging toward the summit.
            G.   Lemma apex minutely bifid .... 2. *Bromus*
            GG. Lemma entire.
              H.   Spikelets usually awned; lemmas pointed... 4. *Festuca*
              HH. Spikelets awnless .... 9. *Poa*
          FF. Nerves of lemma not converging at the summit.
            G.   Upper empty glumes 1-nerved .... 5. *Glyceria*
            GG. Upper empty glumes 3-nerved .... 10. *Puccinellia*

1. Blepharidachne

1. **B. kingii** (Wats.) Hack. Dry rocky places, northern canyons, 5000–7500 ft.: near Trail Canyon, 7000 ft., *D s.n.*

180

2. Bromus

A. Plants annual.
  B. Spikelets strongly flattened; lemma teeth less than 0.5 mm. long
  7. *B. uniloides*
  BB. Spikelets usually terete; lemma teeth more than 0.5 mm. long.
    C. Panicle drooping; first glume 4–6 mm. long........6. *B. tectorum*
    CC. Panicle erect; first glume 7–9 mm. long............5. *B. rubens*
AA. Plants perennial.
  B. First glume 3–5 nerved.
    C. Spikelets strongly flattened; lemmas compressed-keeled; sheaths pilose ....2. *B. marginatus*
    CC. Spikelets terete when young; lemmas not compressed-keeled; sheaths mostly glabrous ....3. *B. porteri*
  BB. First glume 1-nerved.
    C. Leaf blades 5–15 mm. wide; creeping rhizomes present
    1. *B. inermis*
    CC. Leaf blades 3–7 mm. wide; creeping rhizomes absent
    4. *B. richardsonii*

1. **B. inermis** Leyss. Of sporadic distribution, moist areas, upper desert scrub to subalpine forest, 5500–10,000 ft.: Crooked Creek, 9900 ft., under *Populus tremuloides, HM 813*.

2. **B. marginata** Nees. Dry slopes and canyons, throughout the range, desert scrub to subalpine forest, 4500–10,000 ft.: Marble Canyon near Black Canyon, 5700 ft., *D 3022;* Silver Canyon, 4600 ft., *D M101;* Crooked Creek Ranger Station, 9500 ft., *D 1563*.

3. **B. porteri** (Coult.) Nash. Frequent among sagebrush in canyons, less common in alpine, 8000–11,500 ft.: Sagehen Flat, 10,500 ft., *HM 539;* south fork, Cottonwood Creek, 9800 ft., *HM 460;* ¾ mile west of Barcroft gate, *HM 649*.

4. **B. richardsonii** Link. Rocky canyons and flats, pinyon woodland to subalpine forest, 8000–10,500 ft.: 3.7 miles south of Inyo–Mono County Line on White Mountain Road, 9700 ft., *Bacigalupi et al. 8206* (JEPS); Cottonwood Creek, 9500 ft., *D 1621*.

5. **B. rubens** L. Common along roadsides, in washes, and in moist areas throughout the range, desert scrub to pinyon woodland, 4500–8000 ft.: 7.4 miles west of White Mountain Road on Westgard Pass, 5000 ft., *L 2645;* Black Canyon near Black Canyon Mine, 5700 ft., *D 3005;* ca. 1 mile above mouth of Silver Canyon, 4600 ft., *D M40*.

6. **B. tectorum** L.

A. Spikelets pubescent ....6a. var. *tectorum*
AA. Spikelets glabrous...........................6b. var. *glabratus*

6a. Var. **tectorum.** Lower elevations in moist canyons and riparian areas: Antelope Springs, *Raven 7050* (CAS); Silver Canyon, 7100 ft., *L 2860*.

6b. Var. **glabratus** Spenner. Moist canyons and riparian areas below 8100 ft.: Toll House Springs, *L 2698;* Chiatovich Creek, 8050 ft., *D 3067.*

7. **B. uniloides** Kunth. (*B. catharticus* in Munz). Common pasture grass in Owens Valley, escape in western canyons; riparian areas below 6500 ft.: Toll House Springs, *L 2694.*

3. Distichlis

1. **D. spicata** (L.) Greene var. **stricta** (Torr.) Beetle. Common, moist, some-times alkaline soils, Owens Valley, extending up into the southern canyons to 6000 ft.: spring northeast of Antelope Springs, 5680 ft., *L 3019;* Silver Canyon, 4500 ft., *D 3459;* Wyman Creek, 1 mile above mouth, 5450 ft., *D 3130.*

4. Festuca

A.   Plants annual .... 2. *F. octoflora*
AA. Plants perennial.
  B.   Culms 4–10 dm. high; lemmas 5–7 mm. long .... 3. *F. rubra*
  BB. Culms 1–1.5 dm. high; lemmas 3–3.5 mm. long .... 1. *F. brachyphylla*

1. **F. brachyphylla** Schult. Common, dry soils, among sagebrush and on alpine fell-fields, subalpine forest to alpine fell-fields, 9500–14,100 ft.: ½ mile south of Crooked Creek Lab, 10,350 ft., *HM 885;* Crooked Creek Ranger Station, 9500 ft., *D M98;* Cottonwood Creek, 10,000 ft., *D 1659;* McAfee Meadows, 11,700 ft., *D M99;* north of Barcroft Lab, 12,700 ft., *HM 597;* White Mountain Peak, 14,100 ft., *L 3239;* Pellisier Flats, 12,800 ft., *M 2271.*

2. **F. octoflora** Walt. ssp. **hirtella** Piper. Dry slopes, southwest canyons, desert scrub to pinyon woodland: Black Canyon at Marble Canyon, 5700 ft. ,*D 2729;* Silver Canyon, *Heller 8196.* (UC).

3. **F. rubra** L. Riparian areas and meadows, desert scrub to subalpine forest, 4500–10,300 ft.: Chiatovich Creek: 8500 ft., *D 2537;* 10,300 ft., *D 3121.*

5. Glyceria

1. **G. striata** (Lam.) Hitchc. Uncommon, streamsides and meadows, north-eastern canyons, 7000–8500 ft.: Trail Canyon, 8400 ft., *D 2513.*

6. Hesperochloa

1. **H. kingii** (Wats.) Rydb. Hillsides and flats, with sagebrush, aspen, or near meadows, pinyon woodland to subalpine forest, throughout the range, 8000–10,500 ft.: Crooked Creek, 9900 ft., *HM 812;* northwest corner of Sagehen Flats, 10,250 ft., *L 3135;* Cottonwood Creek: 8900 ft., *L 2938;* Chiatovich Creek, 8300 ft. on south slope of Big Meadows, *D 3066.*

7. Melica

A.   Culms bulbous at base .... 1. *M. bulbosa*
AA. Culms not bulbous at base .... 2. *M. stricta*

1. **M. bulbosa** Geyer ex Port. & Coult. Riparian areas, canyons, pinyon wood-

182

land to subalpine forest, throughout the range, 7800–10,500 ft.: Crooked Creek
Lab, 10,200 ft., *Cook s.n.* (UC); Queen Canyon, 7800 ft., *M 2762-A;* also reported from Mustang Mountain, north of Trail Canyon at 9500 ft.

2. **M. stricta** Bol. Rocky washes and canyons, desert scrub to subalpine forest,
throughout the range, 5000–10,500 ft.: White Mountain Road, 7700 ft., *L 3031;*
Black Canyon, 6200 ft., *M 2117;* 2.5 miles below Roberts Ranch, Wyman Creek,
7500 ft., *D 3049;* Crooked Creek Ranger Station, 9500 ft., *D 1566;* north end
of Sagehen Flat, 10,500 ft., *HM 543;* south fork, Cottonwood Creek, 9800 ft.,
HM 467.

8. Phragmites

1. **P. communis** Trin. var. **berlandieri** (Fourn.) Fern. Alkaline soils, eastern
valleys extending into the lower canyons and springs up to about 5000 ft.:
Deep Springs Valley, 4800 ft., *Raven 7023* (CAS); Wyman Creek. ca. 1 mile
above mouth, 4600 ft., *D 3132.*

9. Poa

A. Plants annual ....2. *P. annua*
AA. Plants perennial.
  B. Creeping rhizomes present.
    C. Panicle narrow, dense, 4–7 cm. long; lemmas slightly webbed at base
      3. *P. compressa*
    CC. Panicle open, pyramidal, 5–15 cm. long; lemmas strongly webbed at
      base ....11. *P. pratensis*
  BB. Creeping rhizomes absent.
    C. Lemmas glabrous (not pubescent or puberulent) toward the base.
      D. Spikelets compressed; lemmas keeled.
        E. Lemmas less than 4 mm. long.
          F. Culms only slightly longer than the basal tufts of leaves.
            G. Panicle 1–2 cm. long; spikelets 3–4 mm. long; lemmas 2–3
              mm. long ....9. *P. lettermanii*
            GG. Panicle 2–3 cm. long; spikelets 4–6 mm. long; lemmas 3–5
              mm. long ....14. *P. suksdorfii*
          FF. Culms much exceeding the basal tuft of leaves.. 6. *P. hansenii*
        EE. Lemmas more than 4 mm. long.
          F. Lower lemmas ca. 6 mm. long; culms 2 dm. or less; spikelets
            shining ....12 *P. pringlei*
          FF. Lower lemmas 4–5 mm. long; culms more than 2 dm. tall;
            spikelets purple or green...................4. *P. epilis*
      DD. Spikelets ± not compressed; lemmas rounded and obscurely
        keeled.
        E. Ligule long, acute to acuminate ....10 *P. nevadensis*
        EE. Ligule short, rounded or obtuse.
          F. Blades involute, 10–20 cm. long ....8. *P. juncifolia*
          FF. Blades flat, 20–50 cm. long ....1. *P. ampla*

CC. Lemmas ± pubescent on back toward the base.
  D. Spikelets distinctly compressed; lemmas keeled.
    E. Spikelets 5–7-flowered, 6–10 mm. long . . . . . .5. *P. fendleriana*
    EE. Spikelets 2–4-flowered, 2.5–5 mm. long . . . . . .13. *P. rupicola*
  DD. Spikelets not or only slightly compressed; lemmas rounded
                                                    7. *P. incurva*

1. **P. ampla** Merr. Southeast-facing canyons, up to 8000 ft.: Wyman Creek, 7550 ft., *D M117.*

2. **P. annua** L. Sporadic, meadows and riparian areas, throughout the range. up to 10,000 ft.: highest meadow in Trail Canyon, 9800 ft., *D 3360;* also reported from Toll House Springs.

3. **P. compressa** L. Known only from the head of Crooked Creek in meadows and slopes: Crooked Creek near cave, 10,000 ft., *L 3065;* meadow below Crooked Creek Lab, 10,100 ft., *L 3110, L 3108.*

4. **P. epilis** Scribn. Frequent, in sagebrush and on rocky slopes, subalpine forest to alpine, throughout the range, 9000–13,000 ft.: Cottonwood Creek, 9700 ft., *HM 256;* north of Barcroft Lab, 12,700 ft., *HM 598.*

5. **P. fendleriana** (Steud.) Vasey. Frequent, shrub-covered slopes, open areas, desert scrub to subalpine forest, throughout the range, 5500–10,600 ft.: Black Canyon, 6000 ft., *D 3009;* Silver Canyon, 8700 ft., *L 2842;* Crooked Creek, 9850 ft., *L 2884;* Campito Meadow, 10,600 ft., *L 3171;* Chiatovich Creek, 7500 ft., *D M119.*

6. **P. hansenii** Scribn. Moist meadows and grassy slopes, subalpine forest and alpine: McAfee Meadow, 11,700 ft., *D M114.*

7. **P. incurva** Scribn. & Will. Dry scrub-covered slopes and open areas, pinyon woodland to alpine, throughout the range, 6000–12,600 ft.: 3.8 miles west of White Mountain Road on Westgard Pass, 6450 ft., *L 2750;* Black Canyon 6000 ft., *D 3010;* Cottonwood Creek, 10,500 ft., *D 1660-B;* McAfee Meadow, 11,700 ft., *D M113;* summit of rise above Barcroft Lab, 12,600 ft. *Bacigalupi et al. 8121-B* (JEPS); Queen Canyon, 7100 ft., *D M118.*

8. **P. juncifolia** Scribn. Sporadic, moist-to-dry slopes, somewhat alkaline places, desert scrub to upper subalpine forest, 4800–11,000 ft.: Deep Springs Valley, 4800 ft., *Raven 7015* (CAS); ¾ mile west of Barcroft gate, 11,000 ft., *HM 653.*

9. **P. lettermanii** Vasey. Rare, rocky flats and slopes, above 13,000 ft.: White Mountain Peak, 14,000 ft., *D 2612.*

10. **P. nevadensis** Vasey ex Scribn. Moist flats, meadows and springs, desert scrub to subalpine forest, below 10,100 ft.: Antelope Springs, *Raven 7056* (CAS); southeast rim of Reed Flat, 10,100 ft., *J. & L. Roos 5117* (UC); Chiatovich Creek, 7500 ft., *D 2762;* Trail Canyon, 8300 ft., *D 2508.*

11. **P. pratensis** L. Meadows, riparian areas, desert scrub to subalpine forest, throughout the range, below ca. 10,000 ft.: Antelope Springs, *Raven 7047* (CAS); Wyman Creek, 8300 ft., *L 2790;* Crooked Creek Ranger Station, 9500 ft., *D 1532.* An apomictic segregate, *Poa agassizensis* Boiven & D. Love, differ-

ing from *P. pratensis* in having small, compact tufts with few stems and mostly 2-flowered spikelets with lemmas slightly cobwebby at base, has been collected in Chiatovich Creek, 7500 ft., *D 2763* (CAS).

12. **P. pringlei** Scribn. Dry rocky slopes and meadows, in glaciated canyons, 9000–11,700 ft.: Cottonwood Creek, 10,500 ft., *D 1660-A;* McAfee Meadow, 11,700 ft., *D M115;* These plants appear identical with atypical forms from Mono Co. at 11,300 ft. (see Munz).

13. **P. rupicola** Nash ex Rydb. Common, moist soils of alpine fell-fields, springs, and meadows, 11,400–14,100 ft.: Sheep Mountain, 11,800 ft., *L 3260;* McAfee Meadow, 11,700 ft., *D M114-A;* White Mountain Road near summit, 13,500 ft., *L 3256;* south end of Pellisier Flat, 12,700 ft., *M 2202.*

14. **P. suksdorfii** (Beal) Vasey ex Piper. White Mountain Peak, sandy areas or rocky fell-fields, 12,000–14,246 ft.: 14,000 ft., *J & L Roos 5149a* (RSA): 14,240 ft., *Bacigalupi et al. 8173* (JEPS).

10. Puccinellia

1. **P. distans** (L.) Parl. Infrequent in moist, alkaline places, 4500 to 8500 ft.: Wyman Creek, 7800 ft. common above and along road *L 2775.*

11. Tridens

1. **T. pulchellus** (Kunth) Hitchc. Known only from near Trail Canyon, 7000 ft. *D s.n.*

Tribe 2: HORDEAE

A. Spikelets 1 at each node of the rachis . . . . .12. *Agropyron*
AA. Spikelets 2 to 3 at each node of the rachis.
   B. Spikelets 3 at each node, 1-flowered . . . . .14. *Hordeum*
   BB. Spikelets 2, rarely 3, at each node. 2–6-flowered.
      C. Glumes short-awned; rachis continuous . . . . .13. *Elymus*
      CC. Glumes long-awned; rachis articulating into joints at maturity
                      15. *Sitanion*

12. Agropyron

A. Lemmas with awns 15–25 mm. long . . . . .1. *A. scribneri*
AA. Lemmas without awns or sometimes short-awned.
   B. Glumes short-awned, faintly nerved . . . . .2. *A. smithii*
   BB. Glumes awnless, strongly nerved . . . . .3. *A. trachycaulum*

1. **A. scribneri** Vasey. Rare, high elevations from White Mountain Peak north, above 12,000 ft.: White Mountain Peak, 13,600 ft., *J & L. Roos 5142* (UC).

2. **A. smithii** Rydb. Common, moist, alkaline areas in surrounding valleys, extending up to 6000 ft. in riparian areas of canyons: Antelope Springs, common along marsh, *L 2997.*

3. **A. trachycaulum** (Link) Malte. Rocky canyons and brush-covered slopes, pinyon woodland to alpine, 8000–12,500 ft.: Wyman Creek, 8050 ft., *D s.n.;*

Crooked Creek Ranger Station, 9500 ft., *D 1583;* McAfee Meadow, 11,500 ft., *D 2878;* south of Barcroft Lab, 12,200 ft., *HM 591.*

13. Elymus
A. Rhizomes extensively creeping; culm-nodes glabrous; lemmas glabrous
2. *E. triticoides*
AA. Rhizomes absent; culm-nodes densely fine-pubescent; lemmas pubescent
1. *E. cinereus*

1. **E. cinereus** Scribn. & Merr. Sporadic, moist flats and depressions, occasionally in meadows, desert scrub to subalpine forest, throughout the range, 6000–10,000 ft.: 3.8 miles west of White Mountain Road, Westgard Pass, 6450 ft., *L 2752;* Mollie Gibson Canyon, ½ mile north of Payson Canyon Road, 7100 ft., *L 2949;* Wyman Creek, 8300 ft., *L 2792;* Crooked Creek, 9500 ft., *Bacigalupi et al. 8079* (JEPS); Chiatovich Creek, 8000 ft., *D s.n.*

2. **E. triticoides** Buckl. Infrequent, moist soil and riparian areas, desert scrub to subalpine forest, throughout the range, 5000–10,000 ft.: Toll House Springs, *L 2695;* Roberts Ranch, Wyman Creek, 8000 ft., *D 3161;* north fork, Crooked Creek, 10,000 ft., *Cook s.n.* (UC); south fork, Cottonwood Creek, 9800 ft., *HM 465.*

14. Hordeum
A. Plants annual; auricle well developed ....3. *H. leporinum*
AA. Plants perennial; auricle wanting.
B. Blades pubescent, 1.5–5 mm. wide ....2. *H. californicum*
BB. Blades ± glabrous, 3–9 mm. wide ....1. *H. brachyantherum*

1. **H. brachyantherum** Nevskii. Meadows and springs, desert scrub to subalpine forest, 4500–10,000.: Antelope Springs, *L 3103;* meadow just below Crooked Creek Lab, 10,100 ft., *L 3107;* south fork Cottonwood Creek, 9800 ft., *HM 468.*

2. **H. californicum** Cov. & Stebb. Wet places, meadows, below 10,300 ft.: Crooked Creek Ranger Station, 9500 ft., *D 1530;* Crooked Creek, 10,300 ft., *M 2239.*

3. **H leporinum** Link. Moist waste places, throughout the range: Toll House Springs, 5971 ft., *L 2699.*

15. Sitanion
A. Spikes 8–20 cm. long; glumes linear-lanceolate, 2–4 nerved 1. *S. hansenii*
AA. Spikes 3–10 cm. long, about as broad as long; glumes subulate or narrowly lanceolate, 1–3-nerved.
B. Glumes 3–9-cleft ....3. *S. jubatum*
BB. Glumes entire ....2. *S. hystrix*

1. **S. hansenii** (Scribn.) J. G. Sm. Sporadic, dry rocky places, desert scrub to

subalpine forest, throughout the range, below 13,600 ft.: Wyman Creek, 10,400 ft., *J. & L. Roos 5094* (RSA); White Mountain Peak, 13,600 ft., *J. & L. Roos 5142* (RSA); near Benton Station, 5500 ft., *Robinson & Lindner L-56* (RSA).

2. **S. hystrix** (Nutt.) J. G. Sm. var. **californicum** (J. G. Sm.) F. D. Wilson. Extremely common, dry rocky slopes and flats, desert scrub to alpine fell-fields, throughout the range, 4500–14,000 ft.: 3.8 miles west of White Mountain Road, Westgard Pass, 6450 ft., *L 2744*; mouth of Mollie Gibson Canyon, 6960 ft., *L 2952*; Silver Canyon: 7400 ft., *HM 213*; Crooked Creek Ranger Station, 9500 ft., *D 1554*; White Mountain summit, 14,000 ft., *HM 493*; south end of Pellisier Flats, 12,500 ft., *M 2201*.

3. **S. jubatum** J. G. Sm. Rocky slopes, canyons below 10,000 ft.: 10 miles northeast of Big Pine on Westgard Pass, 6500 ft., *Keck 531* (UC); east side of Westgard Pass, 7000 ft., *Hovanitz s.n.* (UC).

Tribe 3. AVENEAE

A. Florets 2 per spikelet, the lower perfect and awnless; the upper one male and awned . . . . .17. *Holcus*
AA. Florest usually more than 2 per spikelet, similar.
   B. Lemmas convex, awned from near the base . . . . .16. *Deschampsia*
   BB. Lemmas keeled, awned (if present) from near the middle.
      C. Joints of the rachilla villous; lemma-awns 5–6 mm. long
                                     19. *Trisetum*
      CC. Joints of the rachilla not villous; awns short, if present 18. *Koeleria*

16. Deschampsia

1. **D. caespitosa** (L.) Beauv. Common, moist places, meadows, streamsides, etc., pinyon woodland to alpine fell-fields, throughout the range, 8000–14,000 ft.: meadow below Crooked Creek Lab, 10,100 ft., *L 3109*; Cottonwood Creek, 11,700 ft., *D 2588*; Barcroft gate, 11,600 ft., *HM 639*; White Mountain Peak, 14,000 ft., *HM 494*; Pellisier Flats, 12,700 ft., *M 2272*; Trail Canyon, 8300 ft., *D 2510*.

17. Holcus

1. **H. lanatus** L. Adventive, moist places at low elevations: Antelope Springs, 5600 ft., *L 3011*; *Raven 7041* (CAS).

18. Koeleria

1. **K. cristata** (L.) Pers. Very common, dry slopes and flats, pinyon woodland to alpine fell-fields, throughout the range, 7000–13,000 ft.: head of Silver Canyon, 9300 ft., *HM 281*; Wyman Creek, 9500 ft., *L 2820*; northwest corner of Sagehen Flat, 10,250 ft., *L 3168*; east of Campito Mountain, 10,600 ft., *HM 476*; Cottonwood Creek, 10,000 ft., *D 1658*; north of Barcroft Lab, 12,700 ft., *HM 602*; mouth of Queen Canyon, 7100 ft., *D 3250*; also known from Chiatovich Creek at 8000 ft.

19. Trisetum

1. **T. spicatum** (L.) Richt. Rocky slopes and fields, subalpine forest to alpine fell-fields, Mono Co. north, 10,500–14,240 ft.: head of Cottonwood Creek, 11,700 ft., *D 2590;* north slope, White Mountain Peak, 14,240 ft., *HM 552;* Pellisier Flats, 12,800 ft., *M 2273.*

Tribe 4. AGROSTIDEAE

A.   Glumes falling with the spikelet . . . . .25. *Polypogon*
AA. Glumes persistent.
  B.   Lemma hardening and embracing the grain at maturity.
    C.   Awn twisted, persistent . . . . .27. *Stipa*
    CC. Awn not twisted, deciduous . . . . .23. *Oryzopsis*
  BB. Lemma membranous or hyaline, free.
    C.   Glumes exceeding the lemma.
      D.   Keel of the glumes ciliate .24. *Phleum*
      DD. Keel of the glumes eciliate.
        E.   Palea absent or much reduced . . . . .20. *Agrostis*
        EE. Palea well developed, rachilla extending beyond it as a bristle
                           21. *Calamagrostis*
    CC. Glumes shorter than the lemma.
      D.   Lemma 3-nerved . . . . .22. *Muhlenbergia*
      DD. Lemma 1-nerved . . . . .26. *Sporobolus*

20. Agrostis

A.   Palea absent, or tiny and nerveless . . . . .2. *A. scabra*
AA. Palea present, 3-nerved . . . . .1. *A. palustris*

1. **A. palustris** Huds. Moist areas, southern canyons below 7500 ft.: Antelope Springs, 5600 ft., *L 3012;* Silver Canyon, 4600 ft., *D M103;* Wyman Creek, 7300 ft., *D 3148.*
2. **A. scabra** Willd. Moist places, streamsides, etc., pinyon woodland to subalpine forest, eastern canyons, 7000–10,300 ft.: Cottonwood Creek, 9500 ft., *D 1620;* Cabin Creek, 10,300 ft., *D 2549;* Chiatovich Creek, 8500 ft., *D 3114.*

21. Calamagrostis

1. **C. purpurascens** R. Br. Common, rocky slopes and flats, pinyon woodland to alpine fell-fields, throughout the range, 8000–13,000 ft.: hill west of head of Wyman Creek, 10,500 ft., *HM 529;* head of Cottonwood Creek, 11,750 ft., *D 2585;* summit of rise just north of Barcroft Lab, ca. 12,600 ft., *Bacigalupi et al. 8119.* (JEPS); Chiatovich Creek, ca. 8000 ft., *D M102.*

22. Muhlenbergia

A.   Inflorescence an open, finely branched panicle . . . . .1. *M. asperifolia*
AA. Inflorescence a narrow, dense panicle.

B.   Panicles 3 cm. long or less ....2. *M. filiformis*
BB. Panicles mostly greater than 4 cm. long ....3. *M. richardsonis*

1. **M asperifolia** (Nees & Mey.) Parodi. Dry places, eastern desert slopes: near Antelope Springs, 5600 ft., *L 2996*.
2. **M. filiformis** (Thurb.) Rydg. Known only from streamsides, Cottonwood Creek, 9500 ft., *D 1622*.
3. **M. richardsonis** (Trin.) Rydb. Common, moist areas, slopes and meadows, pinyon woodland to subalpine forest, throughout the range, 8000–11,100 ft.: White Mountain Road, 9300 ft., *HM 336;* Crooked Creek Ranger Station, 9500 ft., *D 1543;* Campito Mountain, 10,800 ft., *HM 478;* south of Piute Trail, 11,100 ft., *HM 641;* Trail Canyon, 8300 ft., *D 2505*.

23. Oryzopsis

A.   Lemmas mostly glabrous ....2. *O. micrantha*
AA. Lemmas with long-pilose pubescence.
   B.   Panicle 8–15 cm. long, branching divaricately...... 1. *O. hymenoides*
   BB. Panicle 2–5 cm. long, branches appressed ....3. *O. webberi*

1. **O. hymenoides** (R. & S.) Ricker. Common, rocky places, desert scrub to subalpine forest, 4200–10,400 ft.: 2.9 miles east of Big Pine on Westgard Pass, 4200 ft., *HM 27;* mouth of Mollie Gibson Canyon, 6960 ft., *L 2953;* Silver Canyon, 7350 ft., *HM 108;* Wyman Creek, 9500 ft., *D 1740;* Crooked Creek Ranger Station, 9500 ft., *D M41;* south ridge, Cottonwood Creek, 10,250 ft., *HM 263*.
2. **O. micrantha** (Trin. & Rupr.) Thurb. Sporadic, rocky crevices, throughout the range, 7000–10,300 ft.: Wyman Creek, 8800 ft., *J. & L. Roos 5840* (UC), Station Peak (Crooked Creek), 10,300 ft., *D 1587*.
3. **O. webberi** (Thurb.) Benth. ex Vasey. Common, rocky slopes, pinyon woodland, throughout the range, 7000–9000 ft.: Cedar Flat, 7400 ft., *HM 371;* White Mountain Road, 7800 ft., *HM 348;* Trail Canyon, 8200 ft., *D 3088*.

24. Phleum

A.   Glumes ca. 5.0 mm. long; awns 2 mm. long ....1. *P. alpinum*
AA. Glumes ca. 3.5 mm. long; awns 1 mm. long ....2. *P. pratense*

1. **P alpinum.** L. Wet places, streamsides, and fell-fields, McAfee Creek north: Cabin Creek, 10,300 ft.; *D 2552*.
2. **P. pratense** L. Meadows, riparian areas, pinyon woodland to subalpine forest, 7000–10,000 ft.: Roberts Ranch, Wyman Creek, 8000 ft., *D 3165;* Cottonwood Creek, 9500 ft., *HM 471*.

25. Polypogon

A.   Panicle more or less simple ....1.*P. monspeliensis*
AA. Panicle appearing lobed due to many short, whorled, lateral branches
                                      2. *P. semiverticillatus*

1. **P. monspeliensis** (L.) Desf. Common, disturbed, riparian areas, desert scrub to pinyon woodland, 4500–7000 ft.: Westgard Pass, 6000 ft., *Raven 6994* (CAS); Antelope Springs, 5600 ft., *L 3008;* Black Canyon, 6200 ft., *M 2120;* Montenegro Springs, 7000 ft., *M 2149;* Silver Canyon, 4600 ft., *D M106;* Wyman Creek, 6500 ft., *D 3168.*

2. **P. semiverticillatus** (Forsk.) Hylander. Sporadic, moist areas below 6500 ft.: Toll House Springs, 5971 ft., *L 2690;* Antelope Springs, 5600 ft., *Raven 7046* (CAS); Silver Canyon, 4600 ft., *D M104.*

26. Sporobolus
A. Inflorescence open-spreading at maturity.
   B. Throat of the sheath tufted with hairs . . . . .3. *S. cryptandrus*
   BB. Throat of the sheath glabrous or with a few sparse hairs . . 1. *S. airoides*
AA. Inflorescence spikelike . . . . .2. *S. contractus*

1. **S. airoides** (Torr.) Torr. Sporadic throughout the range below 7000 ft.: moist alkaline flat, 4500 ft. near Shealy, Inyo Co. *D 3241.*

2. **S. contractus** Hitchc. Known only from the mouth of Wyman Creek, rocky places in the canyon bottom, 6000 ft. *D 3315.*

3. **S. cryptandrus** (Torr.) Gray. Low altitudes on the east side of the range in the desert and mouths of canyons: above Deep Springs at 5500 ft. *Buechner C62* (RSA).

27. Stipa
A. Lemma with a crown of long, villous hairs . . . . .5. *S. pinetorum*
AA. Lemma merely scabrous.
   B. Awns (at least some segments) conspicuously plumose or long pubescent.
      C. Hairs at the base of the awn 4–8 mm. long . . . . .6. *S. speciosa*
      CC. Hairs at the base of the awn 2 mm. long or less.
         D. Ligule more than 3 mm. long, hyaline . . . . .7. *S. thurberiana*
         DD. Ligule less than 3 mm. long, opaque.
            E. Hairs of the lemma short, all about the same length
               4. *S. occidentalis*
            EE. Hairs of the lemma longer above.
               F. Culms scabrous below the nodes . . . . .3. *S. nevadensis*
               FF. Culms glabrous below the nodes . . . . .1. *S. californica*
   BB. Awns merely scabrous . . . . .2. *S. comata*

1. **S. californica** Merr. & Davy. Moist flats and hillsides, subalpine forest: north rim of Reed Flat, 10,400 ft.; *J. & L. Roos 5107* (RSA).

2. **S. comata** Trin. & Rupr. Common, dry slopes, desert scrub to subalpine forest, 6500–9500 ft.: 3.8 miles west of White Mountain Road, Westgard Pass, 6450 ft., *L 2748;* east side of Westgard Pass, 7000 ft., *L. 2963;* White Mountain Road, 8600 ft., *HM 167;* Crooked Creek Ranger Station, 9500 ft., *D 1582.*

3. **S. nevadensis** B. L. Jones. Slopes and flats, desert scrub to subalpine forest, 6000–10,400 ft.: 3.7 miles south of Inyo-Mono county line on White Mountain Road, ca. 9700 ft., *Bacigalupi et al. 8205* (JEPS); north rim of Reed Flat, 10,400 ft., *J. & L. Roos 5107* (UC); Indian Creek, 6000 ft., *Lankester 757* (BM).

4. **S. occidentalis** Thurb. Dry slopes and rocky areas, subalpine forest, 9500–11,500 ft.: Crooked Creek Ranger Station, 9500 ft., *D 1584;* head of Cottonwood Creek, 11,300 ft., *D 2605.*

5. **S. pinetorum** Jones. Very common, dry, open areas, desert scrub to subalpine forest, 5500–11,100 ft.: mouth of Mollie Gibson Canyon, 6960 ft., *L 2957;* White Mountain Road, 7700 ft., *L 3030;* Silver Canyon, 7400 ft., *HM 218;* Crooked Creek Lab, 10,200 ft., *Cook s.n.* (UC); Cottonwood Creek, 10,000 ft., *D 1656;* south of Piute Trail, 11,100 ft., *HM 642.*

6. **S. speciosa** Trin. & Rupr. Common, dry rocky places, desert scrub to pinyon woodland, throughout the range, 5000–8000 ft.: Westgard Pass, 5.4 miles west of White Mountain Road, 5900 ft., *L 2687;* Payson Canyon, 6800 ft., *HM 364;* White Mountain Road, 7700 ft., *HM 355;* Black Canyon about 4 miles above Marble Canyon, 7000 ft., *D 3013;* Silver Canyon, 7000 ft., *M 2293;* mouth of Pinchot Creek, 6500 ft., *D 3269.*

7. **S. thurberiana** Piper. Dry rocky slopes, pinyon woodland: 3 miles northwest of Cedar Flat, 8500 ft., *J. & L. Roos 5087* (UC).

Tribe 5. ZOYSIEAE
28. Hilaria

1. **H. jamesii** (Torr.) Benth. Common, dry places, desert scrub to pinyon woodland, 6000–7500 ft.: Westgard Pass: 1.3 miles east of Toll House Springs, 6500 ft., *HM 158, L 2737;* Payson Canyon, 6800 ft., *HM 368;* Silver Canyon, 7350 ft., *HM 109.*

Tribe 6. CHLORIDEAE

A.　Plants 1–4 dm. tall; spikes 2 . . . . .29. *Bouteloua*
AA.　Culms 6–10 dm. tall; spikes 4–8 .30. *Spartina*

29. Bouteloua

1. **B gracilis** (Kunth) Lag. Dry slopes, uncommon in pinyon woodland of northern canyons: Trail Canyon, 8000 ft., *D 3353* (UC).

30. Spartina

1. **S. gracilis** Trin. Alkaline places, below 6500 ft.: near Benton Station, 6437 ft., *Ferris 12582* (DS).

FAMILY 69. LEMNACEAE
1. Lemna

1. **L. minima** Phil. Known only from Antelope Springs, 5600 ft., *L 2986; Raven 7051* (CAS).

FAMILY 70. LILIACEAE

A. Plants not bulbous.
   B.   Leaves scalelike, foliage much-branched ....1. *Asparagus*
   BB. Leaves not scalelike.
      C.   Leaves 5–15 cm. long; seeds 3–4 mm. long ....4. *Smilacina*
      CC. Leaves 25–40 cm. long; seeds 10–12 mm. long ......5. *Veratrum*
AA. Plants bulbous.
   B.   Styles 3, distinct to base ....6. *Zygadenus*
   BB. Styles 1, more or less lobed at summit.
      C.   Perianth segments unlike, flowers cream to yellow-orange
                                                        2. *Calochortus*
      CC. Perianth segments similar, flowers dark purplish, maculate
                                                        3. *Fritillaria*

1. Asparagus

1. **A. officinalis** L. Escape from cultivation, low places: Silver Canyon, 5600 ft., beside stream *M 1996.*

2. Calochortus

A.   Flowers white to purple ....2. *C. nuttallii*
AA. Flowers vermillion to orange ....1. *C. kennedyi*

1. **C. kennedyi** Port. Sporadic, desert scrub on east slope, 5000–6500 ft.: between Deep Springs and Oasis, 6374 ft., *Grinnell 1047a* (UC); reported by D. Powell from mouth of Wyman Creek, 5600 ft.

2. **C. nuttallii** Torr.

A.   Stems 4–6 dm. high; petals not spotted; anthers blue to reddish
                                                        2b. var. *panamintensis*
AA. Stems 2–4 dm. high; petals with red or purple spot above gland; anthers
      yellow to maroon ....2a. var. *bruneaunis*

2a. Var. **bruneaunis** (Nels. & Macbr.) Ownbey. Occasional, hillsides and flats, desert scrub to pinyon woodland, 6000–9500 ft.: Westgard Pass, 7300 ft., *J. & H. Grinnell 1043a* (UC); White Mountain Road, 7900 ft., *M & L 1726;* Silver Canyon, 9300 ft., *HM 291;* Indian Creek, 6000 ft., *Lankester 833* (BM).

2b. Var. **panamintensis** Ownbey. Less frequent than the above variety; dry flats and slopes, pinyon woodland, throughout the range, ca. 8500 ft.: Wyman Creek, 8500 ft., *D 1680;* Chiatovich Creek, 8500 ft., *D 2541.*

3. Fritillaria

A.   Stems slender; bulb without rice-grain bulblets; capsule angular
                                                        1. *F. atropurpurea*
AA. Stems fistulose in region of leaves; bulb with bulblets; capsule with horn-
      like processes at base and top of wings ....2. *F. pinetorum*

1. **F. atropurpurea** Nutt. Sporadic throughout the mountains and valleys, desert scrub to subalpine forest, 6000–11,000 ft.: between Crooked Creek and Sheep Mountain on White Mountain Road, 10,800 ft., *Pawek 58-11* (UC); McCloud Camp, Cottonwood Creek, 9500 ft., *D 1611*.

2. **F. pinetorum** A. Davids. Sporadic, pinyon woodland to subalpine forest, throughout the range, 7000–11,000 ft., often inconspicuous due to flower color: cave, rocky places, Crooked Creek, 10,000 ft., *L 3265*.

4. Smilacina

1. **S. stellata** (L.) Desf. Common, riparian areas, pinyon woodland to subalpine forest, 6000–10,000 ft.: Silver Canyon, *Jepson 7203* (JEPS); Wyman Creek, 7650 ft., *L 2809;* McCloud Camp, Cottonwood Creek, 9500 ft., *D 1619;* Chiatovich Creek, 8000 ft., *D 3074*.

5. Veratrum

1. **V. californicum** Durand. Known only from wet meadows in Trail Canyon and Middle Creek: Trail Canyon, 9800 ft., *D 3350*.

6. Zygadenus

1. **Z. paniculatus** (Nutt.) Wats. Rocky and loose, moist soils, northern canyons 6000–8000 ft.: Chiatovich Creek at Davis Ranch, 7300 ft. *D 3061;* Trail Canyon, open flats at 7500 ft., *D 2747*.

FAMILY 71. AMARYLLIDACEAE
1. Allium

A.   Leaves 2–3, flat ....2. *A. bisceptrum*
AA. Leaves solitary, terete ....1. *A. atrorubens*

1. **A. atrorubens** Wats. var. **inyonis** (Jones) Ownbey & Aase. Locally abundant, in many habitats, sagebrush and pinyon woodland, throughout the range, 6000–10,000 ft.: Cedar Flats, 7000 ft., common on flats, *D 3282;* head of Silver Canyon, 9300 ft., *HM 284;* Wyman Creek, on dry sagebrush hillsides at 2300 m, *D 1936;* Trail Canyon, 7500 ft., *D 2757;* Queen Canyon, 7100 ft., *D s.n.*

2. **A. bisceptrum** Wats. Shady, moist areas and meadows, northern and glaciated canyons, 7500–10,300 ft.: Cabin Creek 10,300 ft., *D M49;* Chiatovitch Creek, 8000 ft., *D 2544;* Middle Creek on east slope of Boundary Peak, 8600 ft., *Train 3941* (UC); Queen Canyon, 7800 ft., *M 2760*.

FAMILY 72. IRIDACEAE

A.   Inflorescence umbellate; sepals 1.0–1.5 cm. long ....2. *Sisyrinchium*
AA. Inflorescence not umbellate; sepals ca. 6 cm. long ....1. *Iris*

1. Iris

1. **I. missouriensis** Nutt. Common, meadows of canyons, 6000–8000 ft.: Silver Canyon, 7500 ft., *Jepson 7208* (JEPS); Trail Canyon, 8000 ft., *D s.n.;* observed in Davis and Chiatovich creeks.

2. Sisyrinchium

1. **S. idahoense** Bickn. Common, wet meadows throughout the range, 6000–9000 ft.: Black Canyon Springs, Black Canyon, 8400 ft. *M 2109;* Wyman Creek, 7800 ft., *L 2769.*

FAMILY 73. AGAVACEAE
1. Yucca

1. **Y. brevifolia** Engelm, var. **jaegeriana** McKelvey. Sporadic and nowhere abundant, washes and alluvia of east-facing canyons: 1 mile up Wyman Creek, *D 3170;* observed at the mouth of Wyman Creek on hillside north of road at 6000 ft.

FAMILY 74. ORCHIDACEAE

A. Flowers purplish; leaves ovate . . . . .1. *Epipactis*
AA. Flowers greenish; leaves oblanceolate . . . . .2. *Habenaria*

1. Epipactis

1. **E. gigantea** Dougl. ex Hook. Sporadic, streambanks and riparian areas of southern mountains: Toll House Springs, edge of stream in meadow ca. 20 meters above road, *L 2721;* Antelope Springs, Deep Springs Valley, 5600 ft., *L 3007;* Marble Canyon of Black Canyon, 5800 ft., *D 2876;* Silver Canyon, 6000 ft., *HM 769.*

2. Habenaria

1. **H. sparsiflora** Wats. Riparian areas throughout the range, 7000–10,000 ft.: just south of Black Canyon Springs, Black Canyon, 8300 ft., *M 2124;* in Marble Canyon of Black Canyon, *D M96;* Roberts Ranch, Wyman Creek, 8000 ft.· *D 3164;* Crooked Creek Ranger Station, 9500 ft., *D 1567;* Meadow of Poison Creek and Cottonwood Creek, 9450 ft., *L 2913;* Trail Canyon, at head of creek, 9700 ft., *D 3352.*

SCIENTIFIC NAMES IN THE ENUMERATION

OF THE FLORA

195